Cognitive Diplomacy and Digital Autonomy

Erman Akıllı

Cognitive Diplomacy and Digital Autonomy

Statecraft in the Age of Artificial Intelligence

palgrave
macmillan

Erman Akıllı
International Relations Department
Ankara Hacı Bayram Veli University
Ankara, Türkiye

ISBN 978-3-032-04469-3 ISBN 978-3-032-04470-9 (eBook)
https://doi.org/10.1007/978-3-032-04470-9

Cover credit: imaginima/GettyImages

This Palgrave Macmillan imprint is published by the registered company Springer Nature Switzerland AG
The registered company address is: Gewerbestrasse 11, 6330 Cham, Switzerland

Foreword

We live in a world increasingly governed by invisible architectures—by code, by data, and by machines that learn. In this world, power no longer flows solely through institutions or borders, but through infrastructures, algorithms, and the ability to shape perception at scale. The international system, once organized around territory and treaties, now pulses within digital ecosystems, where influence is exercised not just through diplomacy, but through design. In *Cognitive Diplomacy and Digital Autonomy: Statecraft in the Age of Artificial Intelligence*, Prof. Erman Akıllı has produced a book of striking clarity and originality. At a time when much of the discourse around AI remains abstract, reactive, or overwhelmed by techno-hype, Akıllı offers something more necessary and rare: a strategic framework for agency.

At the heart of the book lies a critical insight—that digital autonomy has become the defining condition of twenty-first century sovereignty. To lack control over your data, your infrastructures, your algorithms, is to lack the ability to govern. Akıllı structures this autonomy around three interdependent pillars: *presence*, *practice*, and *resilience*. Together, they form not just a theory of autonomy, but a call to action—one that recognizes that sovereignty must now be asserted in both physical and cognitive domains. And yet it is the book's most innovative contribution—*Cognitive Diplomacy*—that truly pushes the boundaries of how we understand international relations in an AI-driven world. Drawing from developments in machine learning, neural networks, and cognitive architectures, Akıllı outlines a paradigm in which human and artificial intelligences operate symbiotically to anticipate, interpret, and influence geopolitical developments.

Cognitive Diplomacy is not about automation. It is about augmentation—the use of AI to support, not supplant, human judgment in the conduct of foreign policy. As we have seen in recent diplomatic crises—from the disinformation campaigns targeting democratic elections, to algorithmically mediated negotiations over cyber norms and climate commitments—the ability to process complexity, extract signal from noise, and forecast emergent threats has become indispensable. But these tasks can no longer be achieved through traditional diplomatic practice alone. What Prof. Akıllı proposes is a model in which AI becomes a strategic enabler: assisting diplomats in real-time sentiment analysis, enabling adaptive narrative engagement, and supporting anticipatory governance in high-uncertainty environments. In an age where misinformation spreads faster than rebuttal, and where alliances may be tested or redefined in the span of a news cycle, Cognitive Diplomacy equips states with the reflexes and foresight to remain agile—and sovereign.

Threaded through Akıllı's analysis is a quiet attentiveness to the ethical undercurrents of digital transformation. While not foregrounded as a normative argument, the book invites the reader to consider how strategic autonomy in the age of AI might be pursued without sacrificing democratic values or diplomatic integrity. In this way, it gestures—delicately but deliberately—toward the broader dilemmas of cognitive asymmetry, algorithmic opacity, and the subtle drift toward techno-authoritarian modes of governance. In a world increasingly defined by what we might call "algorithmic geopolitics," this book is a vital companion for policymakers, diplomats, and scholars seeking to navigate the new realities of power. Whether we are looking at the EU's strategic turn toward "tech sovereignty," the diplomatic challenges posed by generative AI in warfare and peace mediation, or the governance dilemmas faced by the Global South in resisting digital dependency, Digital Autonomy offers not just critique but guidance.

This is what makes the book so timely, and so necessary. It reminds us that autonomy in the Digital Age is not merely about owning infrastructure or passing regulation. It is about cultivating cognitive agency—the ability to think, decide, and act strategically in a world mediated by machines. For those willing to take on the challenges of diplomacy in the AI era, Prof. Akıllı's vision offers not a roadmap, but a compass—one calibrated to a new magnetic north, where sovereignty is no longer just territorial, but technological and cognitive. And in that world, Cognitive Diplomacy may well prove to be the decisive art of our time.

Prof. Corneliu Bjola
Professor of Digital Diplomacy
University of Oxford
Oxford, UK

Preface

We are living through a geopolitical transformation shaped not by treaties or military conquests, but by code, data, and algorithmic infrastructures. The classical Westphalian world order, founded on the primacy of territorial sovereignty, is no longer sufficient to explain the dynamics of global power in the twenty-first century. In the technopolar world, influence is exercised not only through embassies and armies, but through digital infrastructure, AI ecosystems, and control over the architectures of cognition.

This shift requires a fundamental reassessment of how we understand sovereignty, autonomy, and diplomatic agency. Power today lies increasingly in the hands of those who command computational capacity, who set the protocols for digital interaction, and who shape the cognitive environment in which information is created, consumed, and contested. The result is a recalibration of international relations—a domain where traditional statecraft is being rewritten by the imperatives of technological interdependence.

Amid this transformation, two strategic imperatives emerge at the center of this book's argument: digital autonomy and cognitive diplomacy. These are not speculative constructs, but necessary doctrines for survival and relevance in an age defined by data-driven governance and AI-mediated influence. Digital autonomy refers to a state's ability to act independently and securely within the digital sphere—an evolved form of sovereignty appropriate for the algorithmic era. It encompasses control over data flows, technological infrastructure, AI capacity, and regulatory frameworks. Cognitive diplomacy, by contrast, is the exercise of strategic influence within digital information ecosystems, where attention, perception, and trust are the true currency of power.

Critically, digital autonomy must be understood as a direct response to the pervasive condition of digital asymmetry. In the emerging global order, access to strategic technologies such as high-performance computing (HPC), sovereign cloud services, secure telecommunications, and AI research and development capabilities is increasingly concentrated in a handful of states and corporations. This imbalance creates systemic dependencies, limits the strategic choices of digitally excluded nations, and exposes them to vulnerabilities ranging from cyberattacks and surveillance to economic coercion and normative marginalization. If left unaddressed, digital asymmetry will crystallize into a new form of structural subordination, undermining both state agency and global equity.

Therefore, this book advances the thesis that *digital autonomy* is not simply a developmental goal, but a geopolitical necessity. It is the crown of Sovereignty 2.0—an evolved model of state authority tailored for the technopolar era. Yet sovereignty without strategy is hollow. This is where *cognitive diplomacy* becomes indispensable: it is the tool that enables states not just to resist digital asymmetry, but to shape the algorithmic environment through anticipatory governance, strategic communication, and AI-enhanced foresight.

The chapters ahead explore this argument in depth. Throughout the book, the rise of the technopolar world is traced alongside the redefinition of sovereignty in the context of AI and digital infrastructure. The architecture of digital autonomy is examined through three strategic pillars: presence, practice, and resilience. The concept of cognitive diplomacy is then introduced as the keystone of sovereign agency in an era where perception is weaponized and reality increasingly shaped by computational systems. The book concludes with a set of forward-looking policy recommendations, aimed at equipping states, institutions, and diplomatic actors with the strategic tools and normative frameworks necessary to navigate the complexities of AI-driven global politics.

In doing so, *Digital Autonomy and Cognitive Diplomacy* offers not only a theoretical intervention, but also a roadmap for how states can reclaim agency, build strategic capacity, and govern with foresight in the age of artificial intelligence.

Ankara, Türkiye

Erman Akıllı

Acknowledgments As the author, this book has been quite a journey for me. It has been shaped and strengthened by the persistence, tenacity, and generosity of many individuals. Their support, friendship, and belief in this project have been a constant source of encouragement. I feel truly privileged to have had them with me along the way.

I would like to acknowledge the following:

- **Palgrave Macmillan**—for publishing this timely monograph, which addresses the pressing need for an authoritative analysis of Artificial Intelligence and its intersection with International Relations.
- **Dr. Anca Pusca**—for her expert guidance and profound support, without which this book would not have become a reality.
- **Aishwarya Balachandar**—for her valuable technical assistance in preparing the manuscript.
- **Prof. Corneliu Bjola**—for his generosity and intellectual courtesy in writing the foreword.
- **Prof. Nicholas Cull, Prof. Nancy Snow, and Prof. Jon-Hans Coetzer**—for their kind support in writing endorsements and for their long-standing contributions to the field of IR.
- **Sudib Sontoran**—for his meticulous proofreading and thoughtful input on copyediting.
- **Simay Sultan Doğan**—for her help with typesetting and ensuring the manuscript adhered to formatting and writing guidelines.

Most of all, I owe my deepest gratitude to my family. Their patience, encouragement, and unwavering support have sustained me throughout this demanding process. This book is dedicated to them, with heartfelt thanks.

Ankara, Türkiye　　　　Erman Akıllı

Competing Interests The author has no competing interests to declare that are relevant to the content of this manuscript.

Contents

About the Author

Prof. Dr. Erman Akıllı is currently serving as a faculty member in the Department of International Relations at Ankara Hacı Bayram Veli University, Türkiye. His areas of expertise include artificial intelligence in foreign policy, digital diplomacy, the Central Asia region, the Organization of Turkish States, soft power, and its sub-branches. Throughout his academic career, he has published articles in peer-reviewed journals indexed in SSCI and WOS; and has contributed as an author and editor to books published by prestigious publishing houses such as Palgrave MacMillan, Routledge, and Springer Nature. Additionally, he continues his work as an assistant editor for the *Insight Turkey* journal published by SETA.

Abbreviations

ABM	Agent-Based Modeling
AI	Artificial Intelligence
AML	Adversarial Machine Learning
ANN	Artificial Neural Networks
AWS	Amazon Web Services
BRI	Belt and Road Initiative
CBDC	Central Bank Digital Currencies
CCDCOE	Cooperative Cyber Defence Centre of Excellence
CCP	The Chinese Communist Party
CERTs	Computer Emergency Response Teams
CfA	Center for Analytics
CISA	Infrastructure Security Agency
CNNs	Convolutional Neural Networks
CSIRT	Computer Security Incident Response Teams
CSIS	Center for Strategic and International Studies
CSL	The Cybersecurity Law
DID	Decentralized Identifiers
DMA	Digital Markets Act
DNNs	Deep Neural Networks
DSA	Digital Services Act
DSL	The Data Security Law
DSR	Digital Silk Road
EEAS	European External Action Service
EU	The European Union
FCDO	Foreign, Commonwealth and Development Office
FTC	Federal Trade Commission

G7	Group of Seven
GDPR	General Data Protection Regulation
GFCE	Global Forum on Cyber Expertise
GGE	Group of Governmental Experts
HPC	High-Performance Computing
IAEA	International Atomic Energy Agency
ICEWS	Integrated Crisis Early Warning System
IMF	International Monetary Fund
INR	Intelligence and Research
IP	Intellectual Property
IPCEI	Important Projects of Common European Interest (IPCEI)
IR	International Relations
ISAC	Information Sharing and Analysis Centers
ITU	International Telecommunication Union
JASM	Japan Advanced Semiconductor Manufacturing
LAWS	Lethal Autonomous Weapons Systems
LGPD	General Data Protection Law
LLM	Large Language Model
MFAs	Ministries of Foreign Affairs
NATO	North Atlantic Treaty Organization
NEST	New and Emerging Strategic Technologies
NGO	Nongovernmental Organizations
NIS	The Network And Information Systems
NLP	Natural Language Processing
NSCAI	National Security Commission on AI
OECD	Organization for Economic Co-Operation and Development
OEWG	Open-Ended Working Group
PIPL	The Personal Information Protection Law
PLI	Production-Linked Incentive
RAN	Radio Access Network
SAR	Suspicious Activity Reporting
SSI	Self-Sovereign Identity
TSMC	Taiwan Semiconductor Manufacturing Company
TTC	Trade and Technology Council
UAE	United Arab Emirates
UK	The United Kingdom
UNCTAD	United Nations Conference on Trade and Development
UNESCO	United Nations Educational Scientific and Cultural Organization
UNITAR	United Nations Institute for Training and Research
US	The Unites States
VC	Verifiable Credentials
VPP	Virtual Power Plants
WIPO	The World Intellectual Property Organization
WTO	World Trade Organization
XAI	Explainable Artificial Intelligence

PART I

Why "Digital Autonomy" Matters?

CHAPTER 1

Introduction

The international system is at a crossroads today. The illusion of linear progress that briefly animated the post-Cold War imagination has given way to a sobering and far more complex reality. Rather than advancing toward a stable and peaceful global order, the world has entered an era of fragmentation, strategic competition, and pervasive uncertainty. Traditional power distribution has been upended and forces reshaping global order are increasingly diffuse, dynamic, and volatile.

Viewed from the vantage point of 2025, the international landscape can be characterized by deepening instability and rivalry. The succession of crises over the past decades including full-scale wars, persistent regional conflicts, transnational terrorism, global pandemics, climate change, and mass displacement of people has exposed the international system's structural fragilities. Far from stabilizing, the post-Cold War order has revealed new fault lines and revived long-standing insecurities. The international system has undergone and is undergoing profound transformations. It will continue to evolve in ways that fundamentally reshape the distribution of power.

This turbulent reality is not an anomaly, but a structural feature of international politics. In mainstream International Relations (IR) theory, the international arena remains defined by anarchy: a condition where no central authority exists to enforce rules or adjudicate disputes. Realist scholars interpret this anarchy as a perpetual struggle for survival and

E. Akıllı, *Cognitive Diplomacy and Digital Autonomy*,
https://doi.org/10.1007/978-3-032-04470-9_1

relative advantage, where states must prioritize security and power. Constructivist theorists, on the other hand, argue that anarchy is not an immutable reality, but a social construction shaped by the interactions and shared meanings of states. As famously articulated by Alexander Wendt: "*Anarchy is what states make of it*" (1992).

Theoretical orientation aside, one constant persists: challenges to order, stability, and security remain among the enduring features of the international system. States are not passive participants but strategic actors engaged in a perpetual contest where adaptation is imperative and complacency perilous. In this dynamic environment, the capacity to harness transformative technologies has become a critical determinant of national power and strategic relevance. The states that recognize the indivisibility of technological and political sovereignty will shape the twenty-first century. Among these transformative forces, artificial intelligence (AI) has emerged as perhaps the most consequential, redefining the parameters of power, influence, and autonomy in global affairs.

AI represents a constellation of technologies enabling machines to perform tasks that typically require human intelligence, like learning, reasoning, problem-solving, perception, and decision-making (Russell and Norvig, 2021). At its core, AI seeks to replicate or simulate cognitive functions, often leveraging techniques like machine learning, where systems learn from data without explicit programming. It can also utilize deep learning, a subset that uses human brain-inspired complex neural networks to identify intricate patterns. This capacity for autonomous learning and adaptation distinguishes AI from traditional software, making it a transformative force across diverse domains.

The journey of AI has been marked by cycles of ambitious vision, significant breakthroughs, and periodical reassessment. Although its conceptual roots can be traced back centuries, the field formally emerged in the mid-twentieth century. In 1950, Alan Turing introduced the concept of machine intelligence in his seminal paper "Computing Machinery and Intelligence," proposing the Turing Test as a criterion for machine cognition (Turing, 1950). It catalyzed interest in the potential of machines to emulate human thought processes. However, AI as a distinct field was formally established in 1956 with the Dartmouth Summer Research Project on Artificial Intelligence, organized by John McCarthy and colleagues. Besides coining the term "Artificial Intelligence," this conference also set the research agenda for decades to come (McCarthy et al., 1955).

Throughout AI's *Belle Époque*, the following decades were marked by several key milestones. For instance, the development of the Logic Theorist by Newell and Simon in 1956 demonstrated that machines could perform logical reasoning tasks, laying the groundwork for automated problem-solving (Newell and Simon, 1956). Similarly, in 1966, Joseph Weizenbaum's ELIZA program illustrated early natural language processing capabilities by simulating human-like conversations (1966).

The field, however, faced periods of stagnation, notably during the "AI winters" of the 1970s and late 1980s, when it suffered from funding cuts and skepticism over unmet expectations (Crevier, 1993). These periods underscored the inherent challenges of replicating human intelligence. The twenty-first-century resurgence of AI, meanwhile, can be attributed to advancements in computational power, the availability of large datasets, and the development of sophisticated algorithms. Notably, the success of deep learning techniques, such as convolutional neural networks, has driven AI applications' success in image and speech recognition (LeCun et al., 2015).

Today, AI as a comprehensive framework of advanced technologies empowers machines to perform tasks that traditionally required human cognitive abilities, often exceeding human efficiency and capacity. By enabling extensive dataset analysis, refining vast quantities of visual, and textual information, and facilitating decision-making based on complex contextual variables, AI has emerged as a transformative force across various fields, including IR, diplomacy, foreign policy decision-making, and national security.

In the realm of IR and diplomacy, AI offers unprecedented capabilities in real-time data analysis, enabling policymakers to assess geopolitical developments, monitor international trends, and anticipate potential conflicts with unparalleled precision. For foreign policy decision-making, AI-driven models provide strategic insights by synthesizing vast amounts of intelligence, evaluating scenarios, and offering evidence-based recommendations. Similarly, in national security, AI enhances threat detection, cyber-defense mechanisms, and surveillance capabilities, thereby strengthening a state's ability to safeguard its sovereignty and protect critical infrastructure.

AI's integration into these domains redefines the speed and accuracy of decision-making processes. It also introduces new dimensions of strategic autonomy and resilience in addressing global challenges, making it an indispensable modern governance tool. AI technologies hold remarkable potential to transform diplomacy, decision-making, and information analysis. A particularly striking application lies in diplomacy, where AI can significantly improve information gathering and analysis. With the capacity to efficiently process vast amounts of data—from news articles and social media activity to public sentiment—AI provides diplomats with real-time insights and the ability to quickly discern trends. These tools enable policymakers to make more informed decisions and adapt their strategies in response to evolving circumstances.

However, the integration of AI into diplomacy demands a cautious and thoughtful approach, guided by ethical considerations. Diplomacy is inherently rooted in moral judgment, trust-building, and a deep understanding of cultural contexts—elements that machines cannot fully replicate. While AI can improve efficiency and provide valuable analytical support, it should complement human decision-making, rather than attempt to replace it. Ensuring transparency, accountability, and respect for privacy are essential to maintaining the integrity of diplomatic processes when deploying AI tools.

At the same time, AI's limitations raise some critical ethical and practical questions. Consider a scenario where an AI system tasked with making foreign policy decisions concludes that a *casus belli* (justification for war) is the only viable response to a situation, regardless of the potential for diplomatic negotiation and de-escalation. Such an outcome highlights the risks of relying too heavily on AI, which processes information in binary terms and lacks the capacity for moral reasoning. Decisions made solely within the confines of algorithms, risk overlooking the profound human implications of a conflict, including life-and-death consequences. This underscores the critical need for robust safeguards and human oversight to prevent such unintended outcomes. Thus, despite AI's power to revolutionize diplomacy and decision-making, it must be integrated with care. By positioning AI as an aid to human expertise, rather than a substitute, we can harness its strengths while mitigating risks. In doing so, AI can serve as a transformative tool that supports the essential human dimensions of diplomacy and foreign policy in an increasingly complex world.

Consequently, AI has rapidly transitioned from a purely technical discipline into a critical element of the international system and a key determinant of state power. Its applications in national security range from intelligence analysis and autonomous weapons systems to cybersecurity and predictive threat modeling.

Economically, AI drives innovation, reshapes industries through automation, and influences global competitiveness. Furthermore, AI's role in shaping information environments, enabling sophisticated disinformation campaigns, and raising fundamental questions about data governance and algorithmic bias places it squarely at the center of contemporary international relations. It is no longer merely a tool but a strategic asset and a domain of competition, fundamentally altering the landscape of global power dynamics. As AI's capabilities expanded, so did its geopolitical significance. Initially confined to economic and scientific applications, AI has now become deeply embedded in matters of national security, diplomacy, and global governance (Bartoletti, 2020).

Meanwhile, AI's political economy reveals stark disparities between nations. Countries in the Global South often face significant challenges in accessing AI technologies, leading to dependencies on external providers, and exacerbating existing inequalities. This dependency risks entrenching a form of digital colonialism, where technological advancements are unevenly distributed, and decision-making power is concentrated in the hands of a few dominant actors (Research ICT Africa, 2024).

The governance of AI has also become a contested arena. States, international organizations, and private entities vie to establish norms and standards that align with their strategic interests. The lack of a unified global framework has led to fragmented approaches, with some nations advocating for stringent regulations to ensure ethical use, while others have prioritized rapid innovation over comprehensive oversight (Carnegie Endowment for International Peace, 2024).

Private technology firms, particularly those based in the United States (U.S.) and China, have emerged as influential players in AI development and deployment. These companies not only drive technological innovation but also shape the ethical and operational standards of AI applications. Their significant resources and global reach grant them a quasi-sovereign status, allowing them to influence international policies and practices (Transcend, 2024).

The risks of technological dependence are multifaceted. Reliance on foreign AI technologies can expose nations to vulnerabilities, including data breaches, surveillance, and loss of control over critical infrastructure. Such dependencies can undermine national security and limit a state's ability to act autonomously in the digital realm (The Conversation, 2024).

Apart from that, ethical considerations surrounding AI are paramount. Issues such as algorithmic bias, lack of transparency, and potential misuse in surveillance and warfare raise concerns about the societal impacts of AI. Ensuring that AI development aligns with human rights and democratic values is essential to prevent harm and promote equitable outcomes (UNESCO, 2024).

In this context, the concept of technopolarity has gained prominence. Technopolarity refers to a global order where technological capabilities and control over digital infrastructure become primary determinants of power, often surpassing traditional geopolitical factors. This shift underscores the importance of technological sovereignty and the need for states to assert control over their digital ecosystems (Bremmer, 2023).

Advanced technologies are no longer confined to economic or military domains; they constitute the critical infrastructure of governance, influence, and strategic autonomy. From cybersecurity and quantum computing to AI and metaverse, the new frontiers of innovation are the arenas where global hierarchies will be contested and redrawn. States that remain dependent on external technological ecosystems risk exposing themselves to vulnerabilities that compromise national security, economic resilience, and diplomatic agency.

The digital revolution is not a phenomenon of the future, it is actively reshaping the foundations of global power today. According to 2025 statistics, slightly more than 5 billion people are actively participating in digital ecosystems—sharing information, influencing public opinion, organizing collective action, and mobilizing political movements. As a result, societies, economies, and political systems are being reengineered in real-time. Global internet penetration has reached approximately 67% of the world's population, while active social media users represent around 62% (International Telecommunication Union, 2024; DataReportal, 2025). Given that the global population in 2025 is estimated at approximately 8.1 billion (United Nations, Department of Economic and Social Affairs, Population Division, 2022), these figures illustrate that a substantial majority of humanity is now integrated into digital networks.

Considering statistics, digitalization has become the principal axis around which modern statecraft revolves. Digital transformation is no longer merely a matter of economic competitiveness or administrative efficiency, it has become a fundamental question of sovereignty, security, and survival. Moreover, according to North Atlantic Treaty Organization's (NATO) Science and Technology Trends 2025–2045 report, AI and quantum technologies are projected to become two of the most strategically contested domains over the coming decades. These emerging technologies are expected to transform a wide range of sectors, particularly defense, by enabling advanced capabilities in data processing, autonomous decision-making, and ultra-secure communications (NATO, 2025). The report underscores that nations possessing leadership in AI and quantum systems will hold a significant strategic advantage in anticipating and responding to future threats. However, achieving technological supremacy in these fields requires sustained investment in digital infrastructure, access to large-scale and high-quality datasets, and the systematic cultivation of highly skilled technical talent (NATO, 2025).

Consequently, the critical importance of digital autonomy emerges as a strategic imperative. It is within this context of accelerated transformation and heightened contestation that digital autonomy must be understood—not as a luxury or a theoretical aspiration, but as a necessary pillar of national strategy for states seeking to preserve agency and influence in a rapidly fragmenting world. Digital autonomy refers to a state or actor's ability to independently design, govern, and protect its digital ecosystem by its own values, interests, and strategic objectives.

Digital autonomy must be understood not as an abstract aspiration, but as a strategic imperative born in response to the entrenched realities of digital asymmetry. In the evolving global order, critical access to technologies such as high-performance computing (HPC), sovereign cloud infrastructure, secure telecommunications networks, and advanced AI research is increasingly monopolized by a small group of powerful states and corporate actors. This concentration of digital capability generates systemic dependencies that sharply constrain the policy space and technological sovereignty of digitally peripheral nations. Such asymmetries render states vulnerable not only to cyber intrusions and foreign surveillance, but also to forms of economic coercion and normative exclusion in international fora. If left unchecked, digital asymmetry risks solidifying into a new architecture of structural inequality, one in which digitally disenfranchised states are relegated to passive roles in a system governed by the technological preferences and political interests of a privileged few. Addressing this imbalance is therefore essential to reclaiming national agency and reconstituting a more equitable digital international order.

Thus, digital autonomy has evolved from a theoretical aspiration into a strategic imperative. In an international environment increasingly shaped by AI, digital infrastructures, and transnational data flows, digital autonomy can be understood as a state or actor's capacity to independently design, regulate, and safeguard its digital ecosystem in alignment with its own values, interests, and strategic objectives. This form of autonomy may be conceptualized through three interrelated pillars: presence, practice, and resilience.

Presence encompasses more than mere connectivity. It refers to the establishment of a sovereign digital footprint, including ownership or control of critical assets like cloud infrastructure and data centers, as well as the ability to assert national identity and normative values within digital spaces. Practice, on the other hand, denotes the capability to innovate, regulate, and deploy emerging technologies—particularly AI—in a manner that advances national development goals and diplomatic agendas. Finally, resilience refers to the ability to withstand external technological pressures, cyberthreats, and systemic dependencies that may jeopardize political sovereignty and strategic autonomy.

In diplomacy, digital autonomy becomes a force multiplier. AI is not only changing how decisions are made but also who gets to make them. From algorithmically mediated negotiations to AI-driven geopolitical risk assessments, diplomacy is becoming increasingly entangled with technological systems. Without digital autonomy, states risk relying on black-box technologies developed and governed by external powers, potentially embedding foreign interests into their core decision-making processes. Digital autonomy enables states to engage as equals in global tech governance, shape international norms on AI, and protect the integrity of diplomacy itself from manipulation, surveillance, and algorithmic asymmetry. In this sense, digital autonomy is not isolation, but it is the foundation for meaningful participation in the digital global order. As mentioned above, digital autonomy rests upon three interlinked pillars: presence, practice, and resilience.

Presence signifies more than mere participation in digital spaces. It demands the establishment of a sovereign digital footprint, encompassing ownership of critical infrastructures such as cloud networks, data centers, and communication platforms, and the assertion of national identity, values, and norms within the digital ecosystem.

Practice encompasses the capacity to innovate, regulate, and deploy emerging technologies, particularly artificial intelligence, in ways that advance national interests, diplomatic priorities, and societal well-being. States must not rely solely on technologies developed elsewhere, rather, they must foster indigenous ecosystems of innovation that are aligned with their strategic vision.

Resilience refers to the ability to withstand technological coercion, cyberthreats, systemic shocks, dependencies, and disruptions that can undermine political autonomy and strategic flexibility. Building digital resilience is now indispensable for safeguarding national sovereignty.

As the world accelerates into the digital century, digital autonomy will increasingly delineate the boundaries between dependence and sovereignty, between marginalization and influence. In the era where technological mastery and strategic independence are fundamentally intertwined, the ability to assert digital autonomy is not merely advantageous, it is existential. Yet a critical question remains: how can states cultivate and operationalize the three pillars of digital autonomy—presence, practice, and resilience—within a technopolar international system?

The answer lies in the emergence of ***Cognitive Diplomacy***. It represents the convergence of artificial intelligence and international relations, integrating cognitive strategies and advanced AI technologies to enhance diplomatic practice, decision-making processes, and statecraft. Rooted in the architecture of deep learning and artificial neural networks (ANNs), Cognitive Diplomacy mirrors the complex, adaptive functions of biological nervous systems, enabling states to process vast streams of data, recognize patterns, and forecast geopolitical dynamics with unprecedented sophistication.

Through the framework of Cognitive Diplomacy, states can elevate their digital autonomy. It refers to the emerging paradigm of statecraft where human judgment and artificial intelligence operate within a hybrid intelligence ecosystem. This integrative domain is characterized by dynamic and symbiotic interaction between human and machine intelligence—each augmenting the other's cognitive capacities. By fostering the symbiotic integration of human judgment and machine intelligence, Cognitive Diplomacy offers a framework through which governments can unlock enhanced presence, refine practice, and build systemic resilience—the three foundational pillars—in navigating the complexities of an AI-driven global order. Without cognitive diplomacy, it is impossible to reach cognitive presence, practice, and resilience in the digital plane, and thus establishing digital autonomy becomes unachievable. Cognitive Diplomacy offers strategic tools to navigate the complexity of global

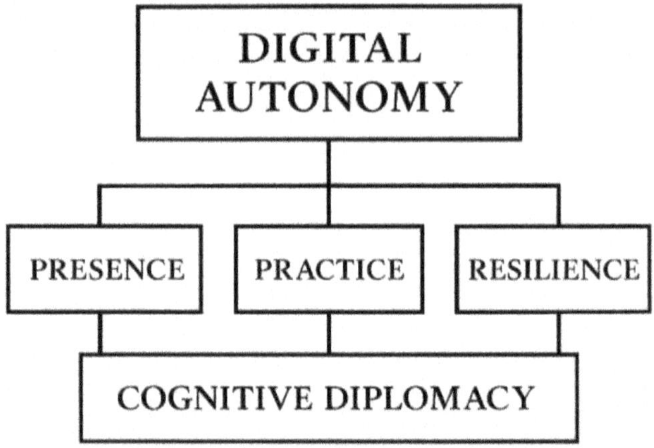

Fig. 1.1 Digital Autonomy Breakdown—Prepared by Author

affairs with greater foresight, anticipate emergent challenges, and exercise agency in a system increasingly shaped by algorithmic processes. It empowers diplomatic actors to engage proactively with the evolving realities of AI-mediated international relations, enhancing both strategic vision and tactical agility (Fig. 1.1).

Cognitive Diplomacy, therefore, is not an ancillary concept, it is the essential keystone that crowns the grand architecture of digital autonomy. In a world where information flows at the speed of light and decision-making is increasingly augmented by artificial cognition, the integration of cognitive diplomatic strategies will define the future contours of sovereign agency, diplomatic influence, and strategic survival. Thus, in a technopolar world, digital autonomy stands as the last resort of power. It is the shield that preserves sovereignty, and Cognitive Diplomacy is the sword of strategic agency.

1.1 Introduction

1.2 AI and Diplomacy: Specialized Academic Literature

The intersection of AI and diplomacy constitutes one of the most urgent and transformative frontiers in international relations today. As states grapple with the far-reaching implications of AI for sovereignty, negotiation, and global power dynamics, both scholars and practitioners have begun to construct a foundational body of literature to interpret, critique, and operationalize these changes.

A coherent body of scholarship has emerged to define how AI reshapes the tools and logic of diplomacy. Among the most empirically grounded contributions is Stanzel and Voelsen's *Diplomacy and Artificial Intelligence: Reflections on Practical Assistance for Diplomatic Negotiations* (2022). This study offers a sophisticated analysis of how AI can support scenario development, data interpretation, and strategic foresight within diplomatic contexts. Drawing on historical case studies—including the German-Austrian customs union negotiations of 1929–1930 and recent UN cybercrime resolutions—the authors demonstrate AI's capacity to model negotiation options. Importantly, they emphasize that while AI can complement decision-making, it cannot replace the nuance and discretion of experienced diplomats.

In a broader conceptual vein, *Artificial Intelligence and Emerging Technologies in International Relations* (Ndzendze and Marwala, 2023) situates AI within a wider technological assemblage that includes blockchain, additive manufacturing, 5G infrastructure, and the Internet of Things. This text examines how these innovations recalibrate global power by altering patterns of trade, conflict, and influence. It highlights the unequal diffusion of such technologies and argues for the urgent need to create multilateral governance frameworks capable of managing these asymmetries in the Fourth Industrial Revolution.

Recent publications aim to connect theory to practice by offering operational frameworks for AI in diplomacy. *AI and Diplomacy: International Relations in the Era of Disruptive Technologies*, produced by SELA (2024), provides a bilingual, practitioner-oriented guide to AI's role in negotiation, cyber diplomacy, and international cooperation. It underscores the importance of capacity-building and diplomatic training in the digital era.

Complementing this is *AI Diplomacy: Insights and Innovations from the Bilateral Navigator* (Grgic, 2025), which explores the transformative potential of AI for bilateral relations. Inspired by experimental diplomatic platforms, it introduces actionable tools to help states apply AI in trust-building, treaty compliance, and dynamic strategy formation. Both publications indicate that AI's value lies not in replacing diplomats, but in augmenting statecraft amid rising complexity and uncertainty.

The forthcoming *Routledge Handbook of Artificial Intelligence and International Relations* (2025) is poised to become a landmark reference for the field. Bringing together leading scholars, technologists, and policymakers, it addresses critical debates on ethical AI governance, algorithmic warfare, predictive diplomacy, and human-machine collaboration in peacebuilding. By assembling interdisciplinary perspectives, the handbook highlights the urgency of rethinking the institutional and normative architectures of global governance in light of intelligent systems.

To anchor these contemporary developments within a broader historical arc, Jovan Kurbalija's *History of Diplomacy and Technology: From Smoke Signals to Artificial Intelligence* (2024) offers a panoramic view of how innovations have shaped diplomacy from ancient times to the present. Kurbalija argues that while each new technology has altered the practice of diplomacy, the core functions of dialogue, negotiation, and mediation remain constant. His work situates AI not as a rupture, but as a continuation of diplomacy's technological evolution—albeit one with unprecedented scale and epistemic consequences.

Wider literature on artificial intelligence offers indispensable insights into the societal and ethical dimensions of emerging technologies. Max Tegmark's *Life 3.0: Being Human in the Age of Artificial Intelligence* (2017), a widely acclaimed popular science text, outlines possible futures shaped by AI, ranging from human flourishing to existential risk. The book examines the role of AI in crime, employment, war, and social order, emphasizing the profound stakes of technological design choices made today.

Stuart Russell's *Human Compatible* (2019) offers a more technical critique of AI's alignment with human values. Russell challenges the dominant model of goal-maximizing AI and proposes a paradigm focused on uncertainty and human preference. His work has become central to global debates on AI safety, ethics, and regulatory innovation.

Kai-Fu Lee's *AI Superpowers* (2018) is a seminal text in understanding the geopolitical dimensions of AI, particularly the accelerating competition between the United States and China. Lee argues that AI is not only an economic force but a geopolitical accelerator, reshaping global hierarchies and labor markets. His predictions about job displacement and techno-nationalism have informed debates about strategic autonomy and digital sovereignty.

Nick Bostrom's *Superintelligence: Paths, Dangers, Strategies* (2014) remains one of the most academically rigorous treatments of long-term AI scenarios. While speculative, it has shaped much of the contemporary literature on risk governance, arguing for proactive institutional safeguards to prevent catastrophic outcomes from future AI systems with general intelligence capabilities.

Critical scholarship has expanded the debate by examining the material, social, and ecological dimensions of artificial intelligence. Kate Crawford's *Atlas of AI* (2021) deconstructs the narrative of AI as purely virtual, exposing the extractive infrastructures—minerals, energy, labor—that underpin data systems. Through ethnographic fieldwork and political analysis, Crawford frames AI as a planetary system of power and inequality, emphasizing the global externalities often hidden in the discourse of innovation.

Ivana Bartoletti's *An Artificial Revolution: On Power, Politics & AI* (2025) offers a feminist and political analysis of algorithmic systems. She examines how AI may entrench racial, gender, and economic biases unless governed by transparent legal frameworks and democratic oversight. Her call for a politicization of AI ethics underscores the importance of protecting human rights in the age of algorithmic governance.

1.3 Positioning the Book in the Literature

While the existing literature offers rich insights into the technological, geopolitical, and ethical implications of AI, this book introduces an original conceptual and strategic framework that extends the field. *Cognitive Diplomacy and Digital Autonomy: "Statecraft in the Age of Artificial Intelligence"* contributes in three distinctive ways.

First, it introduces the concept of cognitive diplomacy, offering a new lens through which to understand diplomacy in the AI age. Unlike most analyses that focus on AI as a tool for data analysis or automation, this book explores how AI reshapes the cognitive environments in which diplomacy is practiced. It examines how perception, strategy formation, and narrative construction are increasingly influenced by machine cognition, transforming the epistemic foundations of statecraft.

Second, the book places the Global South and middle powers at the center of analysis. It addresses how these actors navigate digital asymmetries, build strategic autonomy, and engage in norm entrepreneurship in global AI governance debates. In doing so, it offers a counterbalance to literature dominated by the US-China duality.

Third, this work bridges academic theory with strategic practice. Drawing on real-world case studies, policy blueprints, and institutional innovation, it offers practical guidance for diplomats, technologists, and public officials seeking to responsibly harness AI in service of ethical, inclusive, and resilient diplomacy. By reframing diplomacy as a cognitive practice in a technopolar world, this book advances a novel and actionable paradigm for understanding and shaping the future of global order.

1.4 Objectives and Scope of the Book

The digital revolution has fundamentally reshaped the foundations of global power. The boundaries between the physical and virtual worlds are increasingly porous, and the infrastructure of international relations is now deeply embedded within digital systems, data flows, and algorithmic governance. AI, advanced analytics, and emerging technologies offer states unprecedented capabilities to enhance decision-making, predict risks, and exert strategic influence. In this transformed environment, digital autonomy is not merely advantageous—it is essential for safeguarding sovereignty, ensuring security, and exercising agency on the global stage.

This book, ***Digital Autonomy and Cognitive Diplomacy: Statecraft in the Age of Artificial Intelligence***, offers a comprehensive framework for understanding and navigating the emerging technopolar world. It explores how the global divide in digital infrastructure, intensifying technological rivalries, and the integration of AI into diplomacy and governance are reshaping the international system. At the core of this analysis is the concept of digital autonomy—the ability of states to design, govern, and protect their digital ecosystems in line with their values and strategic interests.

The objectives of this book are threefold:

To Define and Conceptualize Digital Autonomy: Providing a clear, comprehensive understanding of digital autonomy as a foundational pillar of sovereignty in the AI era, and distinguishing it from existing notions of technological power or digital sovereignty.

To Analyze the Role of AI and Digital Infrastructure in Redefining Sovereignty: Investigating how AI, semiconductor supply chains, cloud systems, and data governance regimes are transforming traditional conceptions of sovereignty, influencing how states protect their autonomy in a fragmented digital landscape.

To Establish Cognitive Diplomacy as the Keystone of Strategic Agency: Introducing the concept of cognitive diplomacy—the integration of AI and cognitive strategies into diplomatic practice—and analyzing how cognitive diplomacy serves as the dynamic force that enables states to project influence (presence), adapt rapidly (practice), and survive strategically (resilience) in the competitive arenas of the technopolar world.

1.5 Structure of the Book

This book is organized into five interlinked parts, each addressing a critical dimension of the contemporary struggle for digital autonomy in the age of artificial intelligence and rapid technological change. Together, they offer a comprehensive framework for understanding how states can navigate the profound geopolitical transformations of what may now be called the *technopolar era*.

Part II: The Rise of Technopolarity–Redefinition of Sovereignty in the Digital Age.

After the Part I: Introduction, this opening section lays the conceptual and historical foundation for understanding the structural transformations of global power in the era of artificial intelligence and digital infrastructure. It introduces the notion of the *technopolar world;* a geopolitical landscape increasingly shaped not only by conventional state capabilities, but by technological leadership, control over data ecosystems, and the strategic deployment of AI. In this environment, corporate platforms and algorithmic systems are no longer peripheral actors; they have become central to the exercise of international influence and the negotiation of global norms.

The section then turns to the evolving nature of sovereignty itself. Drawing on the legacy of the Westphalian order, it examines how emerging technologies are eroding the traditional boundaries of state authority. As AI-driven decision-making, transnational data flows, and digital dependencies intensify, the classical model of sovereignty—rooted in territorial control and legal jurisdiction—faces profound challenges. In response, this section argues for a reconceptualization of sovereignty that accounts for informational autonomy, algorithmic agency, and the governance of digital interdependence. Together, these chapters offer a framework for understanding how power, legitimacy, and agency are being reconfigured in the digital age.

Part III: The Pillars of Digital Autonomy presents the essential building blocks required for states to secure and project digital sovereignty. I define digital autonomy through three interdependent pillars: presence, practice, and resilience. Presence concerns the capacity to assert a sovereign digital footprint, encompassing critical infrastructure, cloud sovereignty, and normative identity within cyberspace. Practice refers to the ability to innovate, regulate, and harness emerging technologies, particularly artificial intelligence, in alignment with national interests and diplomatic priorities. Resilience, the final pillar, is understood as the capability to withstand external technological coercion, mitigate cyberthreats, and reduce dependencies that may compromise strategic autonomy. Together, these pillars form a comprehensive model through which states can build institutional, technological, and regulatory strength in an increasingly contested digital landscape.

Part IV: Cognitive Diplomacy—The Sword of Strategic Agency in the Technopolar World establishes cognitive diplomacy as the essential keystone crowning the architecture of digital autonomy. As artificial intelligence increasingly augments cognitive processes through predictive analytics, anomaly detection, and decision-support systems, diplomatic practice itself is being reshaped. This section explores how AI-enhanced cognition enables states to move beyond reactive foreign policy toward proactive strategic leadership. It argues that the strategic deployment of AI-driven insights, combined with adaptive and targeted communication, is redefining influence and agency in global affairs, particularly in contested digital spaces.

Part V: Conclusion.

The conclusion of *Digital Autonomy and Cognitive Diplomacy* reflects on the emergence of a technopolar world, where geopolitical power is increasingly defined by digital infrastructures, AI capabilities, and algorithmic control. As states navigate this shifting terrain, the challenge of ensuring transparency, accountability, and legitimacy in algorithmic governance becomes paramount. The book underscores the need for ethical, human-centric AI systems guided by inclusive norms that reflect global diversity, particularly elevating perspectives from the Global South. It offers a focused set of policy recommendations, including institutional reforms, investment in AI literacy, cross-sector collaboration, digital capacity-building, and the creation of interoperable governance frameworks that balance innovation with sovereignty. Looking ahead, the concept of neurodiplomacy is introduced as a frontier where AI and cognitive science merge to create adaptive, anticipatory diplomatic systems. The final section offers a forward-looking reflection, urging future generations to build a digital order rooted in sovereignty, empathy, and shared responsibility.

Through this comprehensive exploration, the book seeks to establish digital autonomy and cognitive diplomacy as cornerstones of modern statecraft. It aims to equip policymakers, diplomats, scholars, and strategists with the conceptual tools and actionable strategies necessary to thrive in a world where technological sovereignty, cognitive advantage, and resilient diplomacy will determine international standing. As the digital order fragments along new lines of infrastructure, influence, and ideology, mastering the dynamics of technopolarity and building enduring digital autonomy will be among the defining challenges and opportunities of twenty-first-century international relations. Thus, in the technopolar world, ***digital autonomy*** stands as the last resort; the shield that preserves sovereignty while ***cognitive diplomacy*** stands as the sword of strategic agency.

Bibliography

Bartoletti, I. (2020). *An artificial revolution: On power, politics & AI*. The Indigo Press.

Bostrom, N. (2014). *Superintelligence: Paths, Dangers, Strategies*. Oxford University Press.

Bremmer, I. (2023). *Technopolarity: The New Global Order*. Eurasia Group. https://www.eurasiagroup.net/files/upload/Technopolarity.pdf
Carnegie Endowment for International Peace. (2024). *Envisioning a Global Regime Complex to Govern Artificial Intelligence*. https://carnegieendowment.org/2024/03/21/envisioning-global-regime-complex-to-govern-artificial-intelligence-pub-92022
Crawford, K. (2021). *Atlas of AI: Power, politics, and the planetary costs of artificial intelligence*. Yale University Press.
Crevier, D. (1993). *AI: The tumultuous history of the search for artificial intelligence*. Basic Books.
DataReportal. (2025). *Digital 2025: Global Overview Report*. Retrieved April 27, 2025, from https://datareportal.com
Grgic, S. (2025). *AI Diplomacy: Insights and Innovations from the Bilateral Navigator*. [online] Amazon. ISBN 9798305485523. Retrieved June 13, 2025, from https://www.amazon.com/AI-Diplomacy-Innovations-Bilateral-Navigator/dp/B0DS153JVP or https://ssrn.com/abstract=5196262 or https://doi.org/10.2139/ssrn.5196262
International Telecommunication Union. (2024). *Measuring digital development: Facts and figures 2024*. ITU.
Kurbalija, J. (2024). *History of diplomacy and technology: From smoke signals to artificial intelligence*. DiploFoundation.
Latin American and Caribbean Economic System (SELA) (2024). *AI and Diplomacy: International Relations in the Era of Disruptive Technologies*. SELA. ISBN 978–980-6458-31-4. Retrieved June 13, 2025, from https://www.sela.org/wp-content/uploads/2024/11/AI-and-Diplomacy-International-relations-in-the-era-of-disruptive-technologies.pdf
LeCun, Y., Bengio, Y., & Hinton, G. (2015). Deep learning. *Nature, 521*(7553), 436–444.
Lee, K.-F. (2018). *AI superpowers: China, Silicon Valley, and the New World order*. Houghton Mifflin Harcourt.
McCarthy, J., Minsky, M., Rochester, N., & Shannon, C. E. (1955). *A Proposal for the Dartmouth Summer Research Project on Artificial Intelligence*. http://raysolomonoff.com/dartmouth/boxa/dart564props.pdf
NATO. (2025). *Science and Technology Trends 2025–2045: Exploring the S&T Edge*. NATO Science and Technology Organization. Retrieved May 15, 2025, from https://www.nato.int/nato_static_fl2014/assets/pdf/2025/4/pdf/250409-STO-Trends-en.pdf
Ndzendze, B., & Marwala, T. (2023). *Artificial intelligence and international relations theories*. Palgrave. https://doi.org/10.1007/978-981-19-4877-0
Newell, A., & Simon, H. A. (1956). The logic theory machine: A complex information processing system. *IRE Transactions on Information Theory, 2*(3), 61–79.

Research ICT Africa, (2024). *The Political Economy of African AI*. Retrieved June 13, 2025, from https://researchictafrica.net/wp-content/uploads/2024/09/The-Political-Economy-of-African-AI_Research-Paper_AJAI_2405.pdf

Russell, S. (2019). *Human compatible: Artificial intelligence and the problem of control*. Viking.

Russell, S., & Norvig, P. (2021). *Artificial intelligence: A modern approach* (4th ed.). Pearson.

Silver, D., Huang, A., Maddison, C. J., Guez, A., Sifre, L., Van Den Driessche, G., Schrittwieser, J., Antonoglou, I., Panneershelvam, V., Lanctot, M., Dieleman, S., Grewe, D., Nham, J., Kalchbrenner, N., Sutskever, I., Lillicrap, T., Leach, M., Kavukcuoglu, K., Graepel, T., & Hassabis, D. (2016). Mastering the game of go with deep neural networks and tree search. *Nature, 529*(7587), 484–489.

Tegmark, M. (2017). *Life 3.0: Being human in the age of artificial intelligence*. Alfred A. Knopf.

The Conversation, (2024). *There are major risks, but also solutions for AI in the Global South*. Retrieved June 13, 2025, from https://theconversation.com/there-are-major-risks-but-also-solutions-for-ai-in-the-global-south-241172

Transcend. (2024). *Big Tech's Evolving Role in AI Governance: Shaping Ethical Standards*. Transcend. https://transcend.io/blog/big-tech-ai-governance

Turing, A. M. (1950). Computing machinery and intelligence. *Mind, 59*(236), 433–460.

UNESCO, 2024. *Recommendation on the Ethics of Artificial Intelligence*. Retrieved June 13, 2025, from https://www.unesco.org/en/artificial-intelligence/recommendation-ethics

United Nations, Department of Economic and Social Affairs, Population Division. (2022). *World population prospects 2022: Summary of results*. United Nations.

Weizenbaum, J. (1966). ELIZA—A Computer program for the study of natural language communication between man and machine. *Communications of the ACM, 9*(1), 36–45.

Wendt, A. (1992). Anarchy is what states make of it: The social construction of power politics. *International Organization, 46*(2), 391–425.

PART II

The Rise of Technopolarity

CHAPTER 2

Re-Defining Technopolar World

As global politics enters an era of accelerated technological transformation, it is fundamentally restructuring traditional paradigms of power, sovereignty, and governance. To encapsulate this evolving reality, I would like to introduce the concept of the ***technopolar world:*** a systemic and structural reframing of the international order, wherein technological infrastructure, algorithmic authority, and digital sovereignty constitute the primary axes of geopolitical competition and agency (Akıllı, 2025a). This framework departs from and builds upon existing interpretations, most notably Ian Bremmer's ***technopolar moment***, which describes the increasing influence of technology companies ***vis-à-vis*** the state.

Bremmer's "technopolar moment" refers to a transitional period where a handful of powerful technology firms—such as Alphabet, Meta, and Tencent—surpass nation-states in their capacity to shape norms, public opinion, and even geopolitical outcomes (2022). In his account, these firms operate beyond the reach of national regulation and effectively exercise sovereign-like authority over digital public goods. While this insight is crucial in diagnosing the asymmetry between state and corporate power in the digital domain, it remains temporally bounded and actor-specific.

In his article *The Technopolar Moment*, Ian Bremmer (2021) draws attention to the events surrounding the end of Donald Trump's first term as president, particularly the storming of the U.S. Capitol on January 6, 2021. Bremmer highlights how this moment marked a significant shift

E. Akıllı, *Cognitive Diplomacy and Digital Autonomy*,
https://doi.org/10.1007/978-3-032-04470-9_2

in the balance of power between states and technology companies. In response to the events, major tech platforms like Facebook and Twitter (now X under Elon Musk) suspended President Trump's accounts, citing his support for and incitement of the protestors and rioters. Bremmer further notes that Google, Apple, and Amazon collectively de-platformed the social media app Parler, widely used by Trump supporters for organizing and communication. This included removing the app from digital storefronts and cutting off its web-hosting capabilities. In addition to these information-control measures, Bremmer also highlights the financial dimension of this technopolitical response: fintech platforms such as PayPal and Stripe ceased processing payments for Trump-affiliated fundraising efforts. According to Bremmer, these coordinated actions illustrate how technology companies exercised sovereign-like powers in the digital and financial realms, effectively sidelining an elected political leader without state intervention.

As of June 2025, the world is once again witnessing Donald Trump serving a second term as the U.S. President, prompting renewed questions about the stability of democratic institutions and the evolving role of technology companies in political processes. Reflecting on the events of January 6, 2021, Bremmer (2021) argues that major tech platforms acted autonomously—exercising sovereign-like judgment—when they suspended President Trump's accounts and curtailed digital platforms such as Parler, which were used by his supporters. Bremmer interprets these actions as emblematic of a new kind of power: a technopolar moment where private companies exert influence traditionally associated with the state. However, a closer reading suggests that these decisions were not made in a political vacuum. The broader context indicates that the Biden administration, incoming at the time, held greater institutional legitimacy and international backing, which may have influenced these companies' political calculus. In other words, while tech companies displayed a capacity for unilateral action, they were not operating with complete autonomy. Rather, they reflected and facilitated the preferences of dominant political elites.

What I wish to emphasize here is that Big Tech firms—despite their growing influence—are not yet fully autonomous geopolitical actors. They often function as extensions or instruments of state power, aligning with prevailing regulatory environments and political interests. While acknowledging this does not diminish the significant impact they have on political communication, public discourse, and even financial infrastructures, it is equally important to avoid overstating their independence. As of June 2025, it is more accurate to say that the *technopolar world* continues to be state-centric, with governments—particularly those of powerful nation-states—retaining primacy over digital governance and geopolitical agency. Big Tech is influential, but it has not supplanted the state as the central actor in international relations.

This is particularly evident when analyzing the strategic postures of major geopolitical actors like China, the European Union (EU), and the United States. Each case illustrates distinct modes of how state power checks and in many cases subsumes the influence of digital platforms.

In China, the state's dominance over digital actors is institutionalized and absolute. The Chinese Communist Party (CCP) maintains a tight grip on its domestic technology sector, ensuring that companies such as Alibaba, Tencent, and ByteDance operate within the parameters of state-defined strategic goals. The 2021 crackdown on tech firms—from the halted IPO of Ant Group to anti-monopoly investigations—demonstrated the state's readiness to discipline digital giants when their actions diverge from national priorities (Lee et al., 2022). In addition, China's Data Security Law and Cybersecurity Law have formalized the principle that all data generated within China is subject to government control. In this model, Big Tech does not challenge state authority, it is structurally embedded within and subordinate to it. This case illustrates the clearest example of *technopolarity under sovereign command*.

The EU, by contrast, offers a regulatory approach that reasserts state-like functions through supranational law rather than centralized executive power. The EU does not possess tech giants comparable to its U.S. or Chinese counterparts, but it compensates through what Bradford (2012) famously called the "Brussels Effect"—the global export of regulatory norms. Through legislation such as the General Data Protection Regulation (GDPR), the Digital Services Act (DSA), and the Digital Markets Act (DMA), the EU has positioned itself as a regulatory superpower. These frameworks constrain the activities of companies like Meta, Google, and Amazon, requiring compliance with European standards on data privacy, algorithmic transparency, and anti-competitive practices (Celeste et al., 2022). The EU thus leverages law as a geopolitical tool, asserting normative sovereignty in a fragmented digital ecosystem.

In the U.S., meanwhile, the relationship between Big Tech and the state is more ambivalent. On the one hand, firms like Microsoft, Amazon, and Palantir serve as strategic contractors to government agencies, especially in defense and intelligence. On the other hand, there exists an enduring tension over antitrust regulation, data privacy, and content moderation. As the events surrounding Jan. 6, 2021, revealed, technology companies may act assertively in moments of political crisis, suspending a sitting president's digital presence and de-platforming alternative communication channels—but these decisions often reflect broader political alignments rather than corporate autonomy (Bremmer, 2021). Indeed, while platforms exercised significant influence during the transition from the Trump to Biden administrations, they did so in a context that favored the prevailing political consensus. As of June 2025, with President Trump's second term underway, there is no evidence that tech companies have acted in open defiance of executive authority. Instead, they remain entangled with government interests, sometimes in collaboration, sometimes in negotiation, but rarely in true opposition.

In contrast, my conceptualization of the *technopolar world* is not a transient moment but a long-term restructuring of the international system itself. It is not solely about the rise of non-state digital actors, but about how states themselves adapt, contest, and reassert sovereignty through digital means. In this framework, technological sovereignty is not ceded but reimagined, and the core question becomes how states can reclaim strategic autonomy in a landscape shaped by digital infrastructures and algorithmic systems (Akıllı, 2025a). Whereas Bremmer emphasizes corporate power in a moment of governance void, the *technopolar world* foregrounds state agency, institutional adaptation, and the emergence of new forms of diplomatic and technological competition.

I argue that sovereignty in the technopolar world rests on three mutually reinforcing dimensions: **data sovereignty**, **algorithmic capacity**, and **hardware autonomy**. Data sovereignty entails a state's ability to regulate, localize, and secure data generated by its citizens and institutions. Algorithmic capacity refers to the national development and oversight of algorithms that mediate decision-making—from predictive policing to financial regulation. Finally, hardware autonomy denotes the ability to design or procure critical hardware—semiconductors, microchips, and energy infrastructure—without reliance on adversarial supply chains (Akıllı, 2025a). These three pillars form the architecture of *digital autonomy*, which I consider the strategic cornerstone of statehood in the technopolar age.

Importantly, the technopolar world is also defined by the emergence of technological blocks and regulatory fragmentation. This multipolarity of standards challenges the liberal universalism that underpinned earlier digital globalization. As I have written elsewhere, the bifurcation of AI governance between Washington-led and Beijing-led models has forced middle powers to recalibrate their digital alignments (Akıllı, 2025b). The EU's pursuit of a "third way" through digital regulation, what Bradford (2012) has termed the "Brussels Effect," further reinforces the fragmentation of digital norms across jurisdictional spheres.

Moreover, the *technopolar world* cannot be understood without recognizing the symbiosis between AI development and energy infrastructure. AI systems demand immense computational and energy resources, leading to what I have termed the *energy-AI nexus*. In this context, Virtual Power Plants (VPPs) AI-optimized systems that coordinate renewable energy sources emerge as strategic assets. They serve not only ecological sustainability but also national technological capacity. China's rapid deployment of VPPs illustrates how energy infrastructure is now interwoven with AI sovereignty (Akıllı, 2025c).

Finally, the technopolar paradigm reconfigures the grammar of international diplomacy. States must now operate within cognitive architectures, distributed systems where influence is exercised through narrative dominance, algorithmic visibility, and real-time decision-making. To meet this challenge, I am proposing in this book the concept of *cognitive diplomacy*, a strategic model that integrates human and artificial cognition in the formulation and execution of foreign policy. Cognitive diplomacy serves as the enabler of presence, practice, and resilience, the foundational capacities required for digital autonomy and strategic agency in the technopolar world. In conclusion, while Bremmer's *technopolar moment* rightly emphasizes the disruptive power of technology companies, the concept of the *technopolar world* provides a broader, more durable framework that centers on the evolving role of the state. It accounts not only for the agency of Big Tech, but for how states—through regulatory innovation, infrastructural investment, and diplomatic recalibration—can reclaim and reconstruct sovereignty in the digital age. The *technopolar world* is thus not a moment, but a new geopolitical condition.

Bibliography

Akıllı, E. (2025a, April 18). *Rewiring Diplomacy in the Technopolar World*. Daily Sabah (Op-Ed). Retrieved May 11, 2025, from https://www.dailysabah.com/opinion/op-ed/rewiring-diplomacy-in-the-technopolar-world

Akıllı, E. (2025b, February 1). *Trump's Stargate, Biden's Tier List and the Wake of the Techno-Polar World*. Daily Sabah. Retrieved May 5, 2025, from https://www.dailysabah.com/opinion/op-ed/trumps-stargate-bidens-tier-list-and-the-wake-of-the-techno-polar-world

Akıllı, E. (2025c, March 6). *Role of virtual power plants in AI R&D in a technopolar world order*. Daily Sabah. Retrieved May 5, 2025, from https://www.dailysabah.com/opinion/op-ed/role-of-virtual-power-plants-in-ai-rd-in-a-technopolar-world-order

Bradford, A. (2012). The Brussels effect. *Northwestern University Law Review, 107*(1), 1–67.

Bremmer, I. (2021, Octtober 19). *The Technopolar Moment, Foreign Affairs*. Retrieved May 11, 2025, from https://www.foreignaffairs.com/articles/world/ian-bremmer-big-tech-global-order

Celeste, E., Heldt, A., & Iglesias Keller, C. (2022). Introduction. In E. Celeste, A. Heldt, & C. Iglesias Keller (Eds.), *Constitutionalising social media*. Edward Elgar.

Lee, J., Zhang, E., ve Creemers, R. (2022, April). *China's Standardisation System–Trends, Implications and Case Studies*. Leiden Asia Centre. Retrieved May 26, 2025, from https://leidenasiacentre.nl/wp-content/uploads/2022/04/Chinas-standardisation-system.pdf

CHAPTER 3

The Transformation of Sovereignty in the Technopolar World

3.1 Origins and Foundations of the Westphalian Sovereignty

Sovereignty has long stood as the bedrock principle of international order, traditionally understood as the supreme authority of the state over its territory and freedom from external interference. Since the Peace of Westphalia in 1648, this Westphalian conception of state sovereignty has been the cornerstone of the interstate system, enshrining territorial integrity and non-intervention as sacrosanct norms (Kissinger, 2014). For nearly four centuries, the Westphalian model of sovereignty, where each nation-state governs its own affairs and respects the autonomy of others, has provided the legal and normative foundation of world politics. Today, however, the concept of sovereignty is under unprecedented strain.

Forces of globalization and technological disruption are rewiring the very nature of power in what some analysts call a "technopolar world," one in which technological might and digital influence rival the traditional power of states (Akıllı, 2025d; Bremmer & Kupchan, 2022). This chapter explores the evolution of sovereignty from its classical formulation to its current digital age transformation. It lays the theoretical and historical groundwork for understanding how state authority is being reshaped by globalization, interdependence, and the rise of digitalization.

E. Akıllı, *Cognitive Diplomacy and Digital Autonomy*,
https://doi.org/10.1007/978-3-032-04470-9_3

Thus, this chapter aims to set the stage for subsequent chapters on algorithmic governance, data sovereignty, and semiconductor capacity in this emerging "Sovereignty 2.0" era (Akıllı, 2025a).

The modern idea of sovereignty is commonly traced to the treaties of the Peace of Westphalia (1648), which ended the Thirty Years' War in Europe (Philpott, 2001). These treaties are often credited with inaugurating the Westphalian system of independent nation-states (Osiander, 2001). In essence, the Westphalian principle holds that each state possesses exclusive authority within its bounded territory and that no outside power should intervene in another state's domestic affairs. As Henry Kissinger observes, Westphalia amounted to a pragmatic solution after decades of religious conflict: a system of *"independent states refraining from interference in each other's domestic affairs and checking each other's ambitions through a general equilibrium of power"* (Kissinger, 2014, p. 18). In this new order, each state was recognized as sovereign—equal in legal status regardless of size—and free to determine its own religion, laws, and governance within its borders (The Editors of Encyclopaedia Britannica, 2025). The notion of a higher imperial or papal authority imposing universal rule was rejected in favor of a plurality of states, coexisting under the norm of non-intervention (Kissinger, 2014).

De jure sovereignty, under this interpretation, emerges not merely as an attribute of individual states, but as a collectively upheld institution rooted in mutual recognition. As Wendt (1992, p. 280) observes, sovereignty attains institutional character when states acknowledge each other's right to exist as sovereign entities. In this sense, sovereignty transcends from being a mere property of states and becomes embedded within the intersubjective fabric of the international system. Put differently, as Onuf (1991, pp. 430–431) argues, it is precisely this institutional dimension of sovereignty that constitutes states as states, affirming their status and agency within the society of states.

Over time, the Westphalian norms were refined and codified. The principle of territorial integrity and political independence of states became enshrined in international law. For example, Article 2(4) of the United Nations Charter (United Nations, 1945) prohibits the threat or use of force against the territorial integrity or political independence of any state, reflecting Westphalian ideals in the post-World War II order. Likewise, the norm of sovereign equality of states (U.N. Charter Article 2(1)) affirms that no matter how powerful, states in theory have equal rights under international law (United Nations, 1945). Classical theorists like Emer de Vattel in the eighteenth century elaborated that states should not interfere in the internal affairs of others, giving legal-philosophical heft to Westphalian sovereignty (Vattel, 1758). Internally, sovereignty meant a government's exclusive authority over its population and territory, or "domestic sovereignty." Externally, it meant autonomy from foreign control or "external sovereignty." This dual aspect—supreme domestic authority and freedom from outside intervention—became the bedrock of the international system's norms and diplomacy (Philpott, 2001).

It is important to note that even at its zenith, Westphalian sovereignty was as much an ideal as a reality. Strong states frequently violated the norm of non-intervention when it suited their interests, and empires subjected many peoples to foreign rule in the colonial era, belying the principle of equal sovereignty. Nonetheless, the *idea* of sovereignty as absolute authority within a territory remained central. Stephen Krasner (1999) famously termed sovereignty an "organized hypocrisy," routinely breached in practice through interventions, unequal treaties, or covert influence, yet almost always affirmed as an organizing principle of international life. While many within Western academic and policy circles may perceive sovereignty in this rather cynical light, it is important to recognize that Krasner's definition does not exhaust the concept's normative, historical, and existential dimensions. His formulation captures a particular—and predominantly Western-centric—reading of sovereignty as a flexible instrument shaped by power politics. However, for many states and societies, particularly those in the postcolonial world, sovereignty is neither a convenient fiction nor a hypocritical construct. Rather, it is a hard-won and deeply cherished foundation of national identity and self-determination.

The value and significance of sovereignty can only be fully appreciated by those who have fought for it. For peoples who have endured imperial domination, foreign intervention, or violent subjugation, sovereignty represents more than mere legal recognition. It embodies the right to self-governance, dignity, and political agency. In this sense, sovereignty is not simply an abstract principle subject to the whims of powerful states, contrary it is an unshakable cornerstone of national existence and the ultimate expression of collective will.

Thus, while Krasner's critique highlights important tensions in the application of sovereignty in international relations, it risks underestimating the profound normative and emotional resonance the concept holds for much of the world. Sovereignty, in many cases, is an idea worth sacrificing for; a symbol for which countless unnamed individuals have willingly given their lives in the pursuit of national liberation and dignity. To dismiss or trivialize this dimension is to overlook the deep human stakes involved in struggles over sovereign statehood.

This enduring centrality of sovereignty owes much to its utility: it provides a basis for international order (through clear jurisdictional boundaries) and for domestic legitimacy (the state's right to rule). Without the principle of sovereignty, the global system would risk descending into normative ambiguity and unrestrained interventionism. For newly independent or postcolonial states in particular, sovereignty has been indispensable in consolidating national identity and protecting political autonomy against external encroachments. It constitutes both a shield and a platform, protecting states from illegitimate interference while enabling them to participate as equals in the society of states.

Yet, it is precisely this dimension that Krasner's formulation tends to marginalize. While his "organized hypocrisy" thesis rightly exposes the frequent contradictions and selective enforcement of sovereign norms, it implicitly privileges a realist and power-centric perspective rooted in the experiences of established powers. Such a view risks normalizing hegemonic intrusions as inevitable, thereby obscuring the aspirations of states for genuine equality and self-determination. Postcolonial theorists and scholars of IR, such as Acharya (2004) and Barkawi and Laffey (2006), have emphasized that sovereignty is not merely a facade but a deeply contested and lived reality, especially in the Global South.

Sovereignty, therefore, should not be reduced to a strategic fiction manipulated by dominant actors. Rather, it should be understood as a historically situated and normatively rich concept, one that continues to inspire independence movements, resist external domination, and assert national dignity. To those who have fought and continue to fight for it, sovereignty is far from hypocritical. It is foundational, existential, and, for many, sacred.

By the twentieth century, sovereignty had become deeply embedded in international law, from the Montevideo Convention's criteria for statehood (1933) to the U.N. Charter (United Nations, 1945). After World War II, decolonization spread the sovereign state system globally, as nations in Africa, Asia, and the Middle East claimed the Westphalian rights of self-government and non-interference. The world map was filled with dozens of new sovereign states, all rightfully guarding their independence. In sum, classical Westphalian sovereignty—the legal supremacy of the state within its territory and the normative shield against external meddling—stood as the cornerstone of world order from 1648 through the Cold War era.

3.2 Sovereignty in the Twentieth Century: Globalization, Interdependence, and Adaptation

While the formal doctrine of sovereignty persisted, the twentieth century brought profound changes in the context in which states operate. Globalization—the increasing cross-border flow of goods, capital, people, and ideas—challenged the traditional Westphalian notion that states could fully control what happened within their borders. By the late twentieth century, many scholars observed that sovereignty was being redefined, diluted, or pooled, in response to an interdependent world (Mathews, 1997; Strange, 1996). After World War II, the rise of a U.S.-led liberal international order encouraged states to engage in cooperative institutions and rules that voluntarily constrained their sovereignty in specific areas. For instance, by joining the Bretton Woods institutions (the IMF and World Bank) or the General Agreement on Tariffs and Trade (later the WTO), states accepted rules that limited their freedom to unilaterally set trade barriers or monetary policy. European countries took this further, creating the European Community (later European Union) and pooling aspects of sovereignty—agreeing to common policies and supranational governance in exchange for economic integration and peace. Thus, sovereignty in practice became more permeable and negotiated. States were still sovereign in law, but in practice, they were enmeshed in networks of interdependence and international regimes that constrained unilateral action (Keohane & Nye, 1977). As an illustration, a financial crisis in one country could rapidly spread to others, limiting the effective economic sovereignty of states in an age of global finance. Multinational corporations grew in size and influence, at times eclipsing the economic power of smaller states, even pressuring governments to adopt business-friendly policies or risk capital flight (Strange, 1996).

By the 1990s, with the end of the Cold War and a surge in economic globalization, some commentators proclaimed the "erosion" or "end" of Westphalian sovereignty (Radice, 2019). Jessica T. Mathews (1997) argued that power was undergoing a "power shift" away from states toward markets and civil society. Global corporations, nongovernmental organizations (NGOs), and transnational networks were taking on roles once reserved for governments, from providing services to setting standards. Communications technology—satellite TV, and later the internet—enabled information to penetrate borders like never before, empowering non-state actors and citizens. Kenichi Ohmae (1990) provocatively dubbed the modern world a "borderless world," where nation-states would matter less than regional economies and global companies. While these claims were likely overstated (states proved more resilient and adaptable than the most hyperglobalist predictions), it was clear that absolute economic sovereignty was no longer tenable. No state, not even superpowers, could seal itself off from global flows or unilaterally dictate outcomes in the face of complex interdependence. Policy decisions increasingly had international repercussions and often required international coordination (e.g., managing financial markets, climate change, or pandemics). At the same time, new norms and values also challenged the Westphalian stand: international human rights law and the emerging principle of the "Responsibility to Protect" (United Nations, 2005) signaled egregious internal abuses might warrant external action, carving out moral exceptions to non-interference by the early 2000s. In short, by the turn of the twenty-first century, sovereignty had evolved—from the classic model of total Westphalian autonomy toward a more complicated model, wherein states were still the primary authority but frequently bound by external commitments, interdependent constraints, and transnational forces. States had to balance their sovereign prerogatives with the realities of economic globalization and the influence of non-state actors. Yet, despite the diffusion of power, sovereignty remained the organizing concept of world politics as nations continued to fiercely defend their core independence even as they ceded limited control in specific domains.

3.3 Disruptions in the Digital Age: Sovereignty Under Technological Strain

If globalization began the challenge to the Westphalian paradigm, the digital revolution propelled it into a new phase. The advent of the internet, advanced computing, and now artificial intelligence has created a world of borderless digital flows and virtual domains that defy the traditional constraints of geography. Over the past two decades, state authorities have confronted a series of disruptions to their control, from the rise of transnational technology giants, cyber intrusions, and extraterritorial data flows, to the emergence of algorithm-driven governance. These developments have exposed the insufficiency of classical sovereignty concepts in a world where cyberspace transcends physical frontiers (Akıllı, 2025a). A 1996 manifesto by cyberlibertarian John Perry Barlow declared cyberspace independent from the "*Governments of the Industrial World*," reflecting a widespread belief at the time that the internet would undermine state authority and exist largely beyond government reach (Barlow, 1996). That extreme view has not fully materialized and states have reasserted themselves in cyberspace in various ways. However, there is no doubt that the balance of power between states and new digital actors is fundamentally shifting. We now live in an era where digital platforms and infrastructures are critical to economics, social life, and security. Thus, control over these assets has become a source of geopolitical power.

Perhaps the most striking development in the technopolar era is the rise of a handful of gargantuan technology companies with global reach and influence. Firms like Google (Alphabet), Apple, Facebook (Meta), Amazon, Microsoft, Tencent, and Alibaba operate platforms and services used by billions worldwide. They effectively create digital realms that transcend any single state's jurisdiction. These Big Tech companies now perform functions historically associated with government: they mediate communication, and flow of information, set rules for online behavior, manage digital identities and transactions, and even provide quasi-public services. Bremmer and Kupchan has noted that *"a handful of big tech companies, not governments, are the main actors and enforcers"* in much of digital space, exercising a form of private governance over this new domain (Bremmer & Kupchan, 2022). In Bremmer and Kupchan's words, tech giants have attained a kind of de facto sovereignty in cyberspace, setting policies through their terms of service and algorithms that users across the globe must abide by. For example, Facebook's decisions about what speech is permitted on its platform can impact political discourse in dozens of countries, effectively influencing civic life without direct state involvement. Apple and Google's control over smartphone app ecosystems gives them gatekeeping power over digital services in every country where iPhones or Android devices are prevalent.

The growing clout of Big Tech poses a twofold challenge to Westphalian notions of sovereignty. First, it dilutes the authority of states over activities within their territory. National laws still apply to the internet but enforcing them is difficult when the platforms are operated by foreign corporations with headquarters and data centers scattered around the world. We have seen frequent jurisdictional clashes—for instance, when governments demand user data or content removal from platforms that claim to adhere to their own corporate policies or the laws of the home country (e.g., the U.S.) rather than the local law. Second, tech companies themselves sometimes act as geopolitical actors, pursuing quasi-diplomatic roles traditionally reserved for states. They might negotiate directly with governments (as Twitter, Facebook, and Google have done over content or censorship rules), assert neutrality in conflicts, or even influence outcomes of elections and referenda through the flow of information. According to one recent study, Big Tech firms have become "new data sovereigns" and *"a new type of Leviathan,"* leveraging their control of data and technology to challenge the state's exclusive claim to authority (Gu, 2023, p. 128). With access to unprecedented amounts of information, *"the rise of Big Tech poses a challenge to sovereignty's exclusivity … assuming the position of de facto data sovereign"* (Gu, 2023, p. 135). In effect, whoever controls the key networks and databases may wield as much influence as a government—a reality that complicates the traditional state-centric power hierarchy.

States have responded in different ways to this private sector ascendance. In democratic societies, there is an ongoing debate and effort to regulate Big Tech—for instance, the EU's recent Digital Markets Act and Digital Services Act (European Union, 2005) seek to rein in anti-competitive practices and force platforms to moderate content and handle data in line with European standards (Fleming, 2025). These laws represent states reasserting sovereign rule-making power over the digital domain within their jurisdiction, attempting to curb the unfettered reign of tech giants. The U.S., after years of a laissez-faire approach, has also considered antitrust actions and stronger privacy rules to check Big Tech's power, recognizing that corporate concentration can threaten citizens' rights and even national security, and especially, over concerns of social media disinformation (Citron & Pasquale, 2019; Khan, 2017; Wu, 2018). In other parts of the world, the approach has often been to co-opt or contain Big Tech. China, for instance, nurtured its own tech titans behind the Great Firewall, but in recent years has cracked down on them to ensure they align with state objectives and do not become alternative power centers (Hsu, 2021; The Editors of Encyclopaedia Britannica, 2025).

Beijing's concept of "cyber sovereignty" explicitly rejects the idea of the internet as a lawless space, and instead asserts the state's right to control and direct all digital activities within its borders (Chander & Sun, 2021). Meanwhile, U.S. and Chinese authorities alike have recognized that their domestic tech firms are also strategic assets in a geopolitical competition—leading to what some call a tech Cold War. Governments increasingly view leadership in tech innovation, control of data, and dominance in setting technological standards as national security priorities. This dynamic has bound states and their leading corporations into a complex symbiotic relationship: states provide legal protection, funding, and markets for their tech firms, and in return, those firms bolster state power (Gu, 2023). For example, American tech companies benefit from U.S. diplomatic support and often comply with U.S. foreign policy directives such as not selling to blacklisted countries (Akıllı, 2025b). Similarly, Chinese companies like Huawei have been backed by state subsidies and deployed as instruments of Beijing's global influence (Gu, 2023). The result in the technopolar world is a hybrid sovereignty where state authority intersects corporate power. The bargaining power between the two is continually being renegotiated, and the outcome will shape how governance is exercised in the digital age. The key point is that state sovereignty is no longer exercised by governments alone—it is increasingly shared, contested, and constrained by the private rulers of the digital ecosystem. In an era defined by algorithmic governance, transnational data flows, and the pervasive influence of global technology corporations, the locus of authority has become diffused and multilayered. Platforms, AI-driven systems, and digital intermediaries now shape public discourse, mediate access to information, and influence societal cognition at scales once unimaginable. As a result, sovereignty today extends beyond the traditional monopolies over violence and territory. It now implicates control over narratives, data, and cognitive frameworks through which societies perceive themselves and the world.

This subtle yet profound shift signals the emergence of new domains of power that transcend conventional legal and territorial boundaries. Sovereignty, once synonymous with hard borders and juridical authority, increasingly coexists with softer yet equally potent forms of influence exercised in the cognitive and informational spheres. These developments do not merely erode traditional state power, they reconfigure it. They compel states to engage in more sophisticated forms of negotiation and assertion to retain relevance and legitimacy in the digital age. While this chapter highlights the tension between traditional and emergent understandings of sovereignty, the full implications of this transformation—particularly in the realm of perception, knowledge production, and cognitive influence—will be explored in greater depth in subsequent parts of this book. There, we will address how diplomacy itself must adapt to operate effectively within this evolving landscape, where minds and narratives have become critical arenas of contestation.

3.4 Cyberthreats and the Erosion of Territorial Security

Another major disruption to classical sovereignty comes from the realm of cybersecurity. In the Westphalian paradigm, controlling one's territory and defending it against external aggression is fundamental to sovereignty. But how does a state defend itself when malicious actors can penetrate its critical infrastructure, steal secrets, or disrupt services from thousands of miles away through fiber-optic cables and computer code? The rise of cyberwarfare and transnational hacking has severely tested the traditional notion that borders and geographic distance provide security. Cyber vulnerabilities expose states to incursions that do not fit neatly into the established frameworks of warfare or law enforcement. State-sponsored hackers and non-state cybercriminals alike can operate globally with relative anonymity, blurring the line between domestic and foreign threats. A small group of hackers in one country can, for instance, shut down portions of another country's power grid or banking system without ever physically crossing a border—effectively violating sovereignty in a new way. Notable instances include the 2007 cyberattacks on Estonia's government and banks (Haataja, 2017) and the 2010 Stuxnet computer worm, (Farwell & Rohozinski, 2011) which sabotaged Iran's nuclear facilities. Such events demonstrated that even core sovereign functions like protecting infrastructure and enforcing law and order can be subverted remotely via cyberspace. Conventional military power offers limited protection against these threats. A state might have a formidable army, yet find itself paralyzed by a cyberattack launched by an unseen adversary.

The challenge is exacerbated by the difficulty of attribution, identifying with certainty who is behind a cyberintrusion. Attackers often obfuscate their origin, making it hard for a victim state to invoke self-defense or retaliation under international law, which traditionally requires knowing the aggressor. This undermines a key aspect of sovereignty: the ability to respond to violations of one's territorial integrity. Moreover, because cyberspace is a domain that intermingles civilian and military elements (the same internet supports both civilian networks and defense systems), states struggle to establish clear rules of engagement or red lines. Efforts are underway to develop norms. For instance, NATO has declared cyberspace an operational domain and indicated that a serious cyberattack could trigger collective defense obligations, treating it akin to an armed attack (NATO, 2024). Yet, overall, global governance of cyberspace remains nascent.

However, achieving a global consensus on cyber norms remains elusive. Western nations have advocated voluntary norms aimed at protecting critical infrastructure in cyberspace. Notably, the 2015 United Nations Group of Governmental Experts (U.N. GGE) report outlined such norms, including refraining from targeting critical infrastructure during peacetime (U.N. GGE, 2015). In contrast, Russia and China promote the principle of "information sovereignty," which emphasizes extensive state control over internet content for "national security." This approach allows these states to regulate and censor online information within their borders, often justifying such measures as necessary for maintaining social stability and security (Deibert, 2019; Klimburg, 2017).

The absence of borders in cyberspace effectively means sovereignty must be reconceptualized not as control over a physical space but as control over one's digital networks and information systems. Nations are now investing heavily in cyber-defense and resilience (technical capabilities and strategies to secure networks) as an essential aspect of sovereign security. They are also engaging in a quiet cyber arms race—building both offensive and defensive cyber tools—raising questions about how traditional concepts like deterrence apply (Akıllı, 2025c).

Crucially, cyberthreats have forced states to collaborate as well as compete. Because the internet is globally interconnected, no state can secure its slice of cyberspace entirely on its own. International cooperation is needed to trace criminals, shut down botnets, or establish baselines of responsible behavior (e.g., not harboring cybercriminals). This need for cooperation can sometimes run up against sovereignty sensitivities. For example, when law enforcement from one country requests access to data or suspects located in another. Overall, the proliferation of cyberthreats has revealed a sovereignty gap: states are formally sovereign within their *digital borders*, but those borders are porous and often beyond unilateral control. This has led to calls for strengthened "cyber sovereignty," meaning the capacity of a state to manage and secure its own cyber domain. China has been especially vocal in advocating cyber sovereignty, using it to justify tight state regulation of internet traffic and data within its territory (Chander & Sun, 2021). Western liberal democracies have been more hesitant to embrace the term due to its association with censorship, but even they recognize the need for greater sovereign capability in cyber-defense. In summary, the rise of cyber conflict erodes the traditional security pillar of sovereignty and compels states to rethink what defending sovereignty means in the digital era—shifting focus to securing networks, data, and digital infrastructure as vigorously as physical borders.

3.5 Extraterritorial Data Flows and Jurisdictional Dilemmas

Sovereignty has also been upended by the explosion of data flows that cross borders instantly in the digital age. In the Westphalian system, laws and jurisdiction are generally bounded by territory: a country's regulations apply within its borders and to its citizens, and foreign authorities have limited reach inside another state without permission. But what happens when a nation's sensitive information or its citizens' personal data are stored on a cloud server abroad, perhaps in a country with very different laws? Or when intelligence agencies vacuum up data globally, brushing aside national boundaries on the internet? We are confronted with questions of data sovereignty: the idea that a state should have control over data generated within its territory or relating to its people, akin to how it controls land, air, and waters within its borders. In practice, data often flows through transnational corporate networks that are not neatly partitioned by country. For example, a social media post made in Brazil might be stored on U.S. servers, or an Australian company might use a cloud database that replicates information across data centers on multiple continents. This reality creates tension between national jurisdictions. The EU, concerned about privacy and the protection of its citizens' information, has asserted strong data sovereignty claims via regulations like the GDPR (European Union, 2016). GDPR not only governs data within Europe but also asserts extraterritorial reach. If an American company collects data on Europeans, it must abide by EU rules or face penalties. In this way, the EU has tried to project its sovereignty into the digital realm to safeguard personal data (Fleming, 2025). Conversely, the U.S.' CLOUD Act (United States Congress, 2018) asserts that U.S.-based tech companies must comply with valid U.S. warrants for data, even if the data is stored overseas—a claim of American legal authority that potentially conflicts with other countries' sovereignty and privacy laws.

High-profile disputes have highlighted these clashes. After the Snowden revelations in 2013 (Ball & Greenwald, 2013) showed U.S. intelligence accessing vast amounts of global internet data, including data on European citizens, European courts struck down the EU-U.S. "Safe Harbor" and later "Privacy Shield" agreements that allowed data transfers, on the grounds that EU citizens' data was not adequately protected from U.S. government surveillance. This kind of judicial action (the Schrems II ruling by the European Court of Justice in 2020) essentially told the U.S. that its surveillance practices violate Europeans' rights—an extraordinary example of how data interdependence forces two states to reckon with each other's domestic policies in ways that traditional sovereignty would not contemplate.

Meanwhile, countries like Russia and India have introduced data localization laws requiring certain data (like financial or personal data) to be stored on servers physically located inside the country, so that they fall under domestic jurisdiction and control (Captain Compliance, 2025; Ermolina et al., 2025; Reznikova, 2025). These laws are motivated by both economic and security reasons. Keeping data local can support local tech industry and ensure data is accessible to local regulators or security services. However, data localization challenges the borderless nature of the internet and can fragment the global digital economy. We see the emergence of a more fragmented internet, sometimes called the "splinternet" (Akıllı, 2022), as each jurisdiction tries to enforce its own rules on data flows and content.

The concept of digital sovereignty has gained traction as nations grapple with these issues. Broadly, digital or technological sovereignty refers to a nation's ability to control and protect its digital destiny—including data, hardware, and the software/algorithms it relies on (Fleming, 2025). In effect, it means extending the notion of sovereignty to cover the information space and technological infrastructure. Data sovereignty is one pillar of this, emphasizing control over data storage, access, and usage. A country that lacks data sovereignty might feel that its citizens' information is subject to foreign exploitation or that it cannot enforce its laws (for instance, privacy or cybersecurity laws) if data is stored abroad under someone else's control. On the other hand, as legal scholars Chander and Sun (2021) point out, assertions of digital sovereignty are double-edged: they can protect citizens' rights and national security, but they can also be used by governments to censor and surveil, insulating themselves from outside scrutiny under the pretext of "sovereign internet" control. China's Great Firewall is a case in point, it is an exercise of state sovereignty to control data and content, but it also severely restricts citizens' access to global information. Western democracies, for their part, must strike a balance between ensuring data security (e.g., not depending solely on foreign cloud providers or allowing unlimited foreign access to domestic data) and preserving the open, global nature of the internet that enables free expression and commerce.

In summary, extraterritorial data flows have created a jurisdictional conundrum for sovereignty. States are increasingly attempting to reassert control—through regulatory frameworks (like GDPR), legal tools (data localization, cross-border data access agreements), and technological means (developing national cloud services or even satellite internet to bypass foreign networks). This trend reflects a shift from seeing the internet as a global common to treating it as a space that needs sovereign governance. Data has been dubbed "the new oil" in terms of its value, and accordingly, control over data is becoming as strategically important as control over territory or resources. The pursuit of data sovereignty is, at its core, the pursuit of a state's ability to enforce its laws, values, and norms within the digital realm—a twenty-first-century extension of the Westphalian impulse to exercise ultimate authority over one's domain. In an age where data flows effortlessly across borders and is often governed by transnational corporate interests, the desire to regain control over this critical resource has become increasingly pronounced. While this raises profound questions about the nature of sovereignty and governance in the digital era, it also points to emerging strategies aimed at safeguarding national autonomy against external influence. These dynamics, which signal a deeper shift in how power and independence are asserted in the digital age, will be explored in detail in the upcoming chapters of this book.

3.6 Algorithmic Governance and the Challenge of AI

A further disruption to traditional state authority comes from the rise of algorithmic governance and the increasing role of algorithms, particularly AI systems, in decision-making processes that affect societies. Algorithmic governance can refer both to governments using algorithms to govern and to governance *by* algorithms (often operated by private platforms) that shape people's behavior through *coded* narratives. In both senses, it raises questions about accountability, transparency, and the locus of authority.

In the analog era, governance and sovereignty were exercised through human agents—elected officials, bureaucrats, and judges implementing laws and regulations. In the digital age, many decisions are now made or guided by complex algorithms: from social media feeds that govern what information people see and automated systems that approve or deny loans, to predictive policing tools that guide law enforcement attention (Institute for Internet and the Just Society, 2025). When these systems are created by private companies or by foreign entities, a sovereign government may lose a degree of control over crucial processes affecting its citizens. For example, consider Meta's (Facebook) newsfeed algorithm: by prioritizing certain types of content, it can influence public opinion and even election outcomes in a country, effectively governing the information ecosystem without the consent or oversight of that country's authorities. Likewise, Google's search algorithms can shape what information is accessible, which in turn can have societal impacts. These companies typically operate on a global scale with a one-size-fits-all algorithm, which may not align with local laws or norms, thereby causing friction with sovereignty (Bellanova et al., 2022; Srivastava, 2025). We see this when countries demand the removal of extremist or fake news content, and the platforms struggle to adjust their algorithms or policies on a country-by-country basis. The governance power here is shifting toward those who design and control the algorithms, often beyond the reach of any single state.

On the flip side, governments themselves are increasingly deploying algorithms and AI in governance, which transforms how they internally exercise sovereignty. Many states are experimenting with AI-powered tools for tasks like facial recognition surveillance, welfare eligibility, traffic management, and even judicial sentencing recommendations. This trend could enhance the efficiency and reach of state power. For instance, AI can analyze vast datasets for intelligence or fraud detection much faster than humans. However, it also introduces new dependencies and risks. If a government procures its AI systems from a foreign company (say, using an American tech firm's algorithm for smart city management), is the state ceding some sovereignty or exposing itself to external influence through a software backdoor? Even if developed domestically, algorithms can be *opaque* ("black boxes"), making it hard for citizens to understand or challenge decisions. It can weaken democratic accountability, a cornerstone of legitimate sovereignty in a people's eyes. There is also the risk of bias or error in algorithms: for example, biased facial recognition AI could lead to wrongful surveillance or arrests of certain minority groups, effectively undermining the rule of law (Akıllı, 2024). Who is accountable when an algorithm makes a harmful decision (Akıllı, 2023) the state authority deploying it, the private developer, or the algorithm itself? These dilemmas show how governance by algorithm complicates traditional sovereign responsibility.

Recognizing these challenges, some governments, and international bodies are trying to create frameworks for algorithmic accountability and ethics. The EU's proposed AI Act aims to regulate high-risk AI systems (like those used in policing or critical infrastructure) to ensure they meet standards of transparency, safety, and human oversight. This is an assertion of normative sovereignty: the EU is saying that even in the realm of algorithms, its values and regulations will hold sway (Fleming, 2025). In a technopolar context, having *"algorithmic capacity,"* the ability to develop and control the algorithms that shape society is seen as a key dimension of sovereignty (Akıllı, 2025a).

Countries with advanced AI research and robust tech industries will have far more say in how algorithmic governance evolves than those who simply import whatever systems others create. This realization is pushing states to invest in AI development, ensure they have access to data for training algorithms (tying back to data sovereignty), and maintain human-in-the-loop oversight for critical decisions. There is also a geopolitical race on standards, meaning whichever country or bloc sets the standards for AI (be it ethics, technical protocols, or norms for use) could embed its worldview into algorithms globally. The U.S. and EU emphasize individual rights and privacy, whereas China's approach might prioritize state control and collective security. Thus, the contest over algorithmic governance is not just technical but deeply political, with sovereignty implications. It is about whose values and interests will be encoded in the ubiquitous AI systems of the future.

In sum, algorithmic governance represents a frontier where sovereignty is being reimagined. States must ensure they retain or regain control over the algorithms that impact their citizens—whether by developing home-grown systems, rigorously regulating external ones, or collaborating in international governance of AI. At the same time, they face the paradox that to govern effectively in the digital age, they need to leverage algorithms, but doing so can distance or obscure human accountability at the heart of the social contract. How states navigate this will determine the extent to which "Sovereignty 2.0" is compatible with democratic oversight and the rule of law.

Nevertheless, it is essential to establish a clear foundation for the upcoming chapters. A persistent illusion has shaped much of the discourse surrounding the relationship between big technology companies and national governments. This illusion suggests that major technology firms operate independently of state authority, that they are detached from national interests, and possess the capacity to transcend traditional geopolitical boundaries. According to this narrative, technology companies are perceived as advancing far beyond the regulatory reach of states, leading the global technological race through their own autonomous momentum. However, recent developments reveal that this perception of decentralization and independence is fundamentally flawed. The emergence of "technopolarity" as a defining concept of the contemporary international system has exposed the deep entanglement between technology companies and state power. Technopolarity reflects a structural reality in which technological capabilities, innovation trajectories, and global influence are increasingly concentrated within and shaped by the strategic imperatives of nation-states.

Concrete examples vividly illustrate this dynamic. The recent wave of bans against DeepSeek in countries traditionally aligned with the U.S. (Akıllı, 2025d), and the regulatory limitations imposed on NVIDIA's exports to China (Akıllı, 2025b), clearly demonstrate that technology firms are not operating in a vacuum. Rather, they are subjected to and often instrumentalized by the broader geopolitical strategies of their home governments. Such cases highlight that the so-called independence of Big Tech is, in practice, subordinate to national security concerns, economic competition, and strategic alliances. Therefore, the portrayal of big technology companies as neutral patrons of cutting-edge innovation must be critically reassessed. In reality, they function as extensions of their countries of origin, deeply embedded within the political, economic, and strategic frameworks of their respective states. Understanding this embeddedness is crucial for interpreting the evolving nature of international relations in the digital age, where the boundaries between state power and corporate influence are increasingly blurred, and where technological leadership is inseparable from national interest.

Bibliography

Acharya, A. (2004). How ideas spread: Whose norms matter? Norm localization and institutional change in Asian regionalism. *International Organization, 58*(2), 239–275.

Akıllı, E. (2022). The Metaverse Diplomacy: A future vision for Türkiye, *Insight Turkey, 23*(3). Retrieved May 5, 2025, from https://www.insightturkey.com/articles/the-metaverse-diplomacy-a-future-vision-for-turkiye

Akıllı, E. (2023, June 23). *Has the Skynet Moment Finally Arrived?* Daily Sabah. Retrieved May 5, 2025, from https://www.dailysabah.com/opinion/op-ed/has-the-skynet-moment-finally-arrived

Akıllı, E. (2024, April 5). *Artificial Intelligence in Counterterrorism: Navigating the Intersection of Security, Ethics, and Privacy.* SETA Perspective. No. 73. Retrieved May 25, 2025, from https://www.setav.org/en/security/artificial-intelligence-in-counterterrorism-navigating-the-intersection-of-security-ethics-and-privacy

Akıllı, E. (2025a, April 18). *Rewiring Diplomacy in the Technopolar World.* Daily Sabah (Op-Ed). Retrieved May 11, 2025, from https://www.dailysabah.com/opinion/op-ed/rewiring-diplomacy-in-the-technopolar-world

Akıllı, E. (2025b, February 1). *Trump's Stargate, Biden's Tier List and the Wake of the Techno-Polar World.* Daily Sabah. Retrieved May 5, 2025, from https://www.dailysabah.com/opinion/op-ed/trumps-stargate-bidens-tier-list-and-the-wake-of-the-techno-polar-world

Akıllı, E. (2025c, March 6). *Role of virtual power plants in AI R&D in a technopolar world order.* Daily Sabah. Retrieved May 5, 2025, from https://www.dailysabah.com/opinion/op-ed/role-of-virtual-power-plants-in-ai-rd-in-a-technopolar-world-order

Akıllı, E. (2025d, February 14). *AI geopolitics: Power shifts in the techno-polar world.* Daily Sabah. Retrieved May 5, 2025, from https://www.dailysabah.com/opinion/op-ed/ai-geopolitics-power-shifts-in-the-techno-polar-world

Ball, J. and Greenwald, G. (2013, 20 September). *Revealed: how US and UK Spy Agencies Defeat Internet Privacy and Security.* The Guardian. Retrieved

May 5, 2025, from https://www.theguardian.com/world/2013/sep/05/nsa-gchq-encryption-codes-security

Barkawi, T., & Laffey, M. (2006). The postcolonial moment in security studies. *Review of International Studies, 32*(2), 329–352.

Barlow, J. P. (1996). *A Declaration of the Independence of Cyberspace*. Electronic Frontier Foundation (EFF). Retrieved May 5, 2025, from https://www.eff.org/cyberspace-independence

Bellanova, R., Carrapico, H., & Duez, D. (2022). Digital/sovereignty and European security integration: An introduction. *European Security, 31*(3), 337–355. https://doi.org/10.1080/09662839.2022.2101887

Bremmer, I. and Kupchan, C. (2022, January 3). *Top risks 2022: Risk 2—Technopolar world*. Eurasia Group. Retrieved May 5, 2025, from https://www.eurasiagroup.net/live-post/top-risks-2022-2-technopolar-world

Captain Compliance. (2025, January 6). *Russia Data Localization Law: 2025 Essential Guide*. Retrieved May 5, 2025, from https://captaincompliance.com/education/russia-data-localization-law/

Chander, A. and Sun, H. (2021). *Sovereignty 2.0*. Georgetown University Law Center. Retrieved May 5, 2025, from https://scholarship.law.georgetown.edu/facpub/2404

Citron, D. K., & Pasquale, F. (2019). The scored society: Due process for automated predictions. *Washington Law Review., 89*(1), 1–33.

Deibert, R. J. (2019). The road to digital Unfreedom: Three painful truths about social media. *Journal of Democracy, 30*(1), 25–39. https://doi.org/10.1353/jod.2019.0002

Ermolina, D., Bulgakov, I. and Sholokhov, M. (2025). *Tougher Personal Data Localisation Requirements from 1 July 2025*. Denuo Legal. Retrieved May 5, 2025, from https://denuo.legal/en/insights/news/250303/

European Union. (2016). General data protection regulation. *Official Journal of the European Union, 119*, 1–88. Retrieved May 5, 2025, from https://eur-lex.europa.eu/eli/reg/2016/679/oj

European Union. (2005). Digital Markets Act (DMA). Retrieved October 16, 2025, from https://digital-marketsact.ec.europa.eu/index_en

Farwell, J. P., & Rohozinski, R. (2011). Stuxnet and the future of cyber war. *Survival, 53*(1), 23–40. https://doi.org/10.1080/00396338.2011.555586

Fleming, S. (2025, 10 January). *What Is Digital Sovereignty and How Are Countries Approaching It*? World U Forum. Retrieved May 5, 2025, from https://www.weforum.org/stories/2025/01/europe-digital-sovereignty/

Gu, H. (2023). Data, big tech, and the new concept of sovereignty. *Journal of Chinese Political Science, 29*(4), ss. 591–612. https://doi.org/10.1007/s11366-023-09855-1

Haataja, S. (2017). The 2007 cyber attacks against Estonia and international law on the use of force: An informational approach. *Law, Innovation and*

Technology., *9*(2), 159–189. https://doi.org/10.1080/17579961.2017.1377914
Hsu, S. (2021). *China's Regulatory Clampdown on Big Tech*. Chinaus-ICAS. Retrieved May 5, 2025, from https://chinaus-icas.org/research/chinas-regulatory-clampdown-on-big-tech/
Institute for Internet and the Just Society. (2025). *Algorithmic Decision-Making*. Retrieved May 5, 2025, from https://www.internetjustsociety.org/algorithmic-decision-making
Keohane, R. O., & Nye, J. S. (1977). *Power and interdependence: World politics in transition*. Little, Brown and Company.
Khan, L. (2017). Amazon's Antitrust Paradox. *Yale Law Journal.*, *126*(3), 710–805.
Kissinger, H. (2014). *World Order*. Penguin Books.
Klimburg, A. (2017). *The darkening web: The war for cyberspace*. Penguin Press.
Krasner, S. D. (1999). *Sovereignty: Organized hypocrisy*. Princeton University Press.
Mathews, J. T. (1997). Power shift. *Foreign Affairs, 76*(1), 50–66.
NATO. (2024). *Cyber Defence*. Retrieved May 5, 2025, from https://www.nato.int/cps/en/natohq/topics_78170.htm
Ohmae, K. (1990). *The borderless world: Power and strategy in the interlinked economy*. Harper Business.
Onuf, N. (1991). Sovereignty: Outline of a conceptual history. *Alternatives, 16*(4), 425–444.
Osiander, A. (2001). Sovereignty, international relations, and the Westphalian myth. *International Organization, 55*(2), 251–287.
Philpott, D. (2001). *Revolutions in sovereignty: How ideas shaped modern international relations*. Princeton University Press.
Radice, L. C. (2019). *Evolving Conceptions of Sovereignty as Applied to Membership in International Organizations*. Claremont McKenna College. Retrieved May 5, 2025, from https://scholarship.claremont.edu/cmc_theses/2147
Reznikova, A. (2025, 25 March). *New Requirements for Localization of Personal Data in Russia*. Konsu Group. Retrieved May 5, 2025, from https://konsugroup.com/en/news/new-requirements-personal-data-protection-russia-2025-07/
Srivastava, S. (2025, September 15). *Algorithmic Governance and the International Politics of Big Tech*. Political Science Now. Retrieved May 5, 2025, from https://politicalsciencenow.com/algorithmic-governance-and-the-international-politics-of-big-tech/
Strange, S. (1996). *The retreat of the state: The diffusion of power in the world economy*. Cambridge University Press.

The Editors of Encyclopaedia Britannica. (2025). *"Peace of Westphalia", Encyclopedia Britannica*. Retrieved April 29, 2025, from https://www.britannica.com/event/Peace-of-Westphalia

United Nations. (1945). *Charter of the United Nations*. United Nations. Retrieved May 4, 2025, from https://www.un.org/en/about-us/un-charter

United Nations. (2005, 24 October). *2005 World Summit Outcome, UN Doc. A/RES/60/1, 24 October*. Retrieved May 4, 2025, from https://www.un.org/en/development/desa/population/migration/generalassembly/docs/globalcompact/A_RES_60_1.pdf

United Nations Group of Governmental Experts (UN GGE). (2015). *Report of the Group of Governmental Experts on developments in the field of information and telecommunications in the context of international security*. United Nations General Assembly.

United States Congress (2018). *Clarifying Lawful Overseas Use of Data Act (CLOUD Act)*. Public Law. (pp. 115–141). Retrieved June 13, 2025, from https://www.justice.gov/criminal/media/999391/dl?inline

Vattel, E. de. (1758). *The law of nations, or, Principles of the law of nature applied to the conduct and affairs of nations and sovereigns. (Translated by J. Chitty, 1834)*. T. & J.W. Johnson.

Wendt, A. (1992). Anarchy is what states make of it: The social construction of power politics. *International Organization*, *46*(2), 391–425.

Wu, T. (2018). *The curse of bigness: Antitrust in the new gilded age*. Columbia Global Reports.

CHAPTER 4

Sovereignty 2.0: Adapting the Westphalian Principle to the Technopolar Era

The theoretical and historical survey in the previous chapter revealed a clear trajectory—sovereignty, while remaining a foundational concept, has never been static. It has evolved from the territorial, monarch-centric order of Westphalia through the complex interdependence of the twentieth century, and now into a digitally infused paradigm that demands new interpretations of what it means to be a sovereign state (Montevideo Convention on the Rights and Duties of States, 1933). In the technopolar world of the twenty-first century, power is increasingly measured not only in tanks or GDP but in control of technology infrastructure, data, and innovation (Akıllı, 2025a). States find themselves vying not just with each other, but with powerful tech corporations and diffuse cyberthreats, over who governs the digital realm. The classical Westphalian model based on inviolable borders is insufficient in a world of ubiquitous connectivity and algorithmic influence (Akıllı, 2025a). Consequently, we see the emergence of what might be called *Sovereignty 2.0*: a reconceptualization of sovereignty that emphasizes a state's capacity to wield influence and enforce rules in the digital domain and maintain autonomy in critical technologies. This includes data sovereignty—the ability to control and protect data; algorithmic sovereignty—the ability to develop and govern the AI and algorithms that shape society; and hardware or tech sovereignty—the ability to secure supply chains and production of key technologies like semiconductors (Akıllı, 2025a; Larsen, 2022). In this

E. Akıllı, *Cognitive Diplomacy and Digital Autonomy*,
https://doi.org/10.1007/978-3-032-04470-9_4

view, sovereignty is becoming as much about infrastructural and digital capability as it is about legal authority. As one analyst noted, there is a shift "from juridical control to infrastructural capability"—states are now competing over the architectures of the digital future, not just territory (Akıllı, 2025a).

However, as states pursue Sovereignty 2.0, they walk a tightrope. On one side, lies the imperative to adapt and protect sovereignty: to prevent undue dependence on foreign tech, to ensure that local laws can be enforced in cyberspace, and to guard against external manipulation or data exploitation. On the other side, lies the risk of fragmentation and authoritarianism (Kokas, 2023): taken to extremes, digital sovereignty drives could balkanize the internet and provide cover for repressive control over information (Chander & Sun, 2021). The technopolar world thus forces a rebalancing of values (Bremmer, 2023). Democratic states are challenged to uphold openness and universal rights while still securing their digital flank—a theme that will recur in discussions of data governance and AI ethics. (Bremmer and Suleyman, 2023). Meanwhile, developing countries fear being left behind as digital dependence could translate into new forms of digital colonialism by richer states or tech firms (Gu, 2023). International diplomacy is beginning to grapple with these issues, as seen in forums, from the U.N. to the Antalya Diplomacy Forum, which stresses inclusivity and cooperation in technology governance (Akıllı, 2025a).

Sovereignty remains central but its expression is transforming. The Westphalian ideal of absolute control within territorial borders is yielding to a nuanced reality where effective sovereignty means building resilient digital infrastructure, asserting normative frameworks for cyberspace, and sometimes partnering with or counterbalancing powerful non-state actors. The historical arc from 1648 to today demonstrates that the resilience of sovereignty as a principle lies in its ability to adapt to new power dynamics.

In this chapter, we will delve deeper into three critical facets of this transformation: how states are dealing with algorithmic governance, redefining data sovereignty in an age of information ubiquity, and securing semiconductor production and technological autonomy as a linchpin of national power. Each of these domains illuminates the opportunities and perils for state sovereignty in the technopolar era. The theoretical foundation laid in this chapter underscores a pivotal insight:

to thrive in the current global system, states must rewire the traditional sovereignty doctrine for the digital age—crafting and advancing Sovereignty 2.0 in a manner that preserves the core values of the international order while embracing the realities of technological change.

4.1 Data Sovereignty and the Control of Digital Economies

To say, "*data is the new oil*," has become a *cliché* but the analogy underscores how vital data has become to national power in the digital economy. Data: information about individuals, businesses, natural resources, and virtually every facet of life is now a key input for economic activity, scientific research, governance, and military intelligence. The ability to collect, store, and analyze large datasets gives rise to competitive advantages in AI (which learns from data), targeted advertising, health care, urban planning, and more. Countries with rich data resources and the capacity to exploit them can spur innovation and growth, whereas those without access to data (or dependent on others for data processing) may fall behind. Moreover, certain types of data are highly sensitive: personal data implicates privacy and civil liberties; government data can affect national security; and industrial data (like proprietary designs or geological surveys) bears on economic competitiveness. Hence, controlling data—who owns it, where it is located, and who can use it—has become a strategic matter for states (Akıllı, 2025a).

Data sovereignty refers to the principle that data is subject to the laws and governance of the nation where it is collected or pertains and that nations have the right to control data generated within their borders (Akıllı, 2025a). In practice, data sovereignty means a country asserting that its domestic data (especially personal data of its citizens, or data critical to national interests) should be stored and processed on servers physically located on its territory or at least under its legal jurisdiction. By doing so, the state can enforce its privacy laws, data protection regulations, and security requirements on that data, rather than having it reside in foreign jurisdictions where it might be accessible to foreign governments or beyond the reach of local law. The push for data sovereignty has grown as a reaction to the earlier period of unfettered data globalization. In the 1990s and 2000s, companies freely moved data across borders to maximize efficiency—for instance, storing data in large cloud computing centers in whatever country offered the best cost and connectivity. However, this led to situations where a great deal of, say, European user data might be stored in the U.S. and thus subject to U.S. law (like the Patriot Act), or the emails of Brazilian citizens might be handled by servers in California and thus accessible to U.S. subpoenas. Governments grew uncomfortable with the idea that their citizens' information was effectively under foreign jurisdiction (Conceptboard, 2023; De Mooy, 2017; Lowitja Institute, 2024).

Major catalysts for data sovereignty efforts included revelations of extensive U.S. government surveillance programs. After the Snowden revelations in 2013 showed how intelligence agencies accessed global data flows, countries like Germany and Brazil were alarmed that data of their citizens (often stored by U.S. tech firms) had been vacuumed up (Hill, 2014). This spurred calls to keep data at home. For example, Brazil proposed legislation to force internet companies to store Brazilian data on Brazilian soil (though it later softened that requirement), and Germany mulled a "Schengen cloud" for European data. The fear was clear: *if* data is stored abroad, a nation's sovereignty could be "threatened by their inability to exert full control over data stored outside their borders" (Wu, 2021). Thus, data localization, mandating that certain data stay within the country, was promoted as a way to reassert control. Data localization and sovereignty measures are now on the books in many jurisdictions. Russia, for instance, passed a law in 2015 requiring that personal data on Russian citizens be stored on servers located in Russia. China's cybersecurity law in 2017 (Standing Committee of the National People's Congress, 2017; Wagner, 2017) and Data Security Law in 2021 (Standing Committee of the National People's Congress, 2021) likewise impose strict rules on transferring data abroad and require certain data to be held domestically. India has debated and introduced rules around local storage of payment data and draft personal data protection bills that include localization provisions. Even The EU, which generally supports a free and open internet, has taken steps toward what it calls "digital sovereignty," encouraging European cloud infrastructure and passing regulations to keep European data subject to EU privacy standards.

4.2 National Data Governance and Localization Examples

Different countries have adopted varying models of data governance (Srivastava and Bullock, 2024) in line with their sovereignty aims. China operates perhaps the world's most comprehensive system of national data governance: all major internet firms must house data on domestic servers, authorities conduct security reviews before certain data can be exported, and laws ensure the government can access data for national security or law enforcement. This gives China extensive sovereign control over domestic data—at the cost of tight surveillance and restrictions on cross-border information flow. Western countries have been more selective, trying to balance openness with sovereignty. The EU's GDPR, enacted in 2018, is primarily a privacy law, but it has an important sovereignty dimension as well. It asserts that any company anywhere in the world handling EU residents' personal data must adhere to EU standards. Moreover, after a legal challenge (Schrems II case), the EU struck down the EU–U.S. "Privacy Shield" arrangement because U.S. law was deemed inadequate to protect Europeans' data from U.S. government surveillance. In effect, the EU is saying: that unless data transferred to foreign jurisdictions gets an equivalent level of protection as under EU law, those transfers can be limited—a sovereignty-based stance to protect citizens' fundamental rights. Additionally, European leaders have promoted the idea of a "European cloud" or initiatives like Gaia-X—a federated cloud infrastructure project aiming to ensure European data is hosted in Europe and governed by European rules, rather than being reliant on American providers alone. France, for instance, launched a "Trusted Cloud" label and partnerships to encourage cloud services that are immune from extraterritorial foreign laws (meaning, for instance, not subject to the U.S. CLOUD Act) to preserve French control over sensitive data (Frenus, 2025; Gaia-X, 2024; Gaia-X, 2025).

In other cases, data sovereignty drives specific legislation such as data localization laws. These laws require certain categories of data to be stored on servers within the country. For instance, India's financial and payment data. Its central bank in 2018 ordered payment processors (like Visa or MasterCard) to store transaction data of Indians only in India (Basatwar, 2025; S.S. Rana & Co. Advocates, 2022; Reserve Bank of India, 2018).

Likewise for health and genomic data, some countries consider these so sensitive that they restrict foreign access. Government data is often mandated to be hosted on domestic cloud servers or data centers to prevent foreign jurisdiction over state information. The motivations are often couched in terms of security and privacy (Digital Agency Japan, 2025; GOV.UK, 2025). National digital economy strategies increasingly highlight sovereignty. In Australia, for example, debates have arisen about ensuring government data is stored in locally owned clouds, and the term "digital sovereignty" appears in policy papers about balancing engagement in global digital services with control over national data (Mueller, 2017). In the EU, the concept of "technological or digital sovereignty" has broadened to encompass not just data, but also control over technologies and standards—yet data sovereignty remains a core pillar.

A notable manifestation of data sovereignty is the development of sovereign cloud infrastructures (Akıllı, 2025a). These are cloud computing services that are either operated by local companies or operated by foreign companies in such a way that the data they hold is under the effective control of the local jurisdiction. For example, in Germany a few years ago, Microsoft set up a special cloud in partnership with Deutsche Telekom acting as a "data trustee" to ensure that Microsoft could not move data out or comply with foreign requests without Telekom's consent, thereby aligning with German sovereignty concerns (Deutsche Telekom, 2015; Digitalisation World, 2015; Judge, 2015). Similarly, France's government has backed cloud services by domestic firms (or collaborations like Thales with Google under a secure arrangement) to create options where French data is shielded from U.S. legal reach (Thales and Google Cloud, 2022). These efforts reflect a desire to cultivate domestic or regional capabilities in data storage and processing, reducing reliance on U.S. tech giants like Amazon Web Services, Google Cloud, and Microsoft Azure, which currently dominate the cloud industry.

4.3 Benefits and Rationale of Data Sovereignty

Proponents of data sovereignty argue that such measures strengthen national security, protect citizens' privacy, and ensure economic benefits from data accrue locally. By keeping personal data on local servers, governments can more easily enforce privacy laws and prevent foreign intelligence or law enforcement from accessing that data without permission. Localizing data can also force multinational companies to invest in local data centers (creating jobs and infrastructure). Furthermore, if data is a valuable resource for AI and innovation, countries reason that localizing it can help domestic companies and researchers utilize it, rather than having it all flow to Silicon Valley or elsewhere. Countries like Indonesia and Vietnam, for instance, have cited the need to develop their own digital industries as a justification for data localization requirements, hoping to nurture homegrown data centers and analytics firms.

From a sovereignty perspective, having critical datasets under national control is akin to having critical commodities or industries under national control. Just as some nations don't want to rely entirely on foreign oil or foreign electricity grids, they may not want to rely on foreign data services for vital information processing. The COVID-19 pandemic illustrated this point: health data, vaccination data, and mobility data became crucial to managing the crisis, and many countries built national dashboards and databases, sometimes hesitating to use foreign cloud providers for these out of concern for autonomy (European Court of Auditors, 2021; OECD, 2022; NHS England, 2021; U.S. Department of Health and Human Services, 2021). Another rationale is avoiding "data colonization." Scholars have used this term to describe how tech firms from a few countries, notably the U.S. and China (Mayer and Afterman, 2023), extract vast amounts of data from users in other countries, especially developing countries, and then monetize that data with little benefit returning to those users or their states (Global Partnership for Sustainable Development Data, 2020). In response, some countries in the Global South are asserting data sovereignty to prevent this one-way flow of data value. In Africa, for example, there are discussions about requiring that data collected from Africans stay in Africa or is at least governed by African consent, to avoid a new form of digital age dependency (TechAfricaNews, 2025; Abagun, 2025; Africa Practice, 2025; Macdonald, 2025; Benamara, 2025).

4.4 Challenges and Criticisms of Data Sovereignty Efforts

Despite the intuitive appeal of data sovereignty, critics argue that heavy-handed data localization can backfire. For one, forcing companies to store data in every country where they operate can fragment the internet, leading to a "*Balkanization*" of cyberspace (Hill, 2014). It undermines the efficiencies of global cloud computing—instead of centralized hubs serving many markets, data might require needless duplication, raising costs. Studies have shown that data localization can hurt especially smaller economies by isolating them from global services and innovation. For example, businesses in a country with strict localization may not be able to use global cloud platforms or might face higher prices, slowing their digital economy (Institute of International Finance, 2020; OECD, 2023; Cory et al., 2022; Bauer et al., 2014).

An analysis by the Belfer Center noted that such policies are often "ineffective at improving security" and can cause economic harm while not necessarily delivering the sovereignty benefits promised (Chander & Le, 2015). For instance, storing data in-country doesn't automatically shield it from foreign hackers or espionage—strong encryption and cybersecurity practices do and are needed regardless of data location. Furthermore, if every country demanded all data be stored locally, companies would face a maze of compliance, potentially reducing the availability of some online services across borders. Indeed, there have been instances where companies chose to withdraw services rather than comply with local data mandates (Chander & Le, 2015). When states press too hard, it can deter foreign investment in the tech sector.

Another challenge is that *mere localization does not equal absolute control*. Data can be encrypted or transmitted surreptitiously and jurisdictional control can be bypassed if companies or individuals use technological means to route data abroad (virtual private networks, etc.). Thus, data sovereignty is only as strong as the enforcement and the broader cyber capabilities of a nation. Additionally, striking the balance between sovereignty and freedom is delicate. In liberal democracies, policies inspired by data sovereignty still must respect free speech and an open internet. There is a risk that under the banner of "sovereignty," governments could enact measures that censor online content or surveil domestic opponents. Civil liberty advocates often warily note that authoritarian governments use the same language of digital sovereignty to justify internet shutdowns or data hoarding for repression. The double-edged nature of digital sovereignty is evident: it can empower a society or entrench authoritarian power (Chander & Sun, 2021). For instance, Russia's assertion of a "sovereign internet" has involved testing RuNet disconnection from the global web and tightening control over internet exchanges—moves that enhance the government's ability to control information in times of political crisis (BBC News, 2019;

OCCRP, 2019; Reuters, 2024; Wilde & Sherman, 2022; Stolyarov and Papachristou, 2024).

4.5 Case Studies of EU, China, India, and Brazil—Data Sovereignty in Action

The EU stands as a leading advocate of digital sovereignty through regulatory and infrastructural initiatives. The GDPR has established a legal regime whereby the personal data of EU citizens retains EU legal protections wherever it is processed. Following the *Schrems II* decision by the Court of Justice of the EU, which invalidated the Privacy Shield framework with the U.S., the EU, and the U.S. negotiated the Trans-Atlantic Data Privacy Framework (2022) to reconcile EU data protection standards with transatlantic data flows (European Commission, 2022b). Simultaneously, Europe has sought to reduce its dependence on foreign technology providers through initiatives like GAIA-X, which promotes a federated, secure cloud infrastructure built on European values and standards (Gaia-X Association, 2021). Furthermore, landmark regulations such as the Digital Markets Act and the Digital Services Act have reinforced the EU's control over large technology platforms, positioning Europe as a global regulator and a sovereign actor in digital governance (Larsen, 2022).

In China, data sovereignty is pursued as a comprehensive and national security-driven project. Since the Cybersecurity Law which implemented in 2017 (Erdenebileg, 2017) and expanded through the Data Security Law in 2021 (NPC, 2021) and the Personal Information Protection Law (China Briefing, 2021), China has mandated data localization and imposes strict rules on cross-border data transfers. Foreign cloud services are required to partner with local firms to ensure state oversight. A vivid example came in 2021 when Chinese regulators blocked ride-hailing giant *Didi* from app stores after its U.S. IPO, citing risks that U.S. authorities could gain access to Chinese user data (Chander & Sun, 2021). Official discourse frames these policies as safeguarding "information security," yet analysts widely interpret them as advancing regime stability and digital self-determination against perceived Western digital hegemony (Belli & Jiang, 2024).

India, meanwhile, represents a democratic yet assertive model of data sovereignty. While earlier drafts of its Personal Data Protection Bill (since replaced by the Data Protection Act 2023) proposed strict localization requirements, the final legislation took a more flexible stance. Nonetheless, it continues to localize certain critical data types, particularly in the financial sector (Government of India, 2023). In 2020, amid geopolitical tensions with China, India banned over 50 Chinese apps, including TikTok and WeChat, on national security grounds. Officials argued these apps risked transmitting Indian user data to Chinese servers, placing sensitive information under foreign jurisdiction. This move underscored India's readiness to restrict foreign services outright as a means of enforcing its sovereign data policy (Patel, 2020).

Brazil, on the other hand, has advanced digital sovereignty through a rights-based approach. Following the 2013 Snowden revelations, then-President Dilma Rousseff championed internet sovereignty at the United Nations and domestically pushed for regulatory reforms. The passage of the Marco Civil da Internet (CGI.br, 2014) enshrined privacy, net neutrality, and freedom of expression in law. Though Brazil considered but ultimately did not implement strict localization, its General Data Protection Law (LGPD), adopted in 2018 and inspired by the GDPR, reinforced national control over personal data processing (Hill, 2014; LGPD, 2018). Brazil's diplomatic and legal push signaled to foreign tech firms that access to its market depends on respecting Brazilian digital governance frameworks.

4.6 Threats to Data Sovereignty

Even with laws in place, maintaining data sovereignty is an ongoing challenge. Two major types of threats stand out: surveillance threats and foreign corporate dominance (Arun, 2024). Surveillance threats come from the intelligence activities of foreign powers as well as potential misuse by private actors. The Snowden episode exemplified how U.S. surveillance jeopardized other countries' data sovereignty, prompting efforts to route internet traffic away from U.S. networks or develop countersurveillance measures (France 24, 2013; Hopkins, 2013). Today, concerns persist that advanced spyware or cyber espionage can exfiltrate a nation's sensitive data despite localization.

Recent revelations about spyware like NSO Group's Pegasus, which can steal data from phones, show that a determined actor can bypass sovereign controls by going directly to the source (the device) rather than a data center (Amnesty International, 2021; Greengard, 2025). Thus, data sovereignty requires robust cybersecurity—a point not lost on policymakers. Many nations are coupling data governance with investment in encryption, secure networks, and "zero-trust" architectures to guard against unauthorized foreign access. Cooperative initiatives among like-minded countries are also emerging to counteract surveillance threats. For example, the EU and the U.S. are negotiating rules for law enforcement access to data (the CLOUD Act agreements) so that each side's sovereignty is respected when the other seeks data for legitimate investigations (Wu, 2021).

Foreign corporate dominance is another challenge. When a handful of big tech companies control large swathes of a country's digital ecosystem, they effectively become gatekeepers of that country's data. For instance, Facebook holds data on tens of millions of citizens in country X, and Amazon's cloud hosts databases for many of country X's companies. This raises the question: can country X's government enforce its laws on those companies effectively, or will it be at the mercy of the companies' policies (or their home country's laws)? There's also the risk of foreign companies deciding unilaterally to cut off services or data flows, which would impact the local economy—a form of leverage over sovereignty. We have seen glimmers of this when tech companies resist government orders. For example, WhatsApp (owned by Facebook parent Meta) has clashed with governments like Brazil and India over demands to trace messages or break encryption for sovereignty/security reasons, at times resulting in temporary service blockages by governments (Business Today, 2025; McCallum, 2022).

Additionally, economic coercion via data is a theoretical threat. If, say, a foreign firm controls critical databases (imagine a global supply chain platform or a dominant e-commerce marketplace), they could conceivably leverage that control in political disputes. This is analogous to how pipeline owners or financial institutions can exert pressure. Therefore, nations are wary of allowing any single foreign entity to become too entrenched in critical data infrastructure. The current debates over 5G networks and whether to allow Chinese companies like Huawei are partly about data sovereignty as well. Since 5G will carry immense data traffic, if that infrastructure is provided by a company subject to Chinese state influence, governments fear their data sovereignty could be compromised (Berman, 2023; Kroet, 2025; Robinson, 2025). This is why many Western countries banned or restricted Huawei in 5G rollouts, preferring suppliers seen as aligned with their own bloc.

In summary, data sovereignty has moved to the center of digital policy. Nations are crafting laws to keep data close and assert legal authority over information, thereby trying to secure their slice of the digital economy and protect citizens. The trend reflects a realization that informational power is national power. However, as this section has shown, executing data sovereignty is complex. It requires careful calibration to avoid stifling the benefits of a global internet, and it must be backed by technical measures such as cyber-defenses, robust local infrastructure and respect for rights. The next chapter will turn to algorithmic sovereignty, a domain deeply intertwined with data. After all, raw data itself has limited value unless one can derive insight or action from it—and that is the role of algorithms and AI. We will see how states are responding to the rise of autonomous and algorithmic decision-making systems, seeking to ensure that the "brains" behind increasingly important decisions are under sovereign oversight and aligned with national values.

4.7 Algorithmic Sovereignty and Autonomous Decision-Making

First and foremost, what is algorithmic sovereignty? As AI and algorithms permeate governance, economics, and daily life, nations are confronted with a new question: who controls the algorithms that shape societal outcomes? *Algorithmic sovereignty* refers to a state's capacity to govern and shape the algorithms—particularly in complex AI systems—that operate within its jurisdiction (Akıllı, 2025a). In essence, it is about ensuring that the power of automated, data-driven decision-making is subject to the will of the sovereign people (through their government), rather than left solely to private companies or foreign developers. Algorithms now curate the news we read, determine credit scores, control critical infrastructure, assist in military targeting, and much more. If these algorithms are opaque "black boxes," created and hosted elsewhere, a government might find itself unable to answer fundamental governance questions: Is an AI-driven system discriminating against certain citizens? Is a foreign adversary subtly influencing what information an algorithm shows our population? Could an algorithmic trading program crash our financial markets? Algorithmic sovereignty seeks to address such concerns by asserting that nations must have insight into, and possibly control over, important algorithms affecting their citizens.

At the core of algorithmic sovereignty is autonomous decision-making—the idea that AI can make decisions or recommendations with minimal human intervention. While autonomy can increase efficiency and scale, it also complicates accountability. Western societies typically insist that important decisions, like who is approved for welfare, or whether a self-driving car should be allowed on the road, be subject to laws and ethical norms established via sovereign processes (Calo, 2016; European Commission, 2021; Mittelstadt, 2019; Wachter et al., 2017).

Thus, algorithmic sovereignty implies the ability of a state to *audit, regulate, and if necessary intervene in or domesticate* algorithmic systems to align them with public policy and values. It also encompasses building indigenous capability. A country may decide it needs its own AI algorithms (for defense or sensitive applications) rather than relying on potentially untrustworthy foreign AI (Anthony et. al., 2024). For example, there is active discussion in Europe about pursuing "AI sovereignty" (Van Oirsouw, 2023) so that European industries and governments are not entirely dependent on AI systems from the U.S. or China, which might embed those countries' values or priorities (European Commission, 2025a; William Fry, 2024; Innovation News Network, 2025).

4.8 The Importance of Algorithmic Sovereignty in Governance and Security

Why does this matter? Consider that algorithms can carry biases or hidden objectives of their creators. If a crime-prediction algorithm (Akıllı, 2024) used by police is developed in another country, it might not reflect local laws or could even be manipulated. In national security, if a military buys a foreign autonomous drone system, can it trust that system not to have a hidden kill switch or a feed of its data back to the seller? These scenarios illustrate how a lack of algorithmic sovereignty could undermine both the fairness of domestic governance and the effectiveness of national security. Even in less extreme cases, countries worry about a kind of cultural or ideological influence through algorithms. Social media algorithms, often designed in the U.S., determine what content millions of foreign users see.

Some governments fear this could erode local culture or amplify unrest, for instance, if the algorithm inadvertently promotes extremist content (Digital Regulation Cooperation Forum, 2022; UNICRI, 2023). In a notable case, the U.S. itself has expressed national security concerns about the algorithm behind TikTok (a Chinese-owned platform), suggesting it could be tweaked to favor or suppress certain narratives within the U.S. population (Filipiak, 2025; Kiely, 2025; Minges, 2025). These concerns show both superpowers and smaller states are treating algorithmic influence as a sovereignty issue.

Moreover, economic competitiveness is at stake. Algorithms and AI drive modern industries—from manufacturing to medicine. If a nation lacks expertise or access to these, it may become economically subordinate to those who own the algorithms. Countries like France and Germany have called for developing homegrown AI solutions to reduce reliance on foreign tech giants—a theme also echoed in the European Commission's digital strategy which emphasizes technological *and* normative sovereignty in AI (Schneider, 2025; Hulkó et al., 2025; European Commission, 2025b). In sum, algorithmic sovereignty is seen as vital to maintaining political autonomy, social cohesion, and economic self-determination in the age of AI.

4.9 State Efforts to Regulate AI and Algorithms

Globally, governments are waking up to the need for AI regulation and oversight. The EU has been a pioneer with its proposed Artificial Intelligence Act (AI Act) (European Commission, 2025c; European Parliament, 2025). This EU AI Act will create a comprehensive legal framework for AI systems, especially those deemed "high-risk." It adopts a risk-based approach: AI used in sensitive areas like hiring, credit, policing, or medical devices will face strict requirements for transparency, risk mitigation, and even prior approval, whereas low-risk uses are largely left alone (Larsen, 2022).

Notably, the AI Act would *ban* certain AI practices outright (for example, social scoring systems like China's, or real-time face surveillance in public places, except in special cases) as an unacceptable risk to fundamental rights (Larsen, 2022). High-risk AI (say, an algorithm used to decide if someone gets a mortgage) will need to be certified for compliance with EU standards, including requirements for explainability and human oversight. This essentially asserts the EU's sovereign right to deem some algorithms incompatible with its societal values and demand modifications to others. In parallel, the EU's Digital Services Act and Digital Markets Act (European Union, 2025) also impose obligations on large online platforms to reveal how their recommender algorithms work and allow user choice, aiming to curtail opaque algorithmic amplification of harmful content (Larsen, 2022). All these laws together exemplify a democratic approach to algorithmic sovereignty: not building algorithms per se but regulating their impact so that *human* sovereignty (through law) still presides over automated decisions.

The U.S., historically more laissez-faire in tech, is also moving in this direction, albeit more slowly. There have been federal proposals like the Algorithmic Accountability Act (Congress.gov, 2022) that would require companies to assess their AI systems for bias and explain their operation (Larsen, 2022). While the U.S. has no single AI law yet, regulators are using existing laws to oversee algorithms in specific sectors. For instance, the Federal Trade Commission (FTC) has warned it will punish deceptive or biased AI under consumer protection laws while the Equal Employment Opportunity Commission is looking at hiring algorithms that may potentially discriminate. Additionally, several U.S. states (e.g., Illinois, and Virginia) have enacted laws around AI in hiring or AI transparency. The approach in the U.S. is currently more decentralized and sector-specific, but there is growing recognition that some level of algorithmic oversight is part of maintaining fair markets and protecting civil rights.

Importantly, the U.S. has also started addressing algorithmic sovereignty in a security sense: export controls introduced in 2022 limit China's access to advanced AI chips and software (Allen & Goldston, 2025; Hmaidi and Arcsati, 2022), which is a way for the U.S. to maintain a technological edge. The National Security Commission on AI (NSCAI), a U.S. government advisory body, framed AI leadership as a "competition" with authoritarian adversaries and stressed investing in domestic AI to ensure U.S. strategic sovereignty in that domain (Larsen, 2022).

China, on its part, has been *rapidly* developing AI regulations, surprisingly (to some) taking the lead in certain areas. In early 2022, China implemented the provisions on the Management of Algorithmic Recommendations, one of the world's first comprehensive laws regulating recommender algorithms (Huld, 2022). These rules require companies to make their recommendation algorithms fair, transparent, and oriented toward spreading "positive energy" (Huld, 2022). They must also allow users to have some control, such as the ability to turn off personalized recommendations. Additionally, China has set up an algorithm registration system, companies had to file details of their algorithms with the

Cyberspace Administration of China (AppInChina, 2023; Sheehan & Du, 2022).

This is a striking exercise of algorithmic sovereignty—the state literally inventorying and reviewing the algorithms in use, something no Western country has yet done at scale. Furthermore, China enacted rules on deepfakes and is drafting regulations on generative AI (TechNode, 2025), requiring they not produce content contrary to state laws and undergo security assessments (Tang, 2025; White & Case, 2024). From Beijing's perspective, these moves ensure that as AI proliferates, it does so under the watchful eye of the state and in line with Chinese social norms and political imperatives. While motivated by regime stability, it also creates a framework where Chinese companies have clearer guidelines for "acceptable AI," effectively localizing algorithmic design to Chinese standards.

Other countries are also taking steps. Canada has an Algorithmic Impact Assessment tool for government agencies deploying AI and is working on the AI and Data Act. Japan and South Korea are considering turning AI ethics guidelines into regulations (Government of Canada, 2025; Kaye, 2024; Kaye, 2025). OECD countries jointly adopted AI Principles (2019) emphasizing human rights and oversight, which, though non-binding, influence national strategies. We also see efforts at the multilateral level: the Group of Seven (G7) has discussed "Trustworthy AI" and an international code of conduct, and UNESCO adopted a global Recommendation on AI Ethics (OECD, 2025; EY Global, 2023; European Commission, 2023; UNESCO, 2021). These show a trend toward establishing norms that algorithms should be transparent, fair, and accountable—essentially inserting sovereign (or collective) values into the algorithmic realm.

4.10 Building Domestic AI Capabilities

While regulation is one side of the coin, the other is fostering indigenous algorithmic expertise. Many states have launched national AI strategies with significant investments in research and development, talent training, and startup incubation. The logic is that to have sovereignty over algorithms, a country must cultivate its own AI developers and industries. For example, France's AI strategy explicitly frames the goal of nurturing French AI research as a matter of sovereignty—ensuring

France does not become just an importer of AI solutions developed elsewhere (Bpifrance, 2024; De Giovanni, 2025; Supra, 2025). Similarly, the European Commission's 200 billion euro ($226.67 billion) digital plan aims at "European digital sovereignty" by funding homegrown tech and reducing dependence on foreign AI products (European Comission, 2022c; William Fry, 2024). China's massive AI investments (billions in AI parks, subsidies to companies like SenseTime and Megvii, etc.) are driven by a desire to lead globally and ***not*** be in a position where it needs to buy critical AI from abroad (World Economic Forum, 2025; Froman, 2025). Notably, Russian President Vladimir Putin said in 2017 that "***whoever leads in AI will rule the world***," encapsulating the belief that leadership in algorithmic tech is a strategic asset (Akıllı, 2024).

Several countries are also pursuing open data and open-source initiatives to boost their algorithmic autonomy. The idea is that if local innovators have access to data and open-source AI tools, they can create solutions tailored to local needs, rather than depending on foreign black-box systems. For instance, there is an international push, especially in Europe, for data-sharing frameworks (like European Data Spaces for industrial data) to give domestic companies a leg up in training AI models. We also see collaborations like the global "Partnership on AI" or regional centers of excellence which indirectly support algorithmic sovereignty by pooling knowledge among allies so they are not all reliant on a few Big Tech sources.

4.11 Challenges in Achieving Algorithmic Sovereignty

Despite progress, states encounter significant challenges in their quest for algorithmic sovereignty. One major issue is the opacity and complexity of AI systems. Modern machine learning models, especially deep neural networks, are notoriously hard to interpret. Even their creators sometimes cannot fully explain why an AI made a particular decision. This "black box" nature can clash with legal principles that demand accountability. For instance, if an AI denies someone a loan or parole, on what grounds can they appeal if neither they nor the regulator can discern the reasoning? Requiring explainability may, in some cases, slow down the deployment of the most advanced AI, or force the use of simpler (more explainable but possibly less accurate) models. States must decide how to balance innovation with the demand for clarity and accountability. The

EU is leaning toward prioritizing accountability by insisting on *some level* of explainability or human review in high-risk cases (Tracking Exposed, 2022).

Bias and fairness are also key challenges. Algorithms trained on real-world data can inadvertently learn and perpetuate societal biases. For example, a hiring algorithm might discriminate against women if it is fed data from a past male-dominated hiring pool. Sovereignty in this context means ensuring the algorithm reflects the nation's anti-discrimination laws and values, not just whatever bias exists in the data. Detecting and correcting bias is technically and socially tricky. It requires normative decisions (what counts as fair?) that may differ by culture. Countries may embed their own views: an algorithm considered fair in one jurisdiction might be seen as biased in another depending on legal standards (consider differing views on affirmative action). Hence, algorithmic sovereignty might lead to the localization of models—AI customized to each jurisdiction's legal definitions of fairness or acceptability.

Foreign influence and dependency remain central concerns. If a country's critical infrastructure relies on algorithms provided by a foreign vendor, there is an inherent vulnerability. That vendor might be subject to its home government's pressures. This is why, many countries insist that the software running critical utilities or defense systems be auditable and locally sourced, if possible. During the Huawei 5G debate, beyond hardware, there was a software aspect: could updates to the equipment (driven by foreign software code) be trusted? Similar debates occur about things like cloud-based government services—if the service's algorithms routing government data are foreign, could that be a channel of foreign influence or espionage? To mitigate this, some states require *source code escrow* (the source code must be deposited with a trusted third party or government, so it can be examined if needed) for foreign software used in sensitive areas.

Algorithmic Sovereignty in Practice—Examples:

One emerging example is autonomous weapons systems. Many nations worry about the ethics and control of AI-driven lethal systems. They are debating a treaty on "lethal autonomous weapons systems" (LAWS). One dimension of sovereignty here is, if an AI makes a kill decision in war, how does a state ensure that decision was lawful under its rules of engagement? Some have suggested there should always be a "human in the loop," which is a kind of sovereign guarantee that a human officer—bound by the state's military law—ultimately controls the trigger.

Without such a policy, a country might delegate life-and-death decisions to a machine, potentially losing a measure of moral and legal sovereignty on the battlefield (Akıllı, 2023).

Another example is smart cities. Cities are deploying AI for traffic management, policing (predictive policing algorithms), and resource allocation. If those algorithms come as proprietary packages from Big Tech companies, the city might be stuck with whatever the algorithm does. To reclaim sovereignty, some cities (like Amsterdam and Helsinki) have launched AI registries that publicly list the algorithms they use and their purposes, inviting citizen feedback, and ensuring the municipality can explain and adjust them. In Barcelona, there's talk of "technological sovereignty" at the city level, promoting open-source alternatives for urban digital services to avoid lock-in to vendor algorithms (Rieder & Sire, 2020).

Algorithmic sovereignty is also tested in content moderation and information control. After years of entrusting it to platforms, governments are finally asserting that moderation of online content (often driven by platform algorithms ranking, recommending, or removing content) cannot be left entirely to Silicon Valley's discretion. Germany's NetzDG law (2018) requires social media to remove illegal content quickly or face fines, effectively forcing platforms to adjust their algorithms and policies to German standards of speech (which, for example, outlaw Nazi propaganda). More recently, India's 2021 IT rules demand that large platforms appoint local grievance officers and potentially trace the originators of certain messages, again imposing sovereign requirements on how an algorithmic messaging service operates. These moves have sometimes been contentious—platforms argue they threaten privacy or freedom of expression—but they exemplify states extending their legal regime into algorithm-governed spaces.

4.12 Balancing Innovation and Control

A persistent theme is how to not stifle innovation while asserting algorithmic sovereignty. Over-regulation could discourage companies from developing AI or using it domestically, causing them to fall behind globally. The EU has faced critiques that its stringent approach might make Europe less attractive for AI business compared to the U.S. or China. Indeed, a report suggests EU policy "*prioritizes jurisdictional independence over citizens' sovereignty,*" in a way that might emphasize control at the expense of growth (Blancato & Carr, 2024). Policymakers must calibrate interventions—for instance, providing sandboxes where companies can test AI with regulatory guidance rather than punishment, funding local AI research to offset compliance burdens, and engaging in international standard-setting so their regulations become global norms (which levels the field). Europe often uses its market size to export its regulatory approach (the "Brussels effect"), as arguably happened with data privacy and could with AI. If the EU AI Act becomes a de facto standard for any company selling AI in Europe, it could increase transparency and safety worldwide, which in turn reinforces the EU's algorithmic sovereignty by validating its norms on a global stage.

To conclude this chapter, algorithmic sovereignty is about maintaining or reasserting human and national agency over automated systems. It does not mean rejecting AI or algorithms—rather, it means embedding them in a framework of laws, ethics, and domestic capability such that they advance a nation's objectives and values. The pursuit involves regulation (to curb harm and demand accountability) and nurturing domestic innovation (to avoid dependency and lead in setting the pace of AI advances). Achieving this balance is an ongoing process, as technology evolves quickly. Nevertheless, one can observe a clear trend: states are no longer content being passive consumers of algorithmic systems developed elsewhere. They increasingly seek a *say* in how these systems work and a *stake* in their development.

The next chapter shifts focus to the hardware underpinning the entire digital domain—semiconductors. If *data* is the new oil and *algorithms* the new engines, then *semiconductor chips* are the new steel and machinery of the twenty-first century. As we shall explore, ensuring sovereignty over these tiny but mighty components has become a top priority for many nations.

4.13 Semiconductor Sovereignty and Hardware Independence

At the heart of every modern technology—smartphones, computers, automobiles, medical devices, military systems, and power grids—lies the semiconductor chip (Semiconductors.org, 2024; TechBullion, 2024). These tiny slivers of silicon etched with complex circuits are often referred to as the "brains" of modern electronics. Control over semiconductor technology confers significant economic and strategic power. A country with a strong semiconductor industry reaps huge economic benefits as the industry is worth hundreds of billions of dollars and enables trillions more in downstream industries and also gains security advantages; for instance, chips are essential in advanced weapons and intelligence systems. Conversely, a country dependent on foreign sources for chips, especially advanced chips, may find itself vulnerable to supply cut-offs or manipulation in times of crisis (Suhas et al., 2023). Thus, hardware sovereignty, particularly in semiconductors, has become a critical concern for policymakers. It entails the ability to secure a reliable supply of chips and to trust that hardware and by extension the software running on it is free from malicious tampering. In the technopolar era, semiconductors have been dubbed “the new oil” or “the linchpin of global power,” because without cutting-edge chips, a nation’s digital economy and defense capabilities cannot function. For instance, one of former U.S. President Joe Biden’s last executive orders on regulating GPU exports underscores this competitive and strategic approach. These measures are designed to consolidate U.S. influence by introducing a tiered export control system, effectively regulating global access to advanced AI hardware based on geopolitical alignment. Under this framework, countries are classified into three tiers (Akıllı, 2025b):

Tier 1 encompasses 18 countries regarded as close allies of the U.S., including Australia, Belgium, Canada, Germany, Japan, and the United Kingdom (U.K.). These nations theoretically enjoy broader access to AI processors but remain subject to stringent restrictions. For instance, Tier 1 countries are permitted to export only 25% of their imported processors outside the tier, with a further restriction allowing only 3% of exports to any single non-Tier 1 country. This framework demonstrates the U.S.’ cautious approach, even toward its allies, in safeguarding sensitive technologies. Additionally, high-performance AI GPUs (graphics processing units) designated for defense and critical infrastructure use require prior approval from the U.S., reflecting its intent to maintain comprehensive control over the dissemination of advanced technologies.

Tier 2 comprises countries from Eastern Europe, the Middle East, Latin America, and other regions, including Türkiye. These nations face significant limitations in accessing AI-related hardware. For example, between 2025 and 2027, the total allocation for Tier 2 countries is restricted to 50,000 GPUs. Companies within Tier 2 countries may seek enhanced access through “Verified End User” status, contingent upon stringent compliance with U.S.-defined security protocols. These measures underscore the U.S.' intent to maintain robust control over technology flows while reinforcing its geopolitical influence.

Tier 3, meanwhile, includes countries like China, Russia, Iran, and others under various U.S. sanctions and arms embargoes. These nations face near-total export prohibitions on AI hardware. The primary objective is to prevent these states from leveraging AI technologies to bolster military capabilities. This strict approach underscores the U.S. strategy of leveraging its technological dominance as a tool of geopolitical advantage.

This policy not only deepens the U.S.-China technological rivalry but also highlights the centrality of AI and its enabling hardware in shaping the contours of modern geopolitics. Control over such technologies increasingly determines a state's ability to project power, influence global standards, and secure strategic advantage—a theme that will be further explored in subsequent chapters as we turn to the evolving concept of digital autonomy and its critical pillars.

4.14 Global Supply Chain Vulnerabilities

The semiconductor supply chain is famously globalized and specialized. Different countries dominate different stages: Research and design are largely based in the United States, chip fabrication is concentrated in East Asia, while assembly and testing are distributed across various parts of Asia. The supply of critical materials and equipment, meanwhile, is shared among key producers such as Japan, the Netherlands, the United States, and South Korea (Synergy Inc., 2025). This globalization has in the past led to efficiency and innovation through collaboration, but it also introduced fragility (Czerwonko, 2024).

One stark fact highlights this: Taiwan. The Taiwan Semiconductor Manufacturing Company (TSMC) produces about 90% of the world's most advanced chips (those under 10 nanometers feature size) (Berman et.al., 2023). Overall, TSMC alone fabricates nearly 60% of all chips used worldwide (Chen, 2025; MBI Deep Dives, 2024). South Korea's Samsung is the only other manufacturer of cutting-edge chips at scale. This means two locations (Taiwan and South Korea) are an outsized single point of failure for the global electronics supply. A natural disaster, war, or political blockade affecting Taiwan could virtually paralyze the production of high-end chips globally. For example, during 2020-2021, a combination of pandemic disruptions and unexpected demand spikes led to a global chip shortage, which hampered automobile manufacturing in many countries (cars couldn't be finished for lack of certain chips). This was a wake-up call that underscored how vulnerable many economies were to any hiccup in chip supply chains (Akıllı, 2025c).

Geopolitical tensions compound the vulnerability. The fact that China considers Taiwan a renegade province and does not rule out taking it by force is seen as a major risk to chip supply. Policymakers in the U.S. and Europe openly fret that a Taiwan crisis could cut off their access to advanced semiconductors, crippling industries and defense. Additionally, the supply chain has other chokepoints: for instance, the most advanced chip manufacturing equipment (extreme ultraviolet lithography machines) is produced only by a Dutch company, ASML. If ASML's supply or technology is restricted, chip production worldwide is affected. Another example: certain chemicals and gases needed for chipmaking come mostly from Japan or Ukraine (Ukraine produces neon gas critical for lasers used in lithography; disruptions there during conflict can hit the industry). Each of these pinch points represents a potential sovereignty issue—if one country controls a choke point, it can potentially exert pressure on others. The interdependence sovereignty challenge is clear: no single country today is completely self-sufficient in semiconductors, but many are uncomfortably dependent on a few foreign players for crucial elements.

4.15 National Strategies for Semiconductor Independence

Recognizing these risks, major powers and coalitions have launched strategies to regain or bolster semiconductor sovereignty. The goal is not necessarily full self-sufficiency (which may be unattainable in the short term given the complexity and cost), but rather to *reduce dependency* on external, especially single-source, supplies and to *retain access* to the most advanced chip technologies.

The U.S., historically a leader in semiconductor design and intellectual property, experienced a sharp decline in its share of global chip manufacturing, from 37% in 1990 to approximately 12% by 2020 (Kang & Tankersley, 2024). In response, the U.S. enacted the CHIPS and Science Act in 2022, allocating $52.7 billion to strengthen domestic semiconductor production, including $39 billion in manufacturing subsidies and $13 billion for research and workforce training (Berman, 2023). Major private investments followed, including Intel's $20 billion expansion in

Arizona and TSMC's $100 billion commitment to advanced fabs in the U.S. (Reuters, 2024). Washington has also implemented sweeping export controls, first in 2022 and expanded in 2023, to block China's access to advanced semiconductors and manufacturing equipment (Reisinger & Huitt, 2023). Alongside this, the U.S. has organized alliances such as "Chip 4" with Taiwan, Japan, and South Korea, and strengthened coordination with the EU through the Trade and Technology Council. These strategies blend reshoring, allied cooperation, and export restrictions to preserve technological superiority and secure supply chains (Zurich Insurance, 2024).

The EU currently holds about 9% of global semiconductor production capacity (William Fry, 2024). The European Chips Act, announced in 2022, aims to double this figure to 20% by 2030 through mobilizing more than 43 billion euros ($48.76 billion) in public and private investments (European Commission, 2022a). This effort includes significant plans, such as Intel's proposal for a 30-billion-euro ($34.02 billion) fabrication plant in Germany (William Fry, 2024). However, the European Court of Auditors has raised concerns, suggesting Europe may fall short of its goals due to fragmented national efforts and coordination issues (Blancato & Carr, 2024). Still, Europe continues to deepen global partnerships, including with Japan on raw materials and the U.S. on supply chain early warning systems, while maintaining its digital sovereignty agenda (Schneider, 2025).

Meanwhile, China's push for semiconductor sovereignty has intensified as U.S. export controls target its technological advancement. Though Beijing's Made in China 2025 strategy initially set a target of 70% self-sufficiency, estimates suggest only about 30% may be achieved by 2025 (Center for Security and Emerging Technology, 2023). Beijing has responded with substantial investment, including over $50 billion through its "Big Fund" and massive local government support for domestic chipmakers (Ezell, 2023). Companies such as SMIC have reportedly reached limited production of 7 nm chips despite sanctions (White & Case, 2024). Moreover, China has introduced laws like the Algorithm Regulation (2022) and broader AI regulatory frameworks to enhance state control over its digital economy (Huld, 2022; Tang, 2025). While significant gaps remain, especially in cutting-edge logic chips and lithography equipment, China's strategy of import substitution, talent acquisition, and industrial policy underscores its long-term ambition to achieve autonomy (Weinstein, 2022).

Japan, once a semiconductor powerhouse, is regaining strategic relevance by leveraging strengths in materials and equipment. Through the Japan Advanced Semiconductor Manufacturing (JASM), a joint venture with TSMC, Sony, and Toyota, Japan opened a new fab in Kumamoto and planned a second facility (Jacobs, 2024). South Korea remains vital as well, with Samsung pledging $450 billion through 2030 to maintain leadership in memory and advanced chips (Bloomberg, 2021). Taiwan, via TSMC, dominates leading-edge manufacturing and plans to begin 2 nm production in 2025, while balancing global diversification through new fabs in the U.S. and Japan (Focus Taiwan, 2025).

Finally, India also aspires to become a semiconductor hub, offering incentives worth up to $15 billion. Yet its efforts face headwinds, as illustrated by the pause in Adani's $10 billion fab project in partnership with Tower Semiconductor (Vengattil & Kalra, 2025). Nevertheless, India's desire to reduce dependency on foreign chips reflects a growing trend of national strategies to secure digital and technological sovereignty.

4.16 The CHIPS War and Geopolitics

Semiconductor sovereignty has also explicitly entered geopolitical discourse as a "tech war" or "chip war" between the U.S. and China (Akıllı, 2025d). The U.S., as mentioned, has imposed export bans to cap China's semiconductor advancement, effectively leveraging its current control over key choke points (EDA software, chip equipment, high-end GPU chips, etc.) to maintain an edge. It has rallied allies (Japan and Netherlands) to align their export policies to block China from acquiring extreme lithography tools. From one perspective, the U.S. is exercising its sovereignty (and indeed a sort of extraterritorial reach) to try to dictate who can use the world's most advanced hardware tech.

From China's perspective, this is a grave threat to its development—an impetus to redouble sovereignty efforts to never be in such a position of dependency. This tussle indicates that hardware sovereignty is not just a national issue; it's now a central theme in great power competition. Countries in between, like those in Europe or East Asia, may feel pressure to "choose sides" (Akıllı, 2025a) or at least to hedge their bets in supply chains (ensuring they have supply from both Western and Asian sources, for instance). As a result, we may see a partial unwinding of the global integrated supply chain into two or more blocs—sometimes called "decoupling." If this happens, each bloc would aim for self-reliance in chips within itself, which is a sort of collective sovereignty approach.

4.17 Ensuring Hardware Integrity

Beyond producing chips, hardware sovereignty includes ensuring that the hardware used is secure. There have been security scares, such as reports (later disputed) of Chinese implants on server motherboards, and general worries that chips or equipment could have backdoors. Nations are starting to incorporate trust requirements: e.g., defense departments only sourcing chips from vetted fabs, or requiring verification of chips (using techniques like chip certification and reverse engineering checks to ensure no malicious circuitry). Some countries have "trusted foundry" programs—in the U.S., certain fabs (like a GlobalFoundries plant in upstate New York) are designated to produce chips for defense use under secure conditions. This way, even if commercial supply is global, the most sensitive hardware is under tighter national control. European countries too are looking at securing supply for critical infrastructure (for instance, making sure telecom equipment is from trusted vendors).

4.18 Costs and Feasibility

Achieving semiconductor sovereignty or even significant independence is enormously expensive and technically difficult. Cutting-edge fabs cost $10-20 billion each and require a highly skilled workforce and ecosystem. Governments must consider where it's worth investing taxpayer money and where to rely on market purchases. There's an economic trade-off: subsidies can create duplication of capacity, potentially leading to oversupply in the future, or simply be inefficient if done in every country. Smaller countries likely cannot cover the full spectrum (design, fab, materials, and equipment), so they'll focus on niches or align with allies. The CHIPS Act and EU Chips Act (European Comission, 2025c) mark a new era of techno-nationalism, but they also face questions: Will subsidies be enough to overcome the market's gravity (which favored clustering in East Asia)? (Gisonna, 2025). Can government planning keep pace with the rapid innovation cycle of the industry? And could protectionism lead to retaliation or inefficiencies that hurt the global innovation rate? These are debated by economists. Nevertheless, the consensus in policy circles is that some degree of decoupling and on-shoring is prudent for security.

4.19 Implications of Semiconductor Sovereignty

If successful, efforts to regionalize chip production could lead to a more geographically balanced industry. In a decade, we might see a world where the U.S. and Europe produce a larger share of advanced chips domestically, China produces a much larger share of its needs internally, and allies like Japan and India play greater roles—reducing the single-point-of-failure risk. It might also mean higher costs (since duplicating efforts and building in higher-cost locations can increase prices), which could be passed on to consumers or mitigated by government support. Strategically, countries would feel more assured that they can withstand a supply shock or embargo. For example, an EU with 20% of world production (the target) would be in a better position than it is today if, say, an Asian crisis cut off some supply.

However, there are also cooperative angles: recently, shortages have driven home that no one country can alone fix supply issues. This gave impetus to dialogues. For instance, the U.S.-EU Trade and Technology Council set up an early alert mechanism for semiconductor supply chain disruptions, effectively a cooperative sovereignty measure to manage interdependence. Similarly, Japan, South Korea, and the U.S. have discussed coordinating on investing in different parts of the supply chain (so as not to redundantly all invest in the same type of fab). These approaches suggest a *managed interdependence* rather than complete autarky: like-minded nations ensuring collectively they have control, even if individually they don't cover everything. This is sometimes referred to as "ally-shoring" or creating secure supply chain blocs.

In concluding this chapter and the broader work, we see that sovereignty in the technopolar era is multifaceted. **Sovereignty 2.0** is about *much more than defending borders*—it is about defending and cultivating the essential elements of national power and identity in a highly interconnected world. **Data sovereignty** addresses control over the intangible flows of information; **algorithmic sovereignty** addresses control over the invisible decision logic that increasingly governs outcomes; and **hardware sovereignty** addresses control over the tangible foundations of all digital technology. Each pillar comes with its own set of challenges and requires international coordination to some degree, yet all are fundamentally about states adapting the age-old quest for self-determination to the conditions of the twenty-first century.

States today are confronted with profound challenges to their authority, posed not only by geopolitical rivalry but also by the complex architectures of the digital domain. Yet, as this analysis has shown, they are far from powerless. Through law, industrial policy, technological innovation, and diplomatic coalitions, governments are actively reshaping the digital landscape. These efforts go beyond defensive maneuvers. They reflect an emerging recognition that sovereignty in the twenty-first century must be fundamentally reimagined. At the heart of this reimagination lies the strategic imperative of *digital autonomy*.

Digital autonomy is not merely a legal claim or a symbolic aspiration—it is the practical ability to act independently and effectively in the digital realm. Where classical sovereignty emphasizes exclusive control over territory, digital autonomy emphasizes the capacity to operate securely and strategically within interconnected, data-driven environments. In this way, digital autonomy represents the crown of Sovereignty 2.0—the evolved, adaptive sovereignty appropriate for the technopolar world. It does not seek isolation, nor does it deny the realities of global interdependence. Rather, it demands the mastery of that interdependence on national terms.

This mastery rests on three interlinked pillars. The first is **presence**: the ability of a state to cultivate indigenous technological capabilities, ensuring that it maintains a footprint across critical layers of digital infrastructure. Without this, autonomy is hollow, and dependency inevitable. The second is **practice**: the assertion of regulatory power and normative influence over how technologies are designed, deployed, and governed, both domestically and—where possible—globally. Through regulation, standards, and public policy, states embed their values and rules into the digital environment. The third is **resilience**: the capacity to endure shocks, manage dependencies, and maintain freedom of action amid crises or coercive pressures. This requires diversified supply chains, trusted partnerships, and robust institutional frameworks. Together, presence, practice, and resilience constitute the architecture through which digital autonomy is both pursued and sustained.

The technopolar era, where technology firms and transnational platforms increasingly rival states, has forced this sovereign awakening. The outcome will not be a return to rigid Westphalian territoriality. Rather, we are witnessing the formation of a new equilibrium, in which digital borders are drawn and national jurisdictions are reaffirmed, but openness and connectivity are not wholly abandoned. Western countries and the

Global South alike are pursuing digital autonomy, though with different priorities and ethical frameworks. The common thread is unmistakable: no government can afford to cede control over the infrastructures that shape economic competitiveness, social cohesion, and national security.

As Louis Henkin once noted, sovereignty can shield both the good and the bad (Sun and Chander, 2021). The challenge for states today is to wield Sovereignty 2.0 and to build digital autonomy in ways that secure prosperity, uphold values, and preserve the innovation and openness that make the digital-era transformative. Digital autonomy is thus not an endpoint, but a governing logic for the unfolding age.

The next part of this book will turn explicitly to this new logic. Having traced how states are reasserting sovereignty through infrastructure, policy, and alliances, we now shift our focus to how digital autonomy is practiced. This involves examining how the pillars of presence, practice, and resilience are operationalized in state strategy, and what they reveal about the emerging global contest over the governance of artificial intelligence, data flows, and digital infrastructures.

Bibliography

Abagun, T. (2025, April 8). *Data Sovereignty in Africa: A Crucial Conversation*. ITWeb. Retrieved May 5, 2025, from https://www.itweb.co.za/article/data-sovereignty-in-africa-a-crucial-conversation/mYZRXv9gZLRMOgA8

Africa Practice. (2025). *Africa: Tech Policy Trends to Watch in 2025*. Retrieved May 5, 2025, from https://africapractice.com/insights/africa-tech-policy-trends-to-watch-in-2025/

Akıllı, E. (2023, June 23). *Has the Skynet Moment Finally Arrived?* Daily Sabah. Retrieved May 5, 2025, from https://www.dailysabah.com/opinion/op-ed/has-the-skynet-moment-finally-arrived

Akıllı, E. (2024, April 5). *Artificial Intelligence in Counterterrorism: Navigating the Intersection of Security, Ethics, and Privacy*. SETA Perspective. No. 73. Retrieved May 25, 2025, from https://www.setav.org/en/security/artificial-intelligence-in-counterterrorism-navigating-the-intersection-of-security-ethics-and-privacy

Akıllı, E. (2025a, April 18). *Rewiring Diplomacy in the Technopolar World*. Daily Sabah (Op-Ed). Retrieved May 11, 2025, from https://www.dailysabah.com/opinion/op-ed/rewiring-diplomacy-in-the-technopolar-world

Akıllı, E. (2025b, February 1). *Trump's Stargate, Biden's Tier List and the Wake of the Techno-Polar World*. Daily Sabah. Retrieved May 5,

2025, from https://www.dailysabah.com/opinion/op-ed/trumps-stargate-bidens-tier-list-and-the-wake-of-the-techno-polar-world

Akıllı, E. (2025c, March 6). *Role of virtual power plants in AI R&D in a technopolar world order*. Daily Sabah. Retrieved May 5, 2025, from https://www.dailysabah.com/opinion/op-ed/role-of-virtual-power-plants-in-ai-rd-in-a-technopolar-world-order

Akıllı, E. (2025d, February 14). *AI geopolitics: Power shifts in the techno-polar world*. Daily Sabah. Retrieved May 5, 2025, from https://www.dailysabah.com/opinion/op-ed/ai-geopolitics-power-shifts-in-the-techno-polar-world

Akıllı, E. (2025e, 21 March). *Techno-polar reckoning: US vs. China*. Daily Sabah. Retrieved May 12, 2025, from https://www.dailysabah.com/opinion/op-ed/techno-polar-reckoning-us-vs-china

Allen, G.C. & Goldston, E. (2025). *Understanding U.S. allies' current legal authority to implement AI and semiconductor export controls*. Center for Strategic and International Studies (CSIS). Retrieved June 13, 2025, from https://www.csis.org/analysis/understanding-us-allies-current-legal-authority-implement-ai-and-semiconductor-export

Amnesty International. (2021, July 18). *Forensic Methodology Report: How to catch NSO Group's Pegasus*. Retrieved May 5, 2025, from https://www.amnesty.org/en/latest/research/2021/07/forensic-methodology-report-how-to-catch-nso-groups-pegasus/

Anthony, A., Sharma, L. & Noor, E. (2024, April 30). *Advancing a More Global Agenda for Trustworthy Artificial Intelligence*. Carnegie Endowment for International Peace. Retrieved May 4, 2025, from https://carnegieendowment.org/research/2024/04/advancing-a-more-global-agenda-for-trustworthy-artificial-intelligence?lang=en

AppInChina. (2023, July 13). *What is China's AI Algorithm Filing?* Retrieved May 5, 2025, from https://appinchina.co/what-is-chinas-ai-algorithm-filing/

Arun, C. (2024). *Transnational AI and Corporate Imperialism, Carnegie Endowment for International Peace*, 8 October. Retrieved May 4, 2025, from https://carnegieendowment.org/research/2024/10/transnational-ai-and-corporate-imperialism?center=china&lang=en

Basatwar, G. (2025). *Everything You Need to Know About RBI's Data Localization Guidelines*, Doverunner, 19 March. Retrieved May 5, 2025, from https://doverunner.com/blogs/everything-to-know-about-rbi-data-localization-guidelines/

Bauer, M., Lee-Makiyama, H., van der Marel, E. & Verschelde, B. (2014). *The Costs of Data Localisation: Friendly Fire on Economic Recovery*. European Centre for International Political Economy. No: 3. Retrieved May 5, 2025, from http://www.ecipe.org/wp-content/uploads/2014/12/OCC32014__1.pdf

BBC News. (2019). *Russia Internet: Law Introducing New Controls Comes Into Force*, 1 November. Retrieved May 5, 2025, from https://www.bbc.com/news/world-europe-50259597

Belli, L., & Jiang, M. (2024). Digital sovereignty from the BRICS: Structuring self-determination, cybersecurity, and control. In M. Jiang & L. Belli (Eds.), *Digital sovereignty in the BRICS countries: How the global south and emerging power alliances are reshaping digital governance*. Cambridge University Press.

Benamara, A. (2025). *Exclusive Q&A: Africa's Blueprint for a Secure Digital Future*. TechAfricaNews. 27 February. Retrieved May 5, 2025, from https://techafricanews.com/2025/02/27/exclusive-qa-africas-blueprint-for-a-secure-digital-future/

Berman, N. (2023). *What Is the CHIPS Act?* Council on Foreign Relations. 11 May. Retrieved April 29, 2025, from https://www.cfr.org/in-brief/what-chips-act

Berman, N., Maizland, L. & Chatzky, A. (2023). *Is China's Huawei a Threat to U.S. National Security?*, Council on Foreign Relations, 8 February. Retrieved May 5, 2025, from https://www.cfr.org/backgrounder/chinas-huawei-threat-us-national-security

Blancato, F. G., & Carr, M. (2024). The trust deficit: EU bargaining for access and control over cloud infrastructures. *Journal of European Public Policy, 31*(4), 567–586. Retrieved May 5, 2025, from https://papers.ssrn.com/sol3/papers.cfm?abstract_id=4843466

Bloomberg. (2021). *Korea Unveils $450 Billion Push to Seize Global Chipmaking Crown*. Bloomberg, 13 May. Retrieved May 5, 2025, from https://www.bloomberg.com/news/articles/2021-05-13/korea-unveils-450-billion-push-to-seize-global-chipmaking-crown

Bpifrance. (2024). *AI and Sovereignty: Europe's Assets and Objectives to Shape Its Digital Future*. 18 December. Retrieved May 5, 2025, from https://www.bpifrance.com/2024/12/18/ai-and-sovereignty-europes-assets-and-objectives-to-shape-its-digital-future/

Bremmer, I. (2023). *What is a technopolar world?* GZERO Media. 30 August. Retrieved April 30, 2025, from https://www.gzeromedia.com/ai/what-is-a-technopolar-world

Bremmer, I., & Suleyman, M. (2023). The AI power paradox: Can states learn to govern artificial intelligence—Before it's too late? *Foreign Affairs, 102*(5), 58–71.

Business Today. (2025). *FM Nirmala Sitharaman Defends Access to Encrypted WhatsApp Chats Under Income Tax Bill 2025*. 28 March. Retrieved May 5, 2025, from https://www.businesstoday.in/technology/news/story/fm-nirmala-sitharaman-defends-access-to-encrypted-whatsapp-chats-under-income-tax-bill-2025-469743-2025-03-28

Calo, R. (2016). Robotics and the lessons of Cyberlaw. *California Law Review, 103*(3), 513–563. Retrieved May 5, 2025, from https://papers.ssrn.com/sol3/papers.cfm?abstract_id=2374593

Center for Security and Emerging Technology. (2023). *Ask the Experts: Is China's Semiconductor Strategy Working?* Center for Security and Emerging Technology. Retrieved May 5, 2025, from https://cset.georgetown.edu/publication/ask-the-experts-is-chinas-semiconductor-strategy-working

Chander, A. & Le, U.P. (2015). *Sovereignty and Data Localization*. Belfer Center for Science and International Affairs, Harvard Kennedy School. Retrieved May 5, 2025, from https://www.belfercenter.org/publication/sovereignty-and-data-localization

Chander, A. & Sun, H. (2021). *Sovereignty 2.0*. Georgetown University Law Center. Retrieved May 5, 2025, from https://scholarship.law.georgetown.edu/facpub/2404

Chen, C.-h. (2025). *TSMC still top foundry, with 67.6% market share. Taipei Times*. Retrieved October 16, 2025, from https://www.taipeitimes.com/News/biz/archives/2025/06/10/2003838326

China Briefing. (2021). *The PRC Personal Information Protection Law (final): A full translation*. Retrieved October 16, 2025, from https://www.china-briefing.com/news/the-prc-personal-information-protection-law-final-a-fulltranslation/

CGI.br. (2014). *Marco Civil Law of the Internet in Brazil*. Retrieved October 16, 2025, from https://www.cgi.br/pagina/marco-civil-law-of-the-internet-in-brazil/180

Conceptboard. (2023). *US Cloud Act: Threat for European Data Protection, Conceptboard Blog*, 15 Mart. Retrieved May 5, 2025, from https://conceptboard.com/blog/us-cloud-act-european-data-protection/

Congress.gov. (2022). *H.R.6580—Algorithmic Accountability Act of 2022*. Retrieved May 5, 2025, from https://www.congress.gov/bill/117th-congress/house-bill/6580/text

Cory, N., Dascoli, L. & Clay, I. (2022). *The Cost of Data Localization Policies in Bangladesh, Hong Kong, Indonesia, Pakistan, and Vietnam*. Information Technology and Innovation Foundation. December. Retrieved May 5, 2025, from https://www2.itif.org/2022-data-localization-five-asian-economies.pdf

Czerwonko, A. (2024). *Is This a Pivotal Moment for the Rise of the Middle Powers*. World Economic Forum. 22 March. Retrieved April 30, 2025, from https://www.weforum.org/stories/2024/03/pivotal-moment-for-the-rise-of-the-middle-powers

De Giovanni, S. (2025). *The AI race: A few take-aways from the 2025 French AI Summit and the need to develop AI policies*. 30 March. Rimon Law. Retrieved May 5, 2025, from https://www.rimonlaw.com/the-ai-race-a-few-take-away-from-the-2025-french-ai-summit-and-the-need-to-develop-ai-policies/

De Mooy, M. (2017). *Rethinking Privacy Self-Management and Data Sovereignty in the Age of Big Data*. Center for Democracy and Technology. Retrieved May 5, 2025, from https://cdt.org/wp-content/uploads/2017/04/Rethinking-Privacy_2017_final.pdf

Deutsche Telekom. (2015). *Sales of Microsoft Cloud Deutschland Launch at Deutsche Telekom*, 16 March. Retrieved May 5, 2025, from https://www.telekom.com/en/media/media-information/archive/sales-of-microsoft-cloud-deutschland-launch-at-deutsche-telekom-487998

Digital Agency Japan. (2025). *Government Cloud*, 9 May. Retrieved May 5, 2025, from https://www.digital.go.jp/en/policies/gov_cloud

Digital Regulation Cooperation Forum. (2022). *The Benefits and Harms of Algorithms: A Shared Perspective*, UK Government. 23 September. Retrieved May 5, 2025, from https://www.gov.uk/government/publications/findings-from-the-drcf-algorithmic-processing-workstream-spring-2022/the-benefits-and-harms-of-algorithms-a-shared-perspective-from-the-four-digital-regulators

Digitalisation World. (2015). *T-Systems to Act as Data Trustee for Microsoft Cloud in Germany*. 11 November. Retrieved May 5, 2025, from https://digitalisationworld.com/news/46236/t-systems-to-act-as-data-trustee-for-microsoft-cloud-in-germany

Erdenebileg, Z. (2017). *China's new Cybersecurity Law to be implemented on June 1*. China Briefing. Retrieved October 16, 2025, from https://www.china-briefing.com/news/china-new-cybersecurity-law-to-be-implemented-june-1

European Commission. (2021). *Ethics Guidelines for Trustworthy AI*. 8 April. Retrieved May 5, 2025, from https://digital-strategy.ec.europa.eu/en/library/ethics-guidelines-trustworthy-ai

European Commission. (2022a). *European Chips Act*. Retrieved October 16, 2025, from https://commission.europa.eu/strategy-and-policy/priorities-2019-2024/europe-fit-digital-age/european-chips-act_en

European Commission. (2022b). *Proposal for a Regulation Establishing a Framework of Measures for Strengthening Europe's Semiconductor Ecosystem (Chip Act)*. Brussels: COM(2022) 45 final. Retrieved May 6, 2025, from https://eur-lex.europa.eu/legal-content/EN/TXT/PDF/?uri=CELEX:52022DC0045

European Commission. (2022c). *Trans-Atlantic Data Privacy Framework*. Retrieved May 5, 2025, from https://ec.europa.eu/commission/presscorner/detail/en/fs_22_2100

European Commission. (2023). *Commission Welcomes G7 Leaders' Agreement on Guiding Principles and a Code of Conduct on Artificial Intelligence*, 30 October. Retrieved May 5, 2025, from https://ec.europa.eu/commission/presscorner/detail/en/ip_23_5379

European Commission. (2025). *European approach to artificial intelligence.* Retrieved October 16, 2025, from https://digital-strategy.ec.europa.eu/en/policies/european-approach-artificial-intelligence

European Commission. (2025a). *AI Act | Shaping Europe's Digital Future*, 1 May. Retrieved May 5, 2025, from https://digital-strategy.ec.europa.eu/en/policies/regulatory-framework-ai

European Commission. (2025b). *Commission Sets Course for Europe's AI Leadership with an Ambitious AI Continent Action Plan*, 9 April. Retrieved May 5, 2025, from https://ec.europa.eu/commission/presscorner/detail/en/ip_25_1013

European Commission. (2025c). *Digital Markets Act* (DMA). Retrieved October 16, 2025, from https://digital-markets-act.ec.europa.eu/index_en

European Court of Auditors. (2021). *Health Data on Pandemic Management in the First Year of the COVID-19 Pandemic*, 17 December 2021. Retrieved May 5, 2025, from https://www.eca.europa.eu/sites/CC/en/Documents/Covid_19/SAI-reports/SAI_AT_Health_Data_on_Pandemic_Management_EN.pdf

European Parliament. (2025). *EU AI Act: First Regulation on Artificial Intelligence*, 08 June. Retrieved May 5, 2025, from https://www.europarl.europa.eu/topics/en/article/20230601STO93804/eu-ai-act-first-regulation-on-artificial-intelligence

EY Global. (2023). *G7 AI Principles and Code of Conduct*. 1 December. Retrieved May 5, 2025, from https://www.ey.com/en_gl/insights/ai/g7-ai-principles-and-code-of-conduct

Ezell, S. (2023). *How Innovative is China in Semiconductors?* Information Technology and Innovation Foundation, 19 August. Retrieved May 5, 2025, from https://itif.org/publications/2024/08/19/how-innovative-is-china-in-semiconductors

Filipiak, S. (2025). *Banning TikTok: Turning point for U.S. data security or threat to free speech?* Ohio University. 17 January. Retrieved May 5, 2025, from https://www.ohio.edu/news/2025/01/banning-tiktok-turning-point-u-s-data-security-or-threat-free-speech

Focus Taiwan. (2025). *TSMC on Track to Begin 2nm Chip Production in 2025*, 22 March. Retrieved May 5, 2025, from https://focustaiwan.tw/business/202503220008

France 24. (2013). *Germany, Brazil Turn to UN to Restrain NSA Surveillance*. 2 November. Retrieved May 5, 2025, from https://www.france24.com/en/20131102-germany-brazil-surveillance-un-draft-NSA-Snowden-espionage

Frenus. (2025). *Gaia-X: European Initiative for Digital Sovereignty and Data Security*. Retrieved May 5, 2025, from https://frenus.com/gaia-x-european-initiative-for-digital-sovereignty-and-data-security/

Froman, M. (2025). *China, the United States, and the AI Race. Council on Foreign Relations*. Retrieved October 16, 2025, from https://www.cfr.org/article/china-united-states-and-ai-race

Gaia-X. (2024). *Gaia-X Strengthens European Digital Sovereignty at European Parliament Reception*, 20 March. Retrieved May 5, 2025, from https://gaia-x.eu/gaia-x-strengthens-european-digital-sovereignty-at-european-parliament-reception/

Gaia-X. (2025). *Home—Gaia-X: A Federated Secure Data Infrastructure*. Retrieved May 5, 2025, from https://gaia-x.eu

Gaia-X Association. (2021). *Gaia-X: Vision and Mission*. Retrieved May 5, 2025, from https://gaia-x.eu/what-is-gaia-x/vision-and-mission/

Gisonna, N. (2025). *Great Firewall | History, China, Hong Kong, & Facts*. Britannica. Retrieved May 5, 2025, from https://www.britannica.com/topic/Great-Firewall

Global Partnership for Sustainable Development Data. (2020). *Avoiding the Data Colonialism Trap*. Retrieved May 5, 2025, from https://www.data4sdgs.org/blog/avoiding-data-colonialism-trap

GOV.UK. (2025). *Multi-Region Cloud and Software-as-a-Service*, 5 February. Retrieved May 5, 2025, from https://www.gov.uk/government/publications/multi-region-cloud-and-software-as-a-service/multi-region-cloud-and-software-as-a-service-html

Government of Canada. (2025). *Algorithmic Impact Assessment Tool*. Retrieved May 5, 2025, from https://www.canada.ca/en/government/system/digital-government/digital-government-innovations/responsible-use-ai/algorithmic-impact-assessment.html

Government of India. (2023). *The Digital Personal Data Protection Act 2023*. Retrieved May 5, 2025, from https://www.meity.gov.in/

Greengard, S. (2025). *Pegasus (Spyware)*, Encyclopaedia Britannica, 30 January. Retrieved May 5, 2025, from https://www.britannica.com/topic/Pegasus-spyware

Gu, H. (2023). Data, big tech, and the new concept of sovereignty. *Journal of Chinese Political Science, 29*(4), 591–612. https://doi.org/10.1007/s11366-023-09855-1

Hill, J. F. (2014). *The Growth of Data Localization Post-Snowden*. Lawfare Research Paper Series. Retrieved May 5, 2025, from https://www.lawfareblog.com/growth-data-localization-post-snowden

Hmaidi, A. & Arcsati R. (2022) *Why Europe struggles with US export controls on China*. The Diplomat. 27 December. Retrieved May 5, 2025, from https://thediplomat.com/2022/12/why-europe-struggles-with-us-export-controls-on-china/

Hopkins, N. (2013). *NSA Surveillance May Cause Breakup of the Internet, Warns Expert*. The Guardian, 1 November. Retrieved May 5, 2025, from https://www.theguardian.com/world/2013/nov/01/nsa-surveillance-cause-internet-breakup-edward-snowden

Huld, A. (2022). *China Passes Sweeping Recommendation Algorithm Regulations, in Effect March 1*. China Briefing. 6 January. Retrieved May 5, 2025, from https://www.china-briefing.com/news/china-passes-sweeping-recommendation-algorithm-regulations-effect-march-1-2022/

Hulkó, G., Kálmán, J., & Lapsánszky, A. (2025). The politics of digital sovereignty and the European Union's legislation: Navigating crises. *Frontiers in Political Science, 7*, 1548562. Retrieved May 5, 2025, from https://www.frontiersin.org/articles/10.3389/fpos.2025.1548562/full

Innovation News Network. (2025). *Game-Changing Action Plan Launched to Boost European AI Innovation*, 10 April. Retrieved May 5, 2025, from https://www.innovationnewsnetwork.com/game-changing-action-plan-launched-to-boost-european-ai-innovation/57075/

Institute of International Finance. (2020). *Data Localization: Costs, Tradeoffs, and Impacts Across the Economy*. Retrieved May 5, 2025, from https://www.iif.com/portals/0/Files/content/Innovation/12_22_2020_data_localization.pdf

Jacobs, E. M. (2024). *TSMC Opens First Japan Fab in Kumamoto*, Global Taiwan Institute, 6 March. Retrieved May 5, 2025, from https://globaltaiwan.org/2024/03/tsmc-opens-its-first-production-facility-in-kumamoto-japan

Judge, P. (2015). *Microsoft Puts Deutsche Telekom in Charge of German Data*. Data Center Dynamics, 12 November. Retrieved May 5, 2025, from https://www.datacenterdynamics.com/en/news/microsoft-puts-deutsche-telekom-in-charge-of-german-data/

Kang, C., & Tankersley, J. (2024). *How the U.S. is racing to build a semiconductor supply chain. The New York Times*. Retrieved October 16, 2025, from https://www.nytimes.com/interactive/2024/03/20/business/economy/semiconductor-chip-manufacturing-us.html

Kaye, K. (2024). *AI Governance on the Ground: Canada's Algorithmic Impact Assessment Process and Algorithm Has Evolved*. World Privacy Forum. 14 August. Retrieved May 5, 2025, from https://www.worldprivacyforum.org/2024/08/ai-governance-on-the-ground-series-canada/

Kaye, K. (2025). *AI Governance on the Ground: Canada's Algorithmic Impact Assessment Process and Algorithm Has Evolved*. Montreal Ethics, 4 February. Retrieved May 5, 2025, from https://montrealethics.ai/ai-governance-on-the-ground-canadas-algorithmic-impact-assessment-process-and-algorithm-has-evolved/

Kiely, E. (2025). *TikTok and U.S. National Security*, FactCheck.org. 3 February. Retrieved May 5, 2025, from https://www.factcheck.org/2025/02/tiktok-and-u-s-national-security/

Kokas, A. (2023). China's digital authoritarianism: How the CCP shapes the future of the internet. *Journal of Digital Policy, 12*(1), 45–62.
Kroet, C. (2025). *Lawmakers call for binding 5G security measures in wake of Huawei scandal*, Euronews, 19 March. Retrieved May 5, 2025, from https://www.euronews.com/next/2025/03/19/lawmakers-call-for-binding-5g-security-measures-in-wake-of-huawei-scandal
Larsen, B.C. (2022). *The Geopolitics of AI and the Rise of Digital Sovereignty*, Brookings Institution. 8 December. Retrieved May 11, 2025, from https://www.brookings.edu/articles/the-geopolitics-of-ai-and-the-rise-of-digital-sovereignty/
LGPD (2018). Lei Geral de Proteção de Dados Pessoais (LGPD), Lei No. 13.709, de 14 de agosto de 2018. Retrieved from https://iapp.org/resources/article/brazilian-data-protection-law-lgpd-english-translation/
Lowitja Institute. (2024). *Taking Control of Our Data: Indigenous Data Sovereignty Discussion Paper*. Retrieved May 5, 2025, from https://www.lowitja.org.au/wp-content/uploads/2024/01/Taking-Control-of-Our-Data-Discussion-Paper.pdf
Macdonald, A. (2025). *Calls for Africa to Secure Its Tech Sovereignty Amid Digital Transformation Push*. Biometric Update, 29 April. Retrieved May 5, 2025, from https://www.biometricupdate.com/202504/calls-for-africa-to-secure-its-tech-sovereignty-amid-digital-transformation-push
Mayer, M. & Afterman, G. (2023). *Do more clubbing: How forming partnerships can help tech middle powers survive the escalating US-China tech war*, Global Policy Journal, 26 April. Retrieved April 30, 2025, from https://www.globalpolicyjournal.com/blog/26/04/2023/do-more-clubbing-how-forming-partnerships-can-help-tech-middle-powers-survive
MBI Deep Dives. (2024). *TSMC: The most mission-critical company on Earth*. Retrieved October 16, 2025, from https://www.mbi-deepdives.com/tsm/
McCallum. S. (2022). *WhatsApp: We Won't Lower Security for Any Government*, BBC News. 30 July. Retrieved May 5, 2025, from https://www.bbc.com/news/technology-62291328
Minges, M. (2025). *National Security and the TikTok Ban*. American University. 23 January. Retrieved May 5, 2025, from https://www.american.edu/sis/news/20250123-national-security-and-the-tik-tok-ban.cfm
Mittelstadt, B. D. (2019). Principles alone cannot guarantee ethical AI. *Nature Machine Intelligence, 1*(11), 501–507. https://doi.org/10.1038/s42256-019-0114-4
Montevideo Convention on the Rights and Duties of States. (1933). *Signed 26 December, entered into force 26 December*. Retrieved May 5, 2025, from https://www.ilsa.org/Jessup/Jessup15/Montevideo%20Convention.pdf
Mueller, M. (2017). *Will the Internet fragment? Sovereignty, globalization, and cyberspace*. Cambridge, UK: Polity Press.

National People's Congress. (2021). *Data Security Law of the People's Republic of China*. Retrieved October 16, 2025, from http://www.npc.gov.cn/englishnpc/c2759/c23934/202112/t20211209_385109.html

NATO (2024). *Cyber Defence*. Retrieved May 5, 2025, from https://www.nato.int/cps/en/natohq/topics_78170.htm

NHS England. (2021). *How data is supporting the COVID-19 response*. Retrieved May 5, 2025, from https://transform.england.nhs.uk/ai-lab/explore-all-resources/understand-ai/how-data-supporting-covid-19-response/

OCCRP. (2019). *Putin Signs Controversial "Internet Sovereignty Bill into Law*, 3 May. Retrieved May 5, 2025, from https://www.occrp.org/en/news/putin-signs-controversial-internet-sovereignty-bill-into-law

OECD. (2022). *Health data and governance developments in relation to COVID-19*. 22 April. Retrieved May 5, 2025, from https://www.oecd.org/en/publications/health-data-and-governance-developments-in-relation-to-covid-19_aec7c409-en.html

OECD. (2023). *The Nature, Evolution and Potential Implications of Data Localisation Measures*. OECD Trad Policy Paper. November. Retrieved May 5, 2025, from https://www.oecd.org/content/dam/oecd/en/publications/reports/2023/11/the-nature-evolution-and-potential-implications-of-data-localisation-measures_249df37e/179f718a-en.pdf

OECD. (2025). *OECD launches global framework to monitor application of G7 Hiroshima AI Code of Conduct*, 7 February. Retrieved May 5, 2025, from https://www.oecd.org/en/about/news/press-releases/2025/02/oecd-launches-global-framework-to-monitor-application-of-g7-hiroshima-ai-code-of-conduct.html

Patel, N. (2020). *India bans TikTok and 58 other Chinese apps*. The Verge. 29 June. Retrieved May 5, 2025, from https://www.theverge.com/2020/6/29/21307053/india-bans-tiktok-chinese-apps-border-clash

Reserve Bank of India. (2018). *Storage of Payment System Data*. 6 April. Retrieved May 5, 2025, from https://www.rbi.org.in/commonman/english/Scripts/FAQs.aspx?Id=2995

Reuters. (2024). *Intel CEO touts $20 billion Arizona expansion amid chip race*. 1 March. Retrieved May 5, 2025, from https://www.reuters.com/technology/intel-ceo-touts-20-billion-arizona-expansion-2024-03-01

Rieder, B., & Sire, G. (2020). The case for "algorithmic sovereignty": Towards a new regulatory framework for platforms. *Social Media+Society, 6*(2), 1–4.

Reisinger, S. H., & Huitt, C. (2023). US expands export restrictions on advanced semiconductors. Norton Rose Fulbright. Retrieved October 16, 2025, from https://www.nortonrosefulbright.com/dede/wissen/publications/5a936192/us-expands-export-restrictions-on-advanced-semiconductors

Robinson, D. (2025). *London's Poor 5G Blamed on Spectrum, Investment, Huawei Ban*. The Register. 25 March. Retrieved May 5, 2025, from https://www.theregister.com/2025/03/25/london_poor_5g_research/

S.S. Rana & Co. Advocates. (2022). *Guidelines for Storage of Payment Data—India*. Mondaq, 3 August. Retrieved May 5, 2025, from https://www.mondaq.com/india/financial-services/1098560/guidelines-for-storage-of-payment-data

Schneider, I. (2025). *Reclaiming digital sovereignty: The EU's role in the geopolitics of digital governance*. Retrieved May 5, 2025, from https://static.ie.edu/CGC/CGC_ReclaimingDigitalSovereignty_PolicyPaper.pdf

Semiconductors.org. (2024). *Industry Impact*. Retrieved May 5, 2025, from https://www.semiconductors.org/industry-impact/

Sheehan, M. & Du, S. (2022). *What China's Algorithm Registry Reveals About AI Governance*. Carnegie Endowment for International Peace, 9 December. Retrieved May 5, 2025, from https://carnegieendowment.org/posts/2022/12/what-chinas-algorithm-registry-reveals-about-ai-governance?lang=en

Srivastava, S. & Bullock, J. (2024). *AI, Global Governance, and Digital Sovereignty*. arXiv, 23 October. Retrieved May 5, 2025, from https://arxiv.org/html/2410.17481

Standing Committee of the National People's Congress. (2017). *Cybersecurity Law of the People's Republic of China (Adopted on 7 November 2016, Effective from 1 June 2017)*. Retrieved May 5, 2025, from https://www.chinalawtranslate.com/en/cybersecurity-law/

Standing Committee of the National People's Congress. (2021). *Data Security Law of the People's Republic of China (Adopted on 10 June 2021, Effective from 1 September 2021)*. Retrieved May 5, 2025, from https://www.chinalawtranslate.com/en/data-security-law/

Stolyarov, G. & Papachristou, L. (2024). *Russia to spend over half a billion dollars to bolster internet censorship system*. Reuters. 10 September. Retrieved May 5, 2025, from https://www.reuters.com/world/europe/russia-spend-over-half-billion-dollars-bolster-internet-censorship-system-2024-09-10/

Suhas, A. R., Martin, J. & Jhunjhunwala, N. (2023). *Semiconductors—the Next Frontier of Geopolitics: Semiconductor Supply Chain Diversification*. HFS Research. 22 March. Retrieved April 29, 2025, from https://www.hfsresearch.com/research/semiconductor-supply-chain-diversification/

Sun, H. & Chander, A. (2021). *Digital Sovereignty*. Georgetown Law Faculty Publications, Paper 2404. Published Version in Vanderbilt J. Transnat'l Law.

JD Supra. (2025). *AI Action Summit 2025: Can the French AI Sector Still Thrive While Being Limited by EU Regulations?* 12 February. Retrieved May 5, 2025, from https://www.jdsupra.com/legalnews/ai-action-summit-2025-can-the-french-ai-9245848/

Synergy Inc. (2025). *Strengthening the Global Semiconductor Supply Chain: Challenges and Opportunities in 2025.* 19 February. Retrieved May 15, 2025, from https://synergy-inc.com/strengthening-the-global-semiconductor-supply-chain-challenges-and-opportunities-in-2025/

Tang, T. (2025). *China and the U.S.: Different Approaches to Regulating AI*. China Law Vision. 3 April. Retrieved May 5, 2025, from https://www.chinalawvision.com/2025/04/digital-economy-ai/china-and-the-u-s-different-approaches-to-regulating-ai/

TechBullion. (2024). *Unveiling the Hidden Heroes: The Crucial Role of Semiconductors in Advancing Technology*. Retrieved May 5, 2025, from https://techbullion.com/unveiling-the-hidden-heroes-the-crucial-role-of-semiconductors-in-advancing-technology/

TechNode. (2025). *China Approves 346 Generative AI Services Under National Registration Scheme*. 9 April. Retrieved May 5, 2025, from https://technode.com/2025/04/09/china-approves-346-generative-ai-services-under-national-registration-scheme/

Thales and Google Cloud. (2022). *Thales and Google Cloud Announce Strategic Partnership to Jointly Develop a Trusted Cloud Offering in France*. 30 June. Retrieved May 5, 2025, from https://www.prnewswire.com/news-releases/thales-and-google-cloud-announce-strategic-partnership-to-jointly-develop-a-trusted-cloud-offering-in-france-301393410.html

Tracking Exposed. (2022). *Thinking Outside the Blackbox: Towards Algorithmic Sovereignty*. 19 December. Retrieved May 5, 2025, from https://tracking.exposed/v0/post/thinking-outside-the-blackbox/

UNESCO. (2021). *Recommendation on the Ethics of Artificial Intelligence*. 16 May. Retrieved May 21, 2025, from https://www.unesco.org/en/articles/recommendation-ethics-artificial-intelligence

UNICRI. (2023). *Algorithms and Terrorism: The Malicious Use of Artificial Intelligence for Terrorist Purposes*, 19 May. Retrieved May 5, 2025, from https://unicri.org/News/Algorithms-Terrorism-Malicious-Use-Artificial-Intelligence-Terrorist-Purposes

United States Department of Health and Human Services. (2021). *Impact of the COVID-19 Pandemic on Major HHS Data Systems*. Retrieved May 5, 2025, from https://aspe.hhs.gov/sites/default/files/2021-08/impact-of-pandemic-on-major-hhs-data-systems.pdf

Van Oirsouw, T. (2023). *AI, Digital Sovereignty, and the EU's Path Forward: A Case for Mission-Oriented Industrial Policy*. Ash Center for Democratic Governance and Innovation, Harvard Kennedy School. Retrieved May 5, 2025, from https://ash.harvard.edu/resources/ai-digital-sovereignty-and-the-eus-path-forward-a-case-for-mission-oriented-industrial-policy/

Vengattil, M. & Kalra, A. (2025). *Adani pauses talks with Israel's Tower Semiconductor*. Reuters. 1 May. Retrieved May 5, 2025, from https://www.reuters.com/world/india/adani-pauses-talks-with-israels-tower-10-billion-india-chip-foray-sources-say-2025-05-01

Wachter, S., Mittelstadt, B., & Floridi, L. (2017). Why a right to explanation of automated decision-making does not exist in the general data protection regulation. *International Data Privacy Law, 7*(2), 76–99. https://doi.org/10.1093/idpl/ipx005

Wagner, J. (2017). *China's Cybersecurity Law: What You Need to Know*. The Diplomat. 1 June. Retrieved May 5, 2025, from https://thediplomat.com/2017/06/chinas-cybersecurity-law-what-you-need-to-know/

Weinstein, E.S. (2022, September 1). *Is China's Semiconductor Strategy Working?* LSE China Foresight—Ask the Experts. Retrieved April 29, 2025, from https://cset.georgetown.edu/article/ask-the-experts-chinas-semiconductor-strategy

White & Case. (2024, May 29). *AI Watch: Global regulatory tracker — China*. White & Case LLP. Retrieved May 5, 2025, from https://www.whitecase.com/insight-our-thinking/ai-watch-global-regulatory-tracker-china

Wilde, G. & Sherman, J. (2022, May 11). *Putin's internet plan: Dependency with a veneer of sovereignty*, Brookings Institution. Retrieved May 5, 2025, from https://www.brookings.edu/articles/putins-internet-plan-dependency-with-a-veneer-of-sovereignty/

William Fry. (2024, April 14). *Europe's AI ambitions: Inside the EU'S €200 billion digital sovereignty plan*. William Fry LLP. Retrieved May 5, 2025, from https://www.williamfry.com/knowledge/europes-ai-ambitions-inside-the-eus-e200-billion-digital-sovereignty-plan.

World Economic Forum. (2025). *China's Path to AI-Powered Industry Transformation*. Retrieved May 5, 2025, from https://reports.weforum.org/docs/WEF_Blueprint_to_Action_Chinas_Path_to_AI-Powered_Industry_Transformation_2025.pdf

Wu, E. (2021, July). *Sovereignty and data localization*. Belfer Center for Science and International Affairs (Harvard Kennedy School). Retrieved April 29, 2025, from https://www.belfercenter.org/publication/sovereignty-and-data-localization.

Zurich Insurance. (2024, February 12). *What lies ahead for the geopolitics of semiconductors*. Zurich Insurance Group. Retrieved May 5, 2025, from https://www.zurich.com/en/knowledge/articles/2024/02/what-lies-ahead-for-the-geopolitics-of-semiconductors.

PART III

The Pillars of Digital Autonomy

CHAPTER 5

Forging the Digital Autonomy

Digital autonomy, as mentioned earlier, is not merely a legal entitlement or a rhetorical ideal. It is, rather, the realistic capacity of a state to act with strategic independence and operational effectiveness within the digital realm shaped by cutting-edge technologies. While the classical, Westphalian-rooted conceptions of sovereignty, prioritized exclusive dominion over geographic territory, digital autonomy represents an evolved understanding of sovereignty suited for the twenty-first century—one that is networked, data-centric, and technologically embedded (Krasner, 1999; Nye, 2011).

In this reconfiguration, digital autonomy emerges as the crown of Sovereignty 2.0 in the technopolar world. It does not, however, come as a nostalgic return to isolationism, but as a strategic mastery of interdependence on sovereign terms. It acknowledges that global connectivity is not only inevitable but also desirable, so long as it does not come at the expense of state agency, citizen dignity, or systemic resilience (Bradford, 2020; Gasser & Mayer-Schönberger, 2024).

Yet this vision of digitally empowered sovereignty cannot be fully realized without addressing the deeper structural inequities of the current international system. At the heart of the contemporary digital divide lies the persistent condition of digital asymmetry. It is a systemic imbalance in access to strategic technologies such as high-performance computing, sovereign cloud infrastructure, secure telecommunications,

E. Akıllı, *Cognitive Diplomacy and Digital Autonomy*,
https://doi.org/10.1007/978-3-032-04470-9_5

and AI research and development capabilities. These asymmetries are not simply developmental gaps, they also constitute geopolitical vulnerabilities. States excluded from these infrastructures become dependent on foreign platforms, unable to set their own digital norms, and are exposed to external coercion, surveillance, or algorithmic manipulation (Feakin, 2024).

Digital autonomy, therefore, must be understood as both a normative goal and a structural countermeasure to digital asymmetry. It provides a roadmap for overcoming dependency, building indigenous capacity, and engaging in the digital order on equitable terms. This mastery is constructed through three interlinked pillars:

5.1 Presence

This refers to a state's ability to maintain a visible, embedded, and secure footprint across all layers of critical digital infrastructure. It entails nurturing indigenous technological capabilities, including sovereign cloud systems, domestic chip fabrication, and national telecom networks. Without such a presence, digital autonomy remains aspirational—rendered hollow by structural dependence on foreign technologies and external platforms (Feakin, 2024; European Commission, 2020).

5.2 Practice

Sovereignty is also expressed through regulatory power and normative agency—the ability to shape the rules, standards, and ethical principles that govern technology. States assert their influence by regulating data flows, enforcing algorithmic transparency, and codifying human-centric AI principles into law. Through this, digital environments are not left to be solely dictated by corporate logic or foreign powers but they become normatively embedded with national values (Bradford, 2020; Celeste et al., 2022).

5.3 Resilience

Finally, autonomy requires strategic durability—the capacity to absorb systemic shocks, withstand coercion, and preserve freedom of action under stress. This includes securing diversified supply chains, investing in cybersecurity, and building trusted international partnerships. The institutional depth and adaptive governance structures underpin a nation's ability to weather technological disruptions and geopolitical turbulence alike (Gasser & Mayer-Schönberger, 2024; Nye, 2011).

Together, these three pillars—Presence, Practice, and Resilience—constitute the architecture of digital autonomy. They offer a framework through which states can secure their digital sovereignty and also assert meaningful leadership in a world where power is increasingly exercised through technological mediation. The emergence of the technopolar world order has catalyzed a sovereign awakening. The resulting transformation will not reinstate rigid Westphalian boundaries, but it will usher in a new equilibrium. In this equilibrium, digital borders are reasserted, national jurisdictions redefined, and technological dependencies reassessed—not to stifle openness, but to enable secure connectivity anchored in the public interest (Bremmer and Kupchan, 2022; Celeste et al., 2022).

From Ankara to Washington, from Brussels to Brasília, the pursuit of digital autonomy is now a shared imperative. While the ethical frameworks and strategic priorities may differ—liberal rights-based approaches in the West, sovereignty-anchored models in parts of the Global South—the common recognition is clear: no government can afford to cede control over the infrastructures that underpin economic competitiveness, democratic legitimacy, and national security. This part of the book will examine the three distinct yet interconnected pillars that form the very foundation of digital autonomy: presence, practice, and resilience. Together, these pillars articulate the structural capacities and strategic orientations that enable states to maintain agency, security, and influence in the technopolar world.

Bibliography

Krasner, S. D. (1999). *Sovereignty: Organized hypocrisy*. Princeton University Press.

Nye, J. S. (2011). *The future of power*. PublicAffairs.

Bradford, A. (2020). *The Brussels effect: How the European Union rules the world*. Oxford University Press.

Bremmer, I. and Kupchan, C. (2022). *Top risks 2022: Risk 2 — Technopolar world. Eurasia Group.* 3 January. Retrieved 5 May, 2025, from: https://www.eurasiagroup.net/live-post/top-risks-2022-2-technopolar-world

Gasser, U., & Mayer-Schönberger, V. (2024). *Guardrails: Guiding human decisions in the age of AI*. MIT Press.

Feakin, T. (2024). *Navigating the New Geopolitics of Tech*, Harvard Business Review, 11 November. Retrieved May 11, 2025, from https://hbr.org/2024/11/navigating-the-new-geopolitics-of-tech

European Commission. (2020). *A European Strategy for Data*, COM(2020) 66 Final. European Commission. Retrieved May 5, 2025, from https://eur-lex.europa.eu/legal-content/EN/TXT/?uri=celex:52020DC0066

Celeste, E., Heldt, A., & Iglesias Keller, C. (2022). Introduction. In E. Celeste, A. Heldt, & C. Iglesias Keller (Eds.), *Constitutionalising social media*. Edward Elgar.

CHAPTER 6

Digital Asymmetry in the Technopolar World

Before delving into digital autonomy's three foundational pillars, we must establish the strategic rationale behind it. Why has digital autonomy become the last resort for shielding and preserving digital sovereignty? This chapter introduces the concept of ***digital asymmetry;*** not as an exception, but as an entrenched reality born of the chaotic and unequal structure of the technopolar world. It is a structural feature, not an anomaly, and understanding its implications is crucial for grasping why digital autonomy is not optional but imperative.

As detailed earlier, control over data and technological infrastructure has become a primary determinant of geopolitical power in the technopolar world. In this context, I define digital asymmetry as the structural condition in which access to critical digital capabilities like high-performance computing, sovereign cloud systems, AI infrastructure, and foundational software is concentrated within a small group of states and corporations, while the rest of the world remains technologically dependent. This imbalance produces new forms of strategic dependency, systemic vulnerability, and global inequality. In practice, many countries lack the domestic capacity to develop or sustain frontier technologies and are thus compelled to rely on external providers.

This chapter examines the geopolitical consequences of this skewed technopolar order. It draws on recent policy developments, including one of the Biden administration's latest executive orders, establishing

E. Akıllı, *Cognitive Diplomacy and Digital Autonomy*,
https://doi.org/10.1007/978-3-032-04470-9_6

a tiered export control regime for advanced chips and semiconductors (Akıllı, 2025b), as well as persistent data governance disparities and the monopolization of digital infrastructure by transnational technology firms. Together, these trends demonstrate how digital asymmetry undermines sovereignty and entrenches dependency. It is this structural problem to which digital autonomy—as explored in the subsequent chapters—must serve as a strategic response.

6.1 Rise of Digital Asymmetry

According to the definition advanced in this book, the concept of the technopolar world is inherently rooted in the deepening of the digital divide. Technopolarity, in this sense, is not merely a descriptive label but a systemic response by the international order to the uneven distribution of cutting-edge digital capabilities. It reflects how global structures are adapting to a new form of strategic imbalance, which is no longer based on ideological confrontation, as in the Cold War, but rather on asymmetries in technological power.

The Cold War era, which gave rise to the bipolar world order, emerged from the ideological rift between the West and the East. It was structured by NATO and the Warsaw Pact, respectively. That bipolarity divided the world politically and militarily and also created competing global systems of influence. Today, a comparable pattern is unfolding—not along ideological lines, but along technological lines, particularly at the frontier of hardware and software innovation.

In this emerging great techno-rivalry, States are increasingly being pressured to align with one of the competing tech powers. The ongoing strategic competition between the U.S. and China is no longer a latent tension—it is an open contest for global technological dominance. As clearly stated in the 'America's AI Action Plan' document: "The United States is in a race to achieve global dominance in artificial intelligence (AI). Whoever has the largest AI ecosystem will set global AI standards and reap broad economic and military benefits" (U.S. White House, 2025). Moreover, the U.S. has imposed aggressive tariffs and export controls targeting Chinese firms and technologies. China, meanwhile, has responded with diplomatic pushback and reciprocal economic measures. As highlighted in my earlier analysis, a senior Chinese diplomat said that Beijing is "ready for all wars with the United States," framing the confrontation as a technological and geopolitical reckoning (Akıllı, 2025c).

The tiered export control framework initiated by the Biden administration further institutionalized this divide. The export framework for AI hardware divides countries into three categories based on strategic alignment and security concerns. Tier 1 includes close allies like Japan, Germany, and the U.K., who receive preferential access to AI processors but face strict reexport limits and licensing controls, especially for defense use. Tier 2, which includes Türkiye and others from Eastern Europe, the Middle East, and Latin America, is subject to severe quantity caps and must comply with U.S. security protocols to gain limited access. Tier 3, encompassing adversaries like China, Russia, and Iran, faces near-total restrictions, aimed at denying them military advantage. This system reflects the U.S.' use of technological dominance to safeguard national security and exert geopolitical influence (Akıllı, 2025b).

In other words, this policy effectively attempts to restructure global access to critical technologies. This move not only reflects the deepening techno-strategic schism but also echoes Cold War-era block politics, where access to resources, influence, and global networks was determined by one's alignment within the bipolar system (Akıllı, 2025a).

One of the clearest manifestations of digital asymmetry is the differential treatment and access to artificial intelligence technologies across geopolitical blocs. A case in point is Australia's recent ban on the Chinese-developed AI application—specifically, a large language model (LLM) known as DeepSeek—which was deemed to pose an "unacceptable risk" to national security. Australia's decision aligns with actions taken by several Tier 1 countries, including the United States, Italy, Canada, and South Korea, all of which have restricted DeepSeek due to concerns over data privacy, cybersecurity vulnerabilities, and the platform's potential role in disseminating Chinese state-aligned narratives. Notably, India—a Tier 2 country under the U.S. export control framework—has also implemented similar restrictions, underscoring that anxieties surrounding technological influence transcend formal access hierarchies (Akıllı, 2025c).

While Chinese officials have condemned these bans as unjustified extensions of national security discourse and as politicized interventions in the digital marketplace, independent analyses indicate that DeepSeek routinely avoids politically sensitive topics such as the Tiananmen Square massacre and often generates outputs aligned with pro-Beijing messaging. However, this raises a deeper normative question: can the same critique not be extended to U.S.-based platforms like OpenAI's ChatGPT? Similar concerns around agenda-setting, narrative framing, and informational bias could be leveled against Western LLMs, particularly as states increasingly instrumentalize AI tools for strategic communication and soft power projection. In this context, it is not merely access to computational infrastructure that defines digital asymmetry but also control over the informational architectures shaping global discourse. These developments reveal that digital asymmetry operates across both technical and narrative domains, making informational integrity, trust, and epistemic sovereignty central to the evolving contest for power in the technopolar world.

Thus, technopolarity is the geopolitical expression of digital asymmetry. It signals a reordering of international relations around digital power, compelling states to recalibrate their alliances, trade policies, and domestic capabilities. This reconfiguration, in turn, reinforces the urgency of pursuing digital autonomy as a strategy to navigate dependency risks and the pressures of alignment in a divided digital world.

One way or another, even states that seek neutrality or non-alignment in the emerging technopolar order, find themselves structurally disadvantaged. If a state chooses to align with a dominant power, it must conform to the strategic and regulatory logic of that bloc—effectively becoming embedded within Cold War-style technoblock politics. Conversely, states that reject alignment or strive for independent positioning, often face exclusion from vital technologies, markets, or governance frameworks. In both cases, the outcome is a loss of agency.

Henceforth, digital asymmetry is not merely a transitional phase—it constitutes a structural condition of the technopolar world order. It constrains sovereign decision-making by conditioning access to innovation, infrastructure, and influence on a state's geopolitical alignment. Without deliberate and strategic investment in domestic technological capabilities, states risk becoming digitally peripheral. Unless concrete measures are taken to build national capacity and pursue digital autonomy, many governments will be compelled to bandwagon with major technopowers—not out of strategic preference, but due to structural necessity.

As some scholars argue, contemporary tech firms "affect, shape, limit, [and] amplify state power," even if "only states can invade countries and arrest people" (Chander & Sun, 2021). Yet in practice, essential functions of governance—such as communications, finance, transportation, and public administration—often depend on foreign digital platforms. In environments where the majority of data traffic and computational capacity flows through externally controlled infrastructure, especially in the Global South, states lose meaningful operational agency.

Digital asymmetry, therefore, encapsulates more than the digital divide—which merely measures differential access to internet connectivity. It represents a deeper geopolitical inequality over who controls the critical architectures of digital power. It is no longer just about inclusion in the network, but about agency within it. In this respect, digital asymmetry echoes critical discourses on "platform capitalism" and "digital colonialism." One-sided data exploitation and the monopolization of AI infrastructure exacerbate global inequalities, foster technological dependency, and reinforce systemic hierarchies (Couldry & Mejias, 2019). By concentrating AI computing, sovereign cloud infrastructure, and next-generation chips within Western and allied economies, the technopolar order structurally binds less-capable states to external digital regimes, limiting their ability to chart independent developmental and diplomatic trajectories.

6.2 Concentration of Critical Technologies

The technopolar world is defined by the extreme concentration of digital capabilities within a small group of states and corporations. This concentration is evident across four core domains: AI computing power, semiconductor fabrication, cloud infrastructure, and global connectivity systems. Together, these domains form the foundation of digital power—and their concentration exacerbates digital asymmetry.

AI computing power is disproportionately located in the United States and its strategic allies. According to the Carnegie Endowment for International Peace, the Biden administration's AI export control policy explicitly acknowledges that "the majority of global AI compute capacity is already concentrated in the United States," and that American providers "dominate the global market for cloud infrastructure" (Winter-Levy, 2025). This dominance is reflected in the November 2024 TOP500 list, where U.S.-based supercomputers such as *El Capitan* and *Frontier* held the top two positions globally, achieving 1.742 and 1.353 exaflops respectively (TOP500, 2024). This matters because training foundation models and deploying high-end AI applications requires immense computing capacity. States and firms without access to such resources are effectively excluded from next-generation innovation.

Semiconductor fabrication is another highly concentrated domain. The most advanced semiconductors, essential for AI, 5G, defense systems, and quantum computing, are produced by a small number of firms, primarily Taiwan's TSMC and South Korea's Samsung. These chips are designed predominantly by U.S.-based companies such as Nvidia and AMD. The Biden administration's 2025 AI export framework grants unrestricted chip access to 18 designated allies, while imposing strict licensing regimes or outright restrictions on other states. These include a Tier 2 category for conditional partners and a Tier 3 category for "countries of concern," such as China, Russia, Iran, and North Korea (Freifeld, 2025). This export control architecture not only reflects geopolitical tensions but also exemplifies digital asymmetry in action: access to foundational technologies is contingent on geopolitical alignment.

Cloud infrastructure is similarly monopolized. The global cloud market is dominated by three U.S.-based corporations—Amazon Web Services (AWS), Microsoft Azure, and Google Cloud—which together control approximately 75% of the global market. In Europe, their dominance is particularly striking, with the three firms accounting for nearly three-quarters of all cloud services by the end of 2023 (Thorne, 2024). This concentration leaves many states reliant on a small number of external providers for core digital infrastructure. The Green Web Foundation warns that these firms benefit from market practices such as bundling, lock-in mechanisms, and inoperability, creating closed ecosystems that intensify dependence and limit national control (Thorne, 2024). For many states, the absence of strong domestic alternatives translates into strategic exposure and normative dependency.

Connectivity infrastructure, especially submarine cables and satellite networks—is also concentrated in the hands of a few corporations and consortia. The physical backbone of the internet relies heavily on undersea fiber-optic cables, most of which are financed, owned, or operated by consortia of major tech firms and telecoms based in a handful of countries. As maps of global submarine cable routes illustrate, transoceanic connectivity flows through a limited number of corridors, often routed through or near Western-aligned territories (Routley, 2020). This architecture introduces critical vulnerabilities: a single cable cut can isolate entire countries, and the strategic placement of cables allows for the potential of surveillance or coercion. Moreover, reliance on commercial satellite systems—many operated by U.S.-based companies—further entrenches asymmetries in global connectivity.

In sum, the concentration of critical technologies—across AI computing, semiconductors, cloud services, and infrastructure—reveals the systemic character of digital asymmetry in the technopolar world. States without indigenous capacity or trusted access are structurally constrained in their ability to innovate, govern, or secure their digital futures. These asymmetries reinforce dependency and weaken sovereignty. In the next sections, we will examine how these structural imbalances manifest as geopolitical vulnerabilities and how they compel states to pursue digital autonomy as a strategic imperative.

6.3 Geopolitical Consequences of Digital Asymmetry: Vulnerability, Dependency, and Sovereignty

The monopolization of digital infrastructure by major technology firms, which are closely aligned with the political agendas of their home governments, introduces new forms of dependency. A salient example is SpaceX's Starlink service, which has been pivotal for Ukraine's military and civil communications during the ongoing conflict with Russia. However, the unilateral control exercised by its founder, Elon Musk, over service parameters, such as denying coverage in Crimea, underscores the geopolitical risks of relying on privately held infrastructure for national security (Roulette, 2023). This scenario exemplifies how a foreign-entity corporate control over critical digital infrastructure can influence a state's sovereignty and actions. The broader implications of such dependencies are multifaceted:

Nations lacking domestic capabilities in AI infrastructure, semiconductor fabrication, or cloud services are compelled to procure these technologies under terms set by foreign entities. The United States' Framework for Artificial Intelligence Diffusion, introduced in January 2025, exemplifies this dynamic (U.S. Department of Commerce, Bureau of Industry and Security, 2025). The policy mandates that foreign cloud providers maintain at least half of their compute capacity within the U.S. and adhere to stringent security protocols to attain "validated end user" status. Consequently, even allied nations like the UAE must comply with rigorous U.S. oversight to access advanced technologies, reinforcing a hierarchy of technological access (Winter-Levy, 2025).

Digital asymmetry exacerbates global economic disparities. While increased internet penetration can significantly boost GDP in emerging markets, the monopolization of advanced technologies by a few countries limits these benefits. The Global South often becomes a source of data for training AI models developed in the Global North, without equitable participation in the resulting innovations. This dynamic has been characterized as "digital colonialism," where data extraction by powerful firms leads to an increased dependency of Southern societies on imported platforms and services (Ndemo, 2024).

Reliance on foreign technology introduces significant security risks as well. Historical concerns over Huawei's 5G infrastructure illustrate how dependence on external vendors can lead to espionage fears. Additionally, the control of critical communication infrastructures, such as undersea cables and satellite networks, by foreign entities poses risks of surveillance and service disruption. Many African nations, for instance, have limited landing stations for undersea cables, making them susceptible to isolation due to outages or geopolitical tensions (Thorne, 2024).

Digital asymmetry undermines national sovereignty by compelling governments to conform to external data governance frameworks. Countries subject to U.S. sanctions or export controls often find their access to essential technologies curtailed. Developing nations frequently express reluctance to align exclusively with either U.S. or Chinese digital models, seeking instead a hybrid approach. However, the lack of robust local infrastructure forces them to navigate a complex landscape of competing regulations, often without significant influence over the rules governing digital spaces (Ndemo, 2024).

Control over advanced technologies has become a strategic tool in international relations. The U.S.' three-tiered export controls on AI technologies serve not only to maintain technological superiority but also to influence the geopolitical alignments of other nations. Conversely, countries lacking technological capabilities may find themselves compelled to align with dominant powers to secure access to essential technologies. This dynamic creates new spheres of influence defined by technological dependencies rather than traditional ideological alignments (Ndemo, 2024).

6.4 Policy Cases Illustrating Digital Asymmetry

Recent developments underscore how digital asymmetry is not accidental but engineered through strategic policy choices and market structures that favor dominant players. These cases reveal how the technopolar world order is being shaped by both state-driven and corporate actions, often reinforcing global hierarchies of access, influence, and control.

One of the most prominent examples is the United States' tiered export control regime, formalized under the 2025 Framework for Artificial Intelligence Diffusion. This framework stratifies the world into three tiers based on perceived alignment with U.S. security and normative interests. Tier 1 includes close allies, such as EU members, Japan, South Korea, and the Five Eyes countries, which enjoy largely unrestricted access to advanced semiconductors, AI chips, and cloud computing infrastructure. Tier 2 nations may access these technologies only under strict licensing agreements, with conditions that often require hosting data centers on U.S. soil or accepting American oversight. Tier 3 countries—those deemed adversarial or unaligned, such as China, Russia, Iran, and North Korea—are effectively excluded from acquiring high-end computing and related technologies (Akıllı, 2025b). This framework not only operationalizes geopolitical alignment as a condition for technological access but also institutionalizes digital asymmetry as a global norm.

Data governance disparities further complicate the strategic landscape. The U.S. champions open data flows as part of its liberal economic agenda, the European Union enforces stringent privacy protections under the GDPR, and China promotes data localization and cyber-sovereignty. These divergent models create a fragmented and often contradictory global regulatory environment. For developing countries, which frequently lack robust digital institutions or technical capacity, the result is a loss of normative agency. Many are forced to adapt to foreign rules or risk exclusion from global data networks. As Ndemo (2024) notes, the Global South increasingly finds itself in a reactive posture, navigating overlapping frameworks without the power to shape them.

The monopolization of digital infrastructure by Big Tech further reinforces digital asymmetry. U.S.-based firms such as Amazon Web Services, Microsoft Azure, and Google Cloud dominate the global cloud market and have become critical enablers of national digital systems, from health care and education to public administration. Their dominance is not solely based on market efficiency but is maintained through bundling practices, regulatory lobbying, and technological lock-ins that suppress competition. The Green Web Foundation (2024) emphasizes that this consolidation grants these firms quasi-sovereign influence over digital economies and weakens the capacity of smaller nations to build sovereign infrastructure. Even efforts to establish national clouds or local data centers are often reliant on partnerships with these corporations, which set the terms of engagement in ways that prioritize the commercial and geopolitical interests of their countries of origin.

Digital asymmetry represents a systemic imbalance in the global digital ecosystem, where control over critical technologies and infrastructures is concentrated among a few powerful actors. This concentration undermines the sovereignty, security, and economic development of nations lacking indigenous digital capabilities. Addressing this challenge necessitates a concerted effort to build digital autonomy through investment in local infrastructure, the development of sovereign technologies, and the establishment of equitable international frameworks for technology governance.

Collectively, these policy cases illustrate how digital asymmetry is strategically embedded in both the global governance of technology and its material distribution. Technology is no longer a neutral tool of development but a calibrated instrument of power projection, alliance formation, and regulatory control. The implications are profound: without assertive efforts to build autonomous capacities and normative independence, many states risk becoming permanent digital dependents in an increasingly fragmented and hierarchical technopolar world.

This reality underscores the urgent need for a coherent and strategic response. As the following chapters will argue, digital autonomy is not merely aspirational, it is imperative. It offers a path to reclaiming agency, securing digital sovereignty, and ensuring national relevance in the algorithmic age. This response rests on three interdependent pillars:

- *Presence*, the ability to build and maintain critical digital infrastructure;
- *Practice*, the capacity to shape and enforce normative and regulatory frameworks; and
- *Resilience*, the strength to withstand shocks, coercion, and exclusion in a turbulent geopolitical environment.

These three pillars do not guarantee independence overnight, but together they provide a foundation for states to engage the technopolar order on sovereign terms—rather than on terms set by others.

References

Akıllı, E. (2025a). "Rewiring diplomacy in the Technopolar world". *Daily Sabah (Op-Ed)*. 18 April. Available at: https://www.dailysabah.com/opinion/op-ed/rewiring-diplomacy-in-the-technopolar-world (Accessed May 11, 2025).

Akıllı, E. (2025b). "Trump's Stargate, Biden's Tier List and the Wake of the Techno-Polar World". Daily Sabah. 1 February. Available at: https://www.dailysabah.com/opinion/op-ed/trumps-stargate-bidens-tier-list-and-the-wake-of-the-techno-polar-world (Accessed May 5, 2025).

Akıllı, E. (2025c). "Techno-polar reckoning: US vs China". *Daily Sabah*. 21 March. Available at: https://www.dailysabah.com/opinion/op-ed/techno-polar-reckoning-us-vs-china (Accessed May 12, 2025).

Chander, A., & Sun, H. (2021). Sovereignty 2.0. *Georgetown University Law Center.*. https://scholarship.law.georgetown.edu/facpub/2404 (Accessed 5 May, 2025

Couldry, N., & Mejias, U. A. (2019). *The costs of connection: How data is colonizing human life and appropriating it for capitalism*. Stanford University Press.

Freifeld, K. (2025). "US tightens its grip on AI chip flows across the globe". Reuters. 13 January. Available at: https://www.reuters.com/technology/artificial-intelligence/us-tightens-its-grip-ai-chip-flows-across-globe-2025-01-13/ (Accessed May 12, 2025).

Ndemo, B. (2024). "Addressing digital colonialism: A path to equitable data governance", UNESCO Inclusive Policy Lab. 8 August. Available at: https://en.unesco.org/inclusivepolicylab/analytics/addressing-digital-colonialism-path-equitable-data-governance (Accessed May 12, 2025).

Roulette, J. (2023). "SpaceX curbed Ukraine's use of Starlink internet for drones - company president". Reuters. 9 February. Available at: https://www.reuters.com/business/aerospace-defense/spacex-curbed-ukraines-use-starlink-internet-drones-company-president-2023-02-09/ (Accessed 12 May 2025).

Routley, N. (2020). "Wired World: 35 Years of Submarine Cables in One Map". Visual Capitalist, 22 December. Available at: https://www.visualcapitalist.com/wired-world-35-years-of-submarine-cables-in-one-map/ (Accessed 12 May 2025).

TOP500. (2024). "TOP500 List—November 2024." Available at: https://top500.org/lists/top500/list/2024/11/ (Accessed 12 May, 2025).

Thorne, M. (2024). "Critical dependencies: How power consolidation of digital infrastructures threatens our democracies—And what we can do about it." The Green Web Foundation. 23 September. Available at: https://www.thegreenwebfoundation.org/publications/report-critical-dependencies/ (Accessed May 12, 2025).

U.S. Department of Commerce, Bureau of Industry and Security. (2025). "Framework for Artificial Intelligence Diffusion." Federal Register, 90(10), pp. 2674–2682, 15 January. Available at: https://www.federalregister.gov/documents/2025/01/15/2025-00636/framework-for-artificial-intelligence-diffusion (Accessed 12 May 2025).

U.S. White House. (2025, July). America's AI Action Plan. https://www.whitehouse.gov/wpcontent/uploads/2025/07/Americas-AI-Action-Plan.pdf

Winter-Levy, S. (2025). "With its latest rule, the U.S. tries to govern AI'S global spread". Carnegie Endowment for International Peace. 13 January. Available at: https://carnegieendowment.org/emissary/2025/01/ai-new-rule-chips-exports-diffusion-framework (Accessed May 12, 2025).

CHAPTER 7

Presence—Sovereign Identity in the Digital Sphere

In the age of the technopolar world, sovereignty is no longer defined solely by control over physical borders or the assertion of legal authority within territorial confines. Rather, it increasingly hinges on a state's capacity to maintain and project its digital presence: its visibility, agency, and regulatory authority within online and technological domains. This marks a profound transformation in the concept of sovereignty, whereby national power is increasingly determined by control over digital infrastructures, data governance systems, and the architectures of algorithmic influence (Bradford, 2023).

As global interdependence becomes digitally mediated through platforms, cloud ecosystems, and artificial intelligence, the locus of strategic advantage shifts from land acquisition or military supremacy to dominance over technological architectures and innovation ecosystems. These infrastructures are disproportionately concentrated in a few geopolitical blocs—namely the U.S., China, and the EU—giving rise to a trilateral technopolitical rivalry that now shapes the evolving contours of the international digital order (Bjola & Kornprobst, 2024).

Within this competitive matrix, a state's ability to secure its sovereign digital identity—defined by its technological base, normative values, and regulatory sovereignty—has become essential not only for digital autonomy but also for long-term economic resilience and political agency.

E. Akıllı, *Cognitive Diplomacy and Digital Autonomy*,
https://doi.org/10.1007/978-3-032-04470-9_7

The legitimacy of modern statecraft now depends on how effectively a nation can govern its digital ecosystems in line with its strategic interests.

As outlined in the previous chapter, digital asymmetry—marked by exclusion from critical technologies such as high-performance computing, sovereign cloud services, or secure communications infrastructure—creates systemic vulnerabilities. These disparities do more than erode economic competitiveness. They compromise a state's autonomous capacity to act in a world increasingly governed by data flows, machine intelligence, and cognitive infrastructures that operate beyond the reach of classical Westphalian instruments (Gasser & Mayer-Schönberger, 2024; Krasner, 1999).

In response, states are rearticulating sovereignty through *presence*—a proactive and strategic engagement with the digital sphere that transcends traditional notions of jurisdiction. This evolving model rests on four mutually reinforcing pillars. First, infrastructure sovereignty refers to the development and control of national cloud ecosystems, secure data centers, and resilient telecommunications networks. Such capabilities are essential to mitigate strategic dependence on foreign infrastructure and ensure the continuity and integrity of digital governance (DeNardis, 2020; Mueller, 2017). Second, digital identity governance involves constructing secure, state-regulated digital identity systems that anchor legal personhood and citizenship in cyberspace, enabling the extension of sovereign rights and responsibilities into the virtual domain (Couture & Toupin, 2019). Third, value-based regulation empowers governments to impose public interest obligations and democratic oversight on digital platforms operating within their jurisdictions, thereby counterbalancing the normative dominance of transnational tech firms (Bradford, 2023; Gorwa, 2019). Finally, normative and cultural projection allows states to shape the global digital landscape through international standard-setting, multilingual content production, and the promotion of ethical and culturally embedded AI frameworks. In this way, states extend their influence beyond borders by participating in the contest over digital norms, epistemologies, and platform governance (Katzenbach & Bächle, 2021).

Presence, in this context, is not merely a function of technical capacity, it is a diplomatic and strategic imperative. It enables a state not only to defend against technological dependency and external manipulation but also to assert normative agency within global governance forums. As digital governance increasingly reflects the dominance of a few powerful states and transnational technology corporations, cultivating a sovereign digital presence allows smaller and emerging actors to participate meaningfully in the development of ethical, legal, and technical standards that govern digital life (DeNardis, 2020; Mueller, 2017). In this shifting geopolitical terrain, digital presence has emerged as the most immediate and visible expression of national agency in the twenty-first century (Couture & Toupin, 2019).

The redefinition of sovereignty in the digital age is rooted in a critical recognition: control over data flows, digital infrastructures, and online identities have become as central to state power as territorial integrity once was. As argued earlier in this book, global influence is increasingly structured around the command of technological architectures and innovation ecosystems disproportionately concentrated in a handful of geopolitical and corporate hubs (Bradford, 2023). States that lack access to these strategic assets face deepening marginalization within the global digital economy, a condition best described as a digital asymmetrical structural dependency that diminishes both economic resilience and political agency (Gasser & Almeida, 2017).

The classical Westphalian conception of sovereignty premised on territorial control and legal jurisdiction proves inadequate in a world increasingly defined by transnational data flows, platform governance, and algorithmic systems. Instead, sovereignty today must be exercised through digital presence—the infrastructure, regulatory capacity, and normative vision that enable states and citizens to assert identity, rights, and political will within cyberspace. As Nye (2011) noted, power in the information age increasingly derives from the ability to shape preferences and norms through control of digital platforms, networks, and information flows.

This chapter explores these foundations in-depth, analyzing how resilient digital infrastructure, nationally governed identity systems, value-based regulatory frameworks, and cultural-normative projection combine to establish a sovereign presence in the global digital order. Taken together, these components shield states from strategic dependence, while empowering them to co-author the emerging rules and norms of digital governance. In this way, digital sovereignty is not a retreat from globalization, but rather a condition for engaging with it on equitable and autonomous terms.

7.1 Infrastructure Sovereignty in the Digital Domain

A core element of digital presence is infrastructure sovereignty—a nation's control over the physical and virtual infrastructure that underpins its internet and communications ecosystems. This includes data centers and servers, telecommunications networks, cloud computing platforms, and the data itself. Increasingly, states are treating these assets as strategic infrastructure on par with ports, energy grids, and transportation systems (DeNardis, 2020). As detailed earlier in this book, the very notion of sovereignty today depends not only on legal jurisdiction but on a state's ability to exercise control across three interdependent domains: **data sovereignty**, the secure storage and governance of data often through localized or sovereign cloud infrastructure; **algorithmic sovereignty**, the capacity to develop and regulate algorithms that inform economic and administrative decisions; and **hardware sovereignty**, which concerns access to or domestic production of key technological components, such as semiconductors.

This multidimensional framing reflects a paradigmatic shift from sovereignty as legal authority to sovereignty as infrastructural capability. States are no longer simply defending borders, they are "competing over the architectures of the digital future" (Mueller, 2017). In this context, infrastructure sovereignty becomes a prerequisite for digital autonomy, national security, and long-term development.

Digital sovereignty, moreover, centers on a state's control over the data produced by its citizens, institutions, and private sector. This control is increasingly institutionalized through data localization laws that mandate the domestic storage and processing of specific categories of sensitive data—such as personal, health, or financial information—in order to reinforce legal jurisdiction and reduce reliance on foreign cloud service providers.

A notable example is Russia's Federal Law No. 242-FZ, which took effect in 2015 and requires that the personal data of Russian citizens be stored in databases physically located within the Russian Federation. This legislation is part of a broader strategy to assert sovereign control over digital infrastructure and limit the extraterritorial reach of foreign technology companies. As commentators have noted, the law reflects Russia's ambition to construct a "Fortress Russia" approach to data governance—anchoring its digital systems within national borders to reinforce state oversight and reduce foreign influence (Tomaszewski & Priebe, 2015).

In Europe, concerns about U.S. tech companies' dominance over data and the implications of extraterritorial laws like the U.S. CLOUD Act (2018) have spurred initiatives to reclaim digital sovereignty. The European Union broadly defines digital sovereignty as the ability to control one's digital destiny, encompassing the physical infrastructure (data centers, telecom networks, cloud resources), the code layer (technical standards and protocols), and the data layer (ownership and governance) (World Economic Forum 2023; Musoni, 2023) to reduce dependence on U.S. cloud providers—who may be compelled by the CLOUD Act to disclose data regardless of physical location—European leaders accelerated plans for sovereign cloud infrastructures. Gaia-X, launched in 2019 by Germany and France, exemplifies this effort by aiming to create a federated European data infrastructure that ensures transparency, openness, and compliance with European values and data protection laws (Gaia-X, 2025; Niebel & Smoleń, 2023).

France's "cloud of trust" strategy further illustrates this approach. The Bleu project, a joint venture by Capgemini and Orange, seeks to provide cloud services fully compliant with French sovereignty requirements by keeping data under French jurisdiction. This initiative targets sensitive sectors such as government, health care, and regional authorities, ensuring data is processed within a trusted and legally secure environment (Capgemini and Orange, 2023). These efforts underscore the critical intersection of infrastructure sovereignty and data governance: controlling physical infrastructure is essential to enforce data sovereignty, protect privacy, and maintain national security in the digital age (Hummel et al., 2021). Without such control, nations risk exposure to foreign legal regimes and potential misuse or loss of critical data assets.

Control over telecommunications networks has also become a critical aspect of infrastructure sovereignty. It is especially highlighted by the controversy surrounding Huawei's involvement in 5G networks. Many Western countries, including Germany, the U.K., and several EU member states, have imposed restrictions or bans on Huawei equipment in their 5G core networks due to fears that reliance on foreign, potentially adversarial technology could enable espionage or coercion. For instance, Germany plans to remove Huawei and ZTE components from its 5G core networks by the end of 2026 to protect critical infrastructure from hybrid and cyberattacks and reduce dependency on single suppliers (Kroet, 2024). The U.K. similarly banned Huawei from selling new 5G equipment after 2020 and mandated the removal of existing Huawei 5G kit by 2027, citing national security concerns linked to China's potential use of Huawei technology for spying (Bowler, 2020). While some EU countries have resisted outright bans, the general trend emphasizes diversification of suppliers and strengthening domestic telecom capabilities as a matter of national security (Politico.eu., 2023; McDonald, 2020).

Beyond 5G, control over undersea fiber-optic cables that carry global internet traffic is also considered strategic. Some states have invested in domestic consortia to build and manage cable landings, ensuring reliable connectivity under national oversight, thereby safeguarding critical digital infrastructure from foreign control or disruption (Brookings Institution analysis, paraphrased).

Sovereign cloud computing is now a central pillar of infrastructure sovereignty. Sovereign clouds are designed to meet national requirements for data control and compliance with local laws, often operated domestically or through partnerships where foreign providers adhere to strict data residency and encryption standards. Germany's Deutsche Telekom launched the Open Telekom Cloud as a German-operated alternative to U.S. cloud giants AWS and Azure, targeting sensitive data storage and processing within national jurisdiction. France's Bleu project, a joint venture between Capgemini and Orange, and another partnership between Thales and Google Cloud, aim to provide cloud services compliant with French sovereignty requirements, combining advanced technology with local operational control (Capgemini and Orange, 2023).

Other countries also pursue sovereign cloud models: the United Arab Emirates and Saudi Arabia have established government cloud services and regulations to keep sensitive data within their borders. China enforces strict data sovereignty by requiring all cloud providers, including foreign-invested ones, to operate through Chinese entities and comply with stringent data laws, effectively insulating Chinese data from external jurisdiction, as part of its broader cyber-sovereignty doctrine (Creemers, 2023).

The push for infrastructure sovereignty is driven by geopolitical realities, including fears of being cut off from critical digital components like semiconductors and cloud services. The concentration of semiconductor production in a few countries (Taiwan, South Korea, the U.S., and the Netherlands) has strategic implications. They were exemplified by U.S. bans on advanced chips export to China which leverage hardware control to constrain rivals. This has prompted China and others to accelerate efforts toward chip self-reliance. Similarly, reliance on foreign cloud servers, risks data access being cut off or surveilled during diplomatic conflicts. Strengthening domestic digital infrastructure, including data centers, national cloud services, and tech industries, is thus essential to insulate nations from external coercion and ensure the continuity of critical digital services, forming the foundation of national digital identity and sovereignty (Creemers, 2023; Small Wars Journal, 2024).

Many nations have adopted policies to develop national cloud computing infrastructure, often called "sovereign clouds," characterized by domestic control over data, compliance with local laws, and protection from foreign jurisdiction. Approaches differ notably between the EU and the U.S.

7.2 European Union and Member States

The EU is a leading advocate for digital and cloud sovereignty, aiming to foster innovation while building resilient and secure infrastructure. The upcoming Cloud and AI Development Act, expected in 2025, seeks to triple the EU's data center capacity within five to seven years and support public administrations with sovereign cloud solutions, emphasizing sustainability and innovation (European Commission, 2024). This Act will complement EU-wide cloud policies for public procurement, potentially giving preferential access to European cloud providers and facilitating capital access to strengthen the sector (European Commission, 2025).

At the core of Europe's sovereign cloud strategy is Gaia-X, a federated cloud ecosystem initiated by Germany and France to ensure interoperability, transparency, and compliance with European privacy and security standards. Gaia-X is not a single cloud platform but a framework encouraging cloud services that meet EU requirements, preventing vendor lock-in to foreign technology (Forum Europe, 2025).

Individual countries have developed trusted cloud projects aligned with sovereignty goals. For example, France's *Project Bleu*, a joint venture between Orange and Capgemini using Microsoft technology, offers cloud services operated under French law to keep operational control domestic. France also partnered with Thales and Google Cloud to create a "strategic sovereign cloud" where Thales manages encryption and data access, ensuring Google cannot access plaintext data (Capgemini and Orange, 2023). Germany similarly collaborates with SAP and Deutsche Telekom to provide cloud options shielded from extraterritorial reach (Smith, 2025).

These initiatives reflect the EU's determination to ensure cloud computing infrastructure-critical for government, AI, and businesses, remains under European control, reducing dependency on the U.S. and other foreign providers (Eropean Union 2025; (Vogiatzoglou, 2025).

7.3 United States

The U.S. approach to cloud sovereignty is less focused on nationalization and more on market-driven solutions and alliances. U.S. cloud providers like Amazon, Microsoft, and Google dominate globally, and the U.S. government maintains sovereign controls primarily for its own sensitive data. For example, Pentagon cloud programs require hosting sensitive military data on U.S. soil with cleared personnel (Fleming, 2025). To meet foreign sovereignty demands, U.S. companies have developed localized cloud zones, such as Microsoft's "German Cloud" operated via Deutsche Telekom and Oracle's dedicated EU cloud regions, effectively extending national control layers abroad (World Economic Forum 2023).

7.4 China

China's cloud and infrastructure sovereignty is among the strongest globally, anchored in its comprehensive cyber-sovereignty policy. Under this policy, data about Chinese citizens must remain within China's borders, and foreign cloud operators such as AWS or Microsoft are required to partner with Chinese firms that operate the services domestically. Consequently, Chinese cloud providers like Alibaba Cloud, Tencent Cloud, and Huawei Cloud dominate the domestic market and are fully subject to Chinese law.

This approach is enforced through a trio of national laws: the Cybersecurity Law (CSL), the Data Security Law (DSL), and the Personal Information Protection Law (PIPL). These laws collectively regulate data governance, cybersecurity, and state oversight of digital infrastructure, functioning as China's equivalent to Europe's GDPR but with a stronger emphasis on national security and regime control. For example, the DSL mandates that certain categories of data cannot be transferred abroad without government approval, enforcing strict data localization (Fan & Zhou, 2025).

The Cybersecurity Law, originally enacted in 2016 and currently undergoing amendments in 2025, strengthens enforcement by introducing harsher penalties and clearer compliance requirements for network operators and critical information infrastructure providers. It mandates security certifications for products, tightens control over foreign cybersecurity products, and requires cooperation with public security organs, reinforcing China's digital sovereignty (Fan & Zhou, 2025; Khan, 2025).

China's sovereign internet infrastructure is further bolstered by the Great Firewall, controlling external internet gateways, and a state-owned telecommunications backbone. Policymakers have also proposed alternative internet architectures like the "New IP" via the International Telecommunication Union (ITU), aiming to increase state control over networks globally (Sheehan 2023).

Internationally, China exports its cloud infrastructure model through the Digital Silk Road initiative, building data centers and communication networks in partner countries that extend China's governance model beyond its borders, raising concerns about digital sovereignty and geopolitical influence (Lewis, 2021; Sheehan, 2023).

7.5 Digital Identity Frameworks and Sovereign Digital IDs

Digital identity frameworks are a fundamental pillar of sovereign presence in the digital realm, enabling states to verify and manage citizens' identities online securely and efficiently. Estonia exemplifies this with its advanced digital ID system, which underpins nearly 100% of government services accessible online. Every Estonian citizen and resident possesses a state-issued digital ID, linked to a physical smart card and mobile ID, enabling activities such as online voting, tax payments, health record access, and digital prescriptions (e-Estonia, 2025).

Estonia's digital identity system is supported by the X-Road platform, an open-source, secure data exchange layer that connects over 52,000 organizations and facilitates more than 2.2 billion transactions annually. X-Road ensures interoperability between public and private sector information systems while maintaining data sovereignty through encryption, authentication, and comprehensive logging of all data exchanges

(X-Road Global, 2025). This architecture allows citizens to provide data once, reducing redundancy and enhancing service efficiency. Moreover, Estonia has extended its digital ID concept internationally through its e-Residency program, granting non-residents access to Estonian and EU digital business services, thus expanding its sovereign digital presence beyond physical borders (Barlow & Levy-Bencheton 2019).

Other countries have developed similar initiatives. India's Aadhaar system assigns biometric-based digital IDs to over 1.3 billion people, streamlining welfare distribution and service verification, though it has raised privacy concerns. The European Union is advancing interoperability among member states' e-ID systems via the eIDAS regulation and plans for a European Digital Identity Wallet, promoting cross-border recognition and user control consistent with privacy-centric principles (Willemson, 2022).

The design of digital identity systems reflects national governance values. Estonia's model emphasizes user control and transparency, logging every data access to ensure accountability. In contrast, authoritarian regimes like China mandate real-name registration linking online activities to national ID numbers, and facilitating state surveillance and social control mechanisms such as the Social Credit System (Larsen, 2022).

One emerging concept in digital identity is "self-sovereign identity (SSI)" which is an emerging digital identity model that shifts control from centralized authorities, such as states or corporations, to individuals themselves. SSI enables users to own and manage their digital identities independently, often using blockchain or decentralized technologies, to store cryptographic proofs rather than personal data in a central repository. This allows individuals to selectively disclose only the minimum necessary information (e.g., age or citizenship) to verify claims without exposing full identity details, enhancing privacy and autonomy in digital interactions (Dock Labs, 2025; Frontiers in Blockchain, 2024; SEON, 2025).

SSI systems rely on three core components: decentralized identifiers (DIDs), verifiable credentials (VCs), and blockchain technology. DIDs are cryptographically verifiable, globally unique identifiers controlled by the user without dependence on a central authority. Verifiable credentials are tamper-evident digital attestations issued by trusted entities (e.g., governments) that users can present selectively. Blockchain provides the immutable ledger ensuring the integrity and decentralized verification of these credentials (Fields, 2025; Hendrickson, 2025).

While SSI enhances user control, it typically depends on government-issued "root" identities or authoritative attestations to establish trustworthiness. Thus, SSI complements rather than replaces sovereign digital identity frameworks, aligning with democratic values of privacy, consent, and user empowerment. For instance, the European Blockchain Services Infrastructure includes pilots for SSI to provide citizens with certified credentials they control, integrating SSI with existing state digital ID systems (Dock Labs, 2025; IEEE SA, 2025).

SSI also serves as a critical layer for digital sovereignty by enabling secure authentication that reduces cyber fraud and disinformation. Without trusted digital IDs, citizens may resort to less secure or foreign identity providers, exposing them to identity theft or surveillance. Therefore, digital IDs, whether state-issued or SSI-based-extend sovereign protections into cyberspace, embody the state-citizen relationship online (Larsen, 2022).

Different countries illustrate varied digital ID governance philosophies. Estonia's system empowers individuals with state-issued digital IDs used under strict consent rules, while India's Aadhaar system, despite enhancing inclusion, has raised privacy and surveillance concerns. Canada is exploring decentralized digital IDs linked to provincial IDs, reflecting a federated model. Authoritarian states like China tightly integrate digital identity with surveillance technologies, such as facial recognition linked to national ID numbers, enabling extensive social control (Center for Strategic and International Studies, 2021; Larsen, 2022; Willemson, 2022).

7.6 Values-Driven Governance of Digital Presence

Digital sovereignty is not only about infrastructure and identity systems—the "skeleton and skin" of a nation's digital presence—but fundamentally about the values that shape digital governance, which form its "soul." Different political systems embed their societal values-such as privacy, freedom of expression, security, and cultural norms, into their digital policies, thereby defining their sovereign presence online.

In democracies, the protection of individual rights and liberties is paramount. The European Union's General Data Protection Regulation (GDPR) exemplifies this by operationalizing privacy and data protection as core values. It enforces uniform data rights like informed consent and the right to be forgotten, holding even global companies accountable to European standards (Musoni, 2023; World Economic Forum, 2023). This regulatory framework protects European identity in the digital economy by prioritizing human dignity over unrestricted data monetization. As noted by analysts at the Center for Strategic and International Studies (CSIS), GDPR marked a turning point by granting consumers unprecedented control over their data while preserving online freedom and openness (World Economic Forum, 2023).

Moreover, the EU's forthcoming AI Act reflects European values by emphasizing ethics and human rights. It bans harmful AI practices such as social scoring and pervasive biometric surveillance and imposes stringent requirements on high-risk AI systems, underscoring a human-centric and precautionary approach to technology governance (Fleming, 2025).

These examples illustrate how the EU's digital sovereignty agenda is deeply values-driven—balancing innovation with social responsibility, transparency, and accountability (IE University, 2024). The EU's regulatory influence also extends globally through the "Brussels Effect," compelling multinational companies worldwide to adapt to its privacy and ethical standards (IE University, 2024).

In contrast, other geopolitical actors embed different values in their digital governance. The United States tends to prioritize technological innovation and market competition, with less emphasis on regulatory sovereignty (Musoni, 2023). China's approach strongly emphasizes state control, security, and regime stability, embedding authoritarian values into its digital policies and infrastructure sovereignty (Kokas, 2023; Teevan & Domingo, 2023). Thus, digital sovereignty is a multifaceted concept encompassing legal, technological, and normative dimensions. The values a nation chooses to uphold in cyberspace shape not only its policies but also its identity and influence in the global digital order (Mihelj & Jiménez-Martínez, 2021; World Economic Forum 2023).

The United States has traditionally embraced a laissez-faire approach to digital governance, rooted in values of free speech, free markets, and minimal government intervention. This "hands-off approach, relying on corporate self-regulation" allowed U.S. tech firms to thrive globally and spread American cultural influence through their platforms (World Economic Forum 2023). The internet, originating from U.S. research, was heralded as a democratizing force and a major cultural export, with policymakers emphasizing an open, global internet aligned with U.S. values of free expression and open markets, warning that heavy regulation might fragment this openness (World Economic Forum 2023; Musoni, 2023).

However, recent years have seen a shift toward incorporating value-driven governance elements. The White House's AI Bill of Rights (Office of Science and Technology Policy, 2022) articulates principles like privacy protection, avoidance of algorithmic bias, and human oversight in AI systems, signaling a recognition that civil rights and safety must be balanced with innovation (Center for Strategic and International Studies 2021; Fleming, 2025). Under the Biden administration, there has been increased scrutiny of tech companies, including debates on content moderation and antitrust enforcement, though future policy directions remain uncertain (IE University, 2024; World Economic Forum, 2023).

In contrast, authoritarian regimes prioritize order, security, and regime stability over individual liberties. China's governance model emphasizes collective stability and ideological control, implementing extensive censorship via the Great Firewall, and mass surveillance to maintain social harmony and party authority. This approach reflects China's "cyber sovereignty" doctrine, which asserts the right of states to control internet access, censor content, and enforce data localization under the guise of protecting national interests (Chander & Sun, 2021; Musoni, 2023). China promotes these values internationally, advocating for norms that legitimize state control over information flows (Teevan & Domingo, 2023).

Similarly, Russia's digital governance is driven by conservatism and state authority, suppressing content that challenges Orthodox values or Kremlin narratives and building mechanisms to isolate its national internet (Runet) to safeguard sovereign control over information (Musoni, 2023).

In summary, U.S. digital governance champions freedom and innovation with evolving recognition of rights protection, while authoritarian regimes embed state primacy and control into their digital sovereignty frameworks. These divergent value hierarchies shape global digital governance and geopolitical competition (Fleming, 2025; Musoni, 2023). Similarly, France enforces cultural sovereignty through policies requiring streaming platforms to meet quotas for French-language content, protecting French language and culture against Anglo-American media dominance. This normative sovereignty ensures national values and identity are maintained in the digital space.

States implement values-driven governance through legislation, technical standards, administrative oversight, and public messaging. Democracies often establish independent regulators to uphold rights and privacy, whereas authoritarian regimes empower ministries or military units to enforce conformity. For example, Europe's data protection authorities contrast with China's Cyberspace Administration and the People's Liberation Army's cyber units, resulting in vastly different digital environments, one fostering trust and rights, the other control and surveillance (Runde & Ramanujam, 2021).

A country's values-driven digital governance also shapes its global image and soft power. Nations championing a free, open internet, like the U.S., attract allies who share that vision, while those prioritizing tight control, like China, appeal to governments seeking similar tools but face wariness from users and companies fearing repression. This dynamic reflects the broader contest between authoritarian and democratic visions for the future of digital technologies, each imprinting its values on the global digital domain (Runde & Ramanujam, 2021).

7.7 Asserting Cultural and Normative Identity in Global Digital Governance

Nations today actively assert their cultural and normative identities in global digital governance, seeking to shape international digital rules and architectures to reflect their own values and interests. This dynamic is often framed as a contest between a democratic, open internet model, and an authoritarian, state-centric model, potentially fracturing the once unitary global internet into distinct spheres (World Economic Forum, 2023).

International institutions and standard-setting bodies serve as major venues for this normative assertion. The International Telecommunication Union (ITU) has become a focal point of rivalry, with China and Russia advocating for increased state control over internet governance. Western countries, in contrast, defend the existing multi-stakeholder model that includes private sector and civil society participation (DataReportal, 2025). China's proposal of "New IP" to the ITU, aiming to redesign internet protocols to facilitate government management and control, exemplifies efforts to embed authoritarian norms into future internet infrastructure, though it has not been adopted (Colquhoun,

2022). Chinese companies also actively influence 5G and AI standardization committees, pushing standards that accommodate surveillance and content filtering capabilities aligned with Chinese governance models (DataReportal, 2025; DiploFoundation, 2025). Western democracies counter by promoting standards emphasizing cybersecurity, privacy, and human rights (IE University, 2024).

Normative identity is also asserted through alliances and agreements. Democratic countries have formed coalitions such as the U.S.-EU Trade and Technology Council (TTC), which explicitly opposes authoritarian practices like social scoring and promotes human-rights-centered AI governance (World Economic Forum, 2023). Initiatives like the Freedom Online Coalition and the 2022 Declaration for the Future of the Internet further embody collective democratic commitments to an open, free, and global internet (DataReportal, 2025). Conversely, authoritarian-leaning blocs such as the Shanghai Cooperation Organisation endorse "internet sovereignty," affirming each nation's right to control its national internet segment and resist external criticism of censorship or cyber operations (Colquhoun, 2022).

This normative competition reflects broader geopolitical tensions, with digital sovereignty expanding beyond infrastructure control to encompass values and governance models that shape the global digital order (Narayanan, 2025). The rise of sovereign AI initiatives and digital public infrastructure further illustrates how states seek technological self-reliance aligned with their political and cultural priorities (Letort & Linask-Goode, 2025).

China's Digital Silk Road (DSR), a key component of the Belt and Road Initiative (BRI), strategically exports Chinese digital infrastructure and technology to partner countries, thereby extending China's technological, economic, and normative influence globally. The DSR encompasses hard infrastructure like 5G telecom networks, fiber-optic cables, data centers, and satellite internet systems, as well as soft infrastructure including applications, mobile payment platforms, and AI technologies (East Asia Forum, 2025; Gordon, 2022; Reddy, 2023).

By financing and constructing these digital assets across Asia, Africa, Latin America, and the Middle East, China not only deepens commercial and geopolitical ties but also promotes its own technical standards and governance models. For example, Huawei and ZTE have built core digital infrastructure and surveillance systems (e.g., Safe City projects) in many DSR countries, embedding Chinese technology ecosystems that may include censorship capabilities or backdoors (Baark, 2024; Yang 2023). This creates dependencies whereby adopting countries rely on Chinese updates, practices, and regulatory frameworks, potentially constraining their digital sovereignty and aligning them with Beijing's state-centric, authoritarian digital norms (Foreign Policy Research Institute, 2024).

In response, Western nations have launched initiatives such as the U.S. "Clean Network" to exclude Chinese vendors from critical infrastructure and the EU's Global Gateway program to invest in secure and open digital infrastructure in developing countries (Runde & Ramanujam, 2021). This competition resembles a Digital Cold War, with blocs vying for influence over markets, standards, and normative frameworks globally.

The consequence is a "splinternet," a fragmentation of the global internet into competing spheres: one following China's closed, state-controlled model and another adhering to Western open, multi-stakeholder principles (Freedom House, 2024). Countries like Türkiye and India occupy intermediate positions, asserting digital nationalism through content controls and data localization while maintaining some democratic elements.

At the international level, normative battles continue in forums such as the U.N. Group of Governmental Experts (GGE) and the Open-Ended Working Group (OEWG) on cybersecurity. Democracies emphasize norms protecting open societies and critical infrastructure from cyberattacks, while authoritarian states prioritize norms against "propaganda" and "interference," often to justify censorship and information control (Runde & Ramanujam, 2021).

In sum, states project digital sovereignty by governing domestic digital spaces as well as by shaping global digital governance through infrastructure exports, standard-setting, and normative alliances. China's DSR exemplifies this strategy, exporting digital authoritarianism under the guise of modernization. The EU and the U.S., in comparison, promote alternative models grounded in openness, security, and human rights (East Asia Forum, 2025; Wedell, 2020).

The future digital sphere faces a critical crossroads between interoperability with shared rules and fragmentation into clashing sovereign ecosystems. There is a tangible risk that without convergence, the global internet could splinter into semi-disconnected internets, such as a China-led bloc, a Western-led bloc, and several non-aligned networks, each adhering to distinct technical standards and content regulations (Diplo Resource, 2025). Such fragmentation threatens the foundational idea of a universal internet enabling global connectivity, innovation, and free information exchange (Runde & Ramanujam, 2021; UNU, 2022).

Policymakers aware of these risks have initiated dialogues to bridge divides, exemplified by the EU-U.S. Trade and Technology Council (TTC), which aims to foster cooperation despite differing values and regulatory philosophies (Fleming, 2025). The concept of digital sovereignty is evolving beyond isolationism toward enabling autonomy by openness, allowing nations to assert values and protect interests while engaging in a global interoperable internet (GIG-ARTS, 2025).

However, asserting normative identity in digital governance remains a geopolitical endeavor. China and the EU each promote their regulatory models globally: China advocates a Westphalian, state-centric cyberspace order, while the EU champions a rules-based, rights-respecting digital commons (Diplo Resource, 2025; World Economic Forum, 2023). Smaller and Global South countries face pressure to align with these blocs or seek inclusive governance reflecting their developmental and cultural priorities (Buhari, 2025; UNU, 2022). The outcome may be a pluralistic digital order with coexisting models under mutual respect or a bifurcated world of competing techno-blocs (GIG-ARTS, 2025).

In sum, the trajectory of digital sovereignty will shape whether the internet remains a unified global network or fragments into competing spheres defined by divergent values and governance models (Digital Watch Observatory, 2024; Kleinwächter, 2025).

Bibliography

Baark, E. (2024). China's digital silk road: Innovation in a globalized world. *Max Planck Institute for the History of Science..* https://pure.mpg.de/pubman/item/item_3586949_2/component/file_3587108/baark-2024-china-s-digital-silk-road.pdf (Retrieved May 11, 2025

Barlow, M. and Levy-Bencheton, C. (2019). "Estonia: Smart nation on the Baltic Sea", BeeSmart City, 13 February. Available at: https://www.beesmart.city/en/smart-city-blog/estonia-smart-nation-on-the-baltic-sea (Retrieved 11 May, 2025).

Bjola, C., & Kornprobst, M. (2024). *Digital international relations: Technology, agency and order*. Oxford University Press.

Bowler, T. (2020). "Huawei: Why is it being banned from the UK'S 5G network?", BBC News, 14 July. Available at: https://www.bbc.com/news/newsbeat-47041341 (Retrieved May 11, 2025).

Bradford, A. (2023). *Digital empires: The global Battle to regulate technology*. Oxford University Press.

Buhari, M.B. (2025). "2025: The year we decide the internet's future", Global Voices, 8 January. Available at: https://advox.globalvoices.org/2025/01/08/2025-the-year-we-decide-the-internets-future/ (Retrieved May 11, 2025).

Capgemini and Orange. (2023). Capgemini and Orange announce plan to create 'bleu', a company to provide a cloud de Confiance in France. *Capgemini News*. https://www.capgemini.com/news/press-releases/capgemini-and-orange-announce-plan-to-create-bleu-a-company-to-provide-a-cloud-de-confiance-in-france/ (Retrieved May 11, 2025).

Center for Strategic and International Studies. (2021). "U.S. digital governance: A strategy for effective engagement", August. Available at: https://csis-website-prod.s3.amazonaws.com/s3fs-public/publication/210802_Runde_U.S._Digital_Governance.pdf (Retrieved May 11, 2025).

Chander, A. and Sun, H. (2021). "Sovereignty 2.0". Georgetown University Law Center. Available at: https://scholarship.law.georgetown.edu/facpub/2404 (Retrieved May 5, 2025).

Colquhoun, T. (2022). *Authoritarian diffusion and cooperation within quasi-autocratic coalitions*. [online PDF] Available at: https://www.ssoar.info/ssoar/bitstream/handle/document/95325/ssoar-2022-thomas-colquhoun-Authoritarian_Diffusion_and_Cooperation_within.pdf [Retrieved June 13, 2025].

Couture, S., & Toupin, S. (2019). What does the notion of 'sovereignty' mean when referring to the digital? *New Media & Society., 21*(10), 2305–2322.

Creemers, R. (2023). "China's approach to cyber sovereignty". Konrad-Adenauer-Stiftung. Available at: https://www.kas.de/en/single-title/-/content/china-s-approach-to-cyber-sovereignty (Retrieved May 11, 2025).

DataReportal. (2025). Digital 2025: Global Overview Report. Available at: https://datareportal.com (Accessed 27 April 2025).

DeNardis, L. (2020). *The internet in everything: Freedom and security in a world with no off switch*. Yale University Press.

Digital Watch Observatory. (2024). "Tackling internet fragmentation: A global challenge at IGF 2024". Digital Watch Observatory, 19 December. Available at: https://dig.watch/updates/tackling-internet-fragmentation-a-global-challenge-at-igf-2024 (Retrieved May 11, 2025).

DiploFoundation. (2025). Resources. https://www.diplomacy.edu/resources/

Dock Labs. (2025). "Self-Sovereign Identity: The Ultimate Guide 2025", 29 April. Available at: https://www.dock.io/post/self-sovereign-identity (Retrieved May 11, 2025).

East Asia Forum. (2025). "China expands AI globally through the digital silk road", East Asia Forum, 11 April. Available at: https://eastasiaforum.org/2025/04/11/china-expands-ai-globally-through-the-digital-silk-road/ (Retrieved May 11, 2025).

e-Estonia. (2025). "ID-Card", Available at: https://e-estonia.com/solutions/estonian-e-identity/id-card/ (Retrieved May 11, 2025).

European Commission. (2024). "Cloud computing | shaping Europe's digital future", *digital-strategy.ec.europa.eu,* 1 March. Available at: https://digital-strategy.ec.europa.eu/en/policies/cloud-computing (Retrieved May 11, 2025).

European Commission. (2025). Cloud and AI development act-initiative details. *ec.europa.eu*, (9 April) https://ec.europa.eu/info/law/better-regulation/have-your-say/initiatives/14628-Cloud-and-AI-Development-Act_en (Retrieved May 11, 2025).

Fan, C. and Zhou, Q. (2025). "China's cybersecurity law amendments 2025: Second draft". China Briefing. 1 April. Available at: https://www.china-briefing.com/news/china-cybersecurity-law-amendments-2025 (Retrieved May 11, 2025).

Fields, N. (2025). "Blockchain self-sovereign identity: True control of your identity". Komodo Platform. 15 March. Available at: https://komodoplatform.com/en/academy/self-sovereign-identity/ (Retrieved May 11, 2025).

Fleming, S. (2025). "What is digital sovereignty and how are countries approaching it?", World Economic Forum [online], 10 January. Available at: https://www.weforum.org/stories/2025/01/europe-digital-sovereignty/ (Retrieved May 5, 2025).

Foreign Policy Research Institute. (2024). "LEO Wars: China's Orbital Challenge to the US-Led Digital Order", 15 March. Available at: https://www.fpri.org/article/2024/03/leo-wars-chinas-orbital-challenge-to-the-us-led-digital-order/ (Retrieved May 11, 2025).

Forum Europe. (2025). "The European sovereign cloud day", *sovereign-cloud.eu.com*. Available at: https://sovereign-cloud.eu.com. (Retrieved May 11, 2025).

Freedom House. (2024). "Freedom on the Net 2024". January. Available at: https://freedomhouse.org/report/freedom-net/2024 (Retrieved May 11, 2025).

Frontiers in Blockchain. (2024). "Self-sovereign identity on the Blockchain: Contextual analysis and quantification of SSI principles implementation", Frontiers in Blockchain. 30 August. Available at: https://www.frontiersin.org/journals/blockchain/articles/10.3389/fbloc.2024.1443362/full (Retrieved May 11, 2025).

Gaia-X. (2025.) "Together towards a federated & secure data infrastructure" Gaia-X brochure Overview, February 2025. Available at: https://gaia-x.eu/wp-content/uploads/2025/02/Gaia-X-Brochure_Overview_February_2025-v2.pdf (Retrieved May 11, 2025).

Gasser, U., & Almeida, V. A. F. (2017). A layered model for AI governance. *IEEE Internet Computing, 21*(6), 58–62.

Gasser, U., & Mayer-Schönberger, V. (2024). *Guardrails: Guiding human decisions in the age of AI*. MIT Press.

GIG-ARTS. (2025). "The rise of digital sovereignty: Ambiguities and challenges", University of Salerno, 26 May. Available at: https://gig-arts.eu/salerno-2025/ (Retrieved May 11, 2025).

Gordon, D. (2022). "The digital silk road: China's technological rise and global ambitions". International Institute for Strategic Studies, 6 December. Available at: https://www.iiss.org/online-analysis/online-analysis/2022/12/digital-silk-road-introduction/ (Retrieved May 11, 2025).

Gorwa, R. (2019). The platform governance triangle: Conceptualizing the informal regulation of online content. *Internet Policy Review, 8*(2), 1–22.

Hendrickson, L. (2025). "Your Guide to Self-Sovereign Identity (SSI)". Identity.com, 19 May. Available at: https://www.identity.com/self-sovereign-identity/ (Retrieved 11 May, 2025).

Hummel, P., Braun, M., Tretter, M., & Dabrock, P. (2021). Data sovereignty: A review. *Big Data & Society, 8*(1) https://journals.sagepub.com/doi/full/10.1177/2053951720982012 (Retrieved May 11, 2025

IEEE Standards Association. (2025). "Data Sovereignty and Trusted Online Identity". IEEE SA. Available at: https://standards.ieee.org/industry-connections/digital-identity.html (Accessed 11 May 2025).

IE University. (2024). "Reclaiming Digital Sovereignty: The EU's Role in the Geopolitics of Digital Governance". Available at: https://static.ie.edu/CGC/CGC_ReclaimingDigitalSovereignty_PolicyPaper.pdf (Retrieved May 11, 2025).

Katzenbach, C., & Bächle, T. C. (2021). Defining concepts of the digital: Toward productive ambiguity in digital sovereignty. *Internet Policy Review, 10*(4), 1–19.

Khan, S. (2025). New draft amendments to China cybersecurity law. *Securiti.ai*, 28 March. Available at: https://securiti.ai/new-draft-amendments-to-china-cybersecurity-law/ (Retrieved May 11, 2025).

Kleinwächter, W. (2025). "Internet Governance Outlook 2025: Unbordered Spaces vs. Bordered Places". CircleID. 16 January. Available at: https://circleid.com/posts/internet-governance-outlook-2025-unbordered-spacesvs-bordered-places (Accessed 11 May 2025).

Kokas, A. (2023). China's digital authoritarianism: How the CCP shapes the future of the internet. *Journal of Digital Policy., 12*(1), 45–62.

Krasner, S. D. (1999). *Sovereignty: Organized hypocrisy*. Princeton University Press.

Kroet, C. (2024). "Eleven EU countries took 5G security measures to ban Huawei, ZTE", Euronews, 12 August. Available at: https://www.euronews.com/next/2024/08/12/eleven-eu-countries-took-5g-security-measures-to-banhuawei-zte (Accessed 11 May 2025).

Larsen, B.C. (2022). "The geopolitics of AI and the rise of digital sovereignty", Brookings Institution. 8 December. Available at: https://www.brookings.edu/articles/the-geopolitics-of-ai-and-the-rise-of-digital-sovereignty/ (Retrieved May 11, 2025).

Letort, B. and Linask-Goode, K. (2025). "What is sovereign AI and why is it growing in importance?". Digital Realty, 3 April. Available at: https://www.digitalrealty.com/resources/articles/what-is-sovereign-ai (Retrieved May 11, 2025).

Lewis, J. A. (2021). Cybersecurity and the COVID-19 pandemic: Risks and responses. *Center for Strategic and International Studies*. https://www.csis.org/ (Retrieved May 15, 2025).

McDonald, J. (2020). "Huawei 5G Debate Causes Rift Between Western Powers." The Diplomat. 19 February. Available at: https://thediplomat.com/2020/02/huawei-5g-debate-causes-rift-between-western-powers/ (Accessed 11 May 2025).

Mihelj, S., & Jiménez-Martínez, C. (2021). Digital nationalism: Understanding the role of digital media in the rise of 'new' nationalism. *Nations and Nationalism, 27* (1), 1–16.

Mueller, M. (2017). *Will the internet fragment? Sovereignty, globalization and cyberspace*. Polity Press.

Musoni, M. (2023). "Unpacking Digital Sovereignty Through Data Governance", Global Approaches to Digital Sovereignty: Competing Definitions and Contrasting Policy Implications, Discussion Paper 344, Chapter 1. *ECDPM.*. Available at: https://ecdpm.org/application/files/3316/8474/8387/Chapter-1-global-approaches-digital-sovereignty-competing-definitions-contrasting-policy-ECDPM-Discussion-Paper-344-2023.pdf (Retrieved May 11, 2025).

Narayanan, A. (2025). Global digital compact: Charting a new era in digital governance? *Policy Brief. South Centre*. https://www.southcentre.int/wp-content/uploads/2025/05/PB140_Global-Digital-Compact-Charting-a-New-Era-in-Digital-Governance_EN.pdf (Retrieved May 30, 2025

Niebel, C. and Smoleń, A. (2023) "AI and Gaia-X", *Gaia-X Hub Deutschland White Paper 3/2023*, November. Available at: https://gaia-x-hub.de/wp-content/uploads/2023/12/GX-WP-AI.pdf (Retrieved May 11, 2025).

Nye, J. S. (2011). *The future of power*. PublicAffairs.

Office of Science and Technology Policy (OSTP) (2022). *Blueprint for an AI Bill of Rights: Making Automated Systems Work for the American People*. The White House. Available at: https://bidenwhitehouse.archives.gov/ostp/ai-bill-of-rights/ [Retrieved June 13, 2025].
Politico.eu. (2023). "Huawei bribery scandal: What we know so far". 17 March. Available at: https://www.politico.eu/article/huawei-bribery-scandal-eu-chinese-tech-lobby-money-lobbying/ (Retrieved May 11, 2025).
Reddy, R. K. (2023). "Digital Silk Road". *OrcAsia*. "8 February". Available at: https://www.orcasia.org/digital-silk-road (Retrieved May 11, 2025).
Runde, D. F., & Ramanujam, S. R. (2021). Global digital governance: Here's what you need to know. In *Critical questions, 1 October*. Center for Strategic and International Studies (CSIS). https://www.csis.org/analysis/global-digital-governance-heres-what-you-need-know (Retrieved May 10, 2025
SEON. (2025). What is self-sovereign identity?. 10 April. Available at: https://seon.io/resources/dictionary/self-sovereign-identity/ (Retrieved May 11, 2025).
Sheehan, M. (2023). "China's AI regulations and how they get made". Carnegie Endowment for International Peace. 10 July. Available at: https://carnegieendowment.org/research/2023/07/chinas-ai-regulations-and-how-they-get-made?lang=en (Retrieved May 4, 2025).
Small Wars Journal. (2024). "Chip War and the Battle for Technological Sovereignty: A Hybrid Warfare Perspective." Available at: https://smallwarsjournal.com/jrnl/art/chip-war-and-battle-technological-sovereignty-hybrid-warfare-perspective (Retrieved May 11, 2025).
Smith, B. (2025). "European digital commitments", *Microsoft*. 30 April. Available at: https://blogs.microsoft.com/on-the-issues/2025/04/30/european-digital-commitments/ (Retrieved May 11, May 2025).
Teevan, C. and Domingo, E. (2023). "Integrating Digital Sovereignty in EU External Action", Global Approaches to Digital Sovereignty: Competing Definitions and Contrasting Policy Implications, Discussion Paper 344, Chapter 3. *ECDPM*.. Available at: https://ecdpm.org/application/files/2316/8474/8387/Chapter-3-global-approaches-digital-sovereignty-competing-definitions-contrasting-policy-ECDPM-Discussion-Paper-344-2023.pdf (Retrieved May 11, 2025).
Tomaszewski, J. and Priebe, J. (2015). "Fortress Russia—The Russian data localization law". Seyfarth. 4 May. Available at: https://www.globalprivacywatch.com/2015/05/fortress-russia-the-russian-data-localization-law/ (Retrieved May 29, 2025).
United Nations University (2022). "Data sovereignty seminar series: Digital sovereignty in the new era of internet governance." 25 May. Available at: https://cris.unu.edu/data-sovereignty-seminar-series-digital-sovereignty-new-era-internet-governance (Retrieved May 11, 2025).

U.S. Department of Justice. (2018). Clarifying Lawful Overseas Use of Data (CLOUD) Act. https://www.justice.gov/d9/pages/attachments/2019/04/09/cloud_act.pdf

Vogiatzoglou, P. (2025). The EU'S quest for digital sovereignty: A matter of quantum innovation? *Digital Society, 4*(1), 16. https://doi.org/10.1007/s44206-025-00162-1

Wedell L. (2020). "China's Digital Silk Road: Reshaping Global Trade". Hinrich Foundation. 23 July. Available at: https://www.hinrichfoundation.com/research/article/tech/china-digital-silk-road-trade/ (Retrieved May 11, 2025).

Willemson, J. (2022). Digital identity—The Estonian approach. *European Data Protection Supervisor*. https://www.edps.europa.eu/system/files/2022-07/05_-_jan_willemson_-_ipen2022_en.pdf (Retrieved May 11, 2025

World Economic Forum. (2023). "What is digital sovereignty and how are countries approaching it?". 20 March. Available at: https://www.weforum.org/agenda/2023/03/digital-sovereignty-how-countries-are-approaching-it/ (Retrieved May 15, 2025).

X-Road Global (2025). "X-Road®". Available at: https://x-road.global (Retrieved May 11, 2025).

Yang, L. (2023). "China's digital silk road exports internet technology controls". *VOA News,* 28 May. Available at: https://www.voanews.com/a/china-s-digital-silk-road-exports-internet-technology-controls/7626266.html (Retrieved May 11, 2025).

CHAPTER 8

Practice—Governing and Shaping Emerging Technologies

In the digital autonomy framework of this book, "practice" refers to the concrete policies, regulations, and norms through which states operationalize their sovereignty in cyberspace. It is the regulatory and normative dimension of sovereignty—the laws, standards, and institutions that embody a nation's claim to control its data, networks, and technology. In effect, practice transforms sovereignty's abstract ideals into enforceable reality. As Braun and Hummel (2024) note, digital sovereignty debates often aim to create an *"ordered, value-driven, regulated … digital sphere."* This implies that regulatory practice—laws on data, AI, infrastructure, and so on—is central to sovereignty in the digital age. Similarly, Fleming (2025) defines digital sovereignty as the ability to "control your own digital destiny – the data, hardware, and software you rely on and create." These layers of control (infrastructure, software/code, and data) are precisely what states attempt to govern through policy instruments.

In short, practice in digital governance means using regulation and policy to protect rights, assert values, and build capacity. This chapter examines how different governments have turned sovereignty into practice in the areas of AI and emerging tech governance. We analyze diverse national models (EU, US, China, and Global South), contrast responsible innovation frameworks under different regimes, and review the policy tools states use (funding, R&D, startup support, IP, and standards) to build domestic tech capacity. Real-world examples—from the

E. Akıllı, *Cognitive Diplomacy and Digital Autonomy*,
https://doi.org/10.1007/978-3-032-04470-9_8

EU AI Act to Singapore's regulatory sandboxes to Türkiye's indigenous tech strategy—illustrate how practice is essential to operationalizing sovereignty and achieving digital autonomy.

8.1 National Models of AI and Technology Governance

Governments around the world are staking out distinct sovereignty models in AI and emerging technologies, shaped by their political systems and values. The European Union epitomizes a rights- and values-driven approach. In recent years the EU has embraced the rhetoric of "digital sovereignty" to reduce reliance on foreign platforms and embed European norms in law. Under the von der Leyen Commission, regulators rolled out a comprehensive suite of rules (Digital Markets Act, Data Governance Act, EU AI Act, etc.) designed to foster native tech industries and protect fundamental rights. For example, Burwell and Propp (2022) observe that the EU's Chips Act and Data Governance Act "are intended to boost European innovation in key elements of the digital economy." The EU's AI Act exemplifies its model: described by RAND analysts as a "landmark" and "first of its kind globally" regulatory framework, it applies a risk-based system of bans and requirements (banning "unacceptable" applications and imposing strict controls on high-risk AI). Importantly, the EU Act's core goals are legal certainty, safety, and alignment with EU values (privacy, human rights, and non-discrimination) rather than industrial competitiveness. This reflects the European model of sovereignty: the state, acting on behalf of citizens, erects a legal infrastructure to codify its values in technology.

The United States offers a stark contrast. American authorities have favored an innovation-first, "light-touch" model with sectoral rules rather than sweeping new laws. Instead of a comprehensive AI law, the U.S. has relied on executive directives (e.g., the 2023 White House AI Executive Order), agency guidelines (e.g., NIST's voluntary AI Risk Management Framework), and existing sectoral regulations (for example, FTC enforcement of data privacy). This approach aligns with the U.S. tradition of limited federal regulation: as Jelinek (2024) notes, the U.S. Executive Order on AI simply "encompass(es) a broad array of guidelines, recommendations, and specific actions," without creating new blanket mandates. It thus leaves implementation to companies and regulators.

This flexible strategy allows rapid technological deployment and prioritizes economic competitiveness. Indeed, the U.S. explicitly links its AI strategy to innovation and geopolitical competition. The Biden Administration's AI initiatives emphasize fostering talent, research, and industry collaboration to keep U.S. firms at the cutting edge. In practice, Congress has introduced a proliferation of AI-related bills (over 90 by mid-2024) but no single unified law. The notable federal AI policy was the CHIPS and Science Act of 2022. Backed by $52.7 billion, it is a form of state-led industrial policy aimed at reviving domestic semiconductor R&D and manufacturing. Denamiel et al. (2025) highlight that the CHIPS Act is heralded as a "new Washington consensus" to strengthen U.S. geoeconomic leadership and reduce supply chain vulnerabilities. In sum, the U.S. model of sovereignty emphasizes maintaining technological leadership through market incentives and targeted funding, while using persuasion (EOs, non-binding frameworks) rather than heavy-handed controls.

China represents a third archetype: a state-led model where sovereignty means both technological supremacy and ideological control. China's 2017 *New Generation AI Development Plan* set the ambitious goal of global AI leadership by 2030, and successive five-year plans have ramped up R&D funding and industry support. However, Chinese policy strongly embeds Party values. Chinese authorities have implemented detailed regulations for algorithms, generative AI, and data—but always under the banner of "correct guidance" and social stability. As Sprick (2025) reports, China's recent AI content rules explicitly require that AI-generated text or images uphold "correct political direction, public opinion orientation, and value orientation," i.e., conform to "socialist core values." Similarly, Sheehan (2023) notes that information control is a "central goal" of China's sweeping AI rules (for recommendation systems, deep synthesis, and generative models). Thus, in China, governance practice enforces state narratives that AI systems must align with regime imperatives. Chinese regulators also push homegrown technology (for example, rewarding domestic cloud and the chip industries) and exert control through licensing and censorship tools. China's approach to sovereignty is both expansive (digital infrastructure is seen as a national strategic asset) and restrictive (freedom of data/information is tightly constrained).

Countries of the Global South, meanwhile, exhibit diverse hybrid models. Many are striving for digital autonomy within their own parameters. For instance, India has proclaimed an "AI autonomy" strategy focused on local needs and development goals. As Elbashir and Desikachari (2025) describe, India is promoting open-source AI and public-sector deployment to ensure local relevance (e.g., the Bhashini language platform and government RAISE initiative).

In Southeast Asia, nations like Indonesia are accelerating AI use in finance and e-government but with new oversight: Indonesia's Financial Services Authority (OJK) introduced AI governance guidelines in 2025 to steer banks' AI use, signaling both encouragement and regulatory certainty (Nugraha 2025).

Across Latin America and Africa, governments often adopt elements of Western models (data privacy laws inspired by GDPR, and national AI strategies referencing OECD principles), while emphasizing social inclusion. For example, Modern Diplomacy notes that Brazil enacted banking-sector AI rules focused on algorithmic transparency and consumer rights, and India has a national AI roadmap linked to the Reserve Bank's oversight of data protection. South Africa is working on a broad AI framework integrating ethical guidelines and data protection.

Nonetheless, Global South states share common constraints: limited R&D budgets, talent shortages, and dependence on foreign technology. Analysts observe that many of these countries thus seek "adaptive" regulatory approaches tailored to local challenges. Nugraha (2025) aptly concludes that the ultimate aim in these contexts is fostering digital sovereignty grounded in local needs—in other words, shaping technology use so as to protect national values and socio-economic goals.

In summary, national models of digital governance reflect how countries assert sovereignty: the EU's model is rights-centric regulation, the U.S.' is innovation-centric pragmatism, China's is control-centric planning, and the Global South approaches mix these strands to address local priorities. Each model uses law and policy to project national values—be it European fundamental rights, American economic freedom, Chinese state ideology, or developing-country developmentalism. These different "practices" of AI governance are manifestations of each state's sovereignty claims, aimed at protecting citizens, promoting preferred industries, or enforcing regime narratives.

8.2 Responsible and Ethical Innovation Frameworks

Alongside formal laws, many governments and international bodies promote "responsible innovation" frameworks to guide technological development according to social values. In liberal democracies, such frameworks typically emphasize human-centric goals and accountability. For example, the OECD defines responsible innovation as "trustworthy technology development, guided by democratic values, responsive to social needs, and accountable to society." The European Union has institutionalized this notion: its research funding—Horizon 2020—embeds *Responsible Research and Innovation (RRI)* principles. An EU report on Horizon notes that ethics review, gender equality, public engagement, and open access were enshrined as RRI elements in 2014–2020 (European Comission, 2017). In practice, this means EU research projects must consider ethical impacts and involve stakeholders. Similarly, UNESCO's (2021) Recommendation on the Ethics of AI (adopted by 193 nations) provides a "global normative bedrock" for aligning AI with human rights and the rule of law. Soft standards like the U.K.'s PAS 440 (2020) offer guidance to companies on anticipating social risks of innovation. These measures demonstrate the liberal democratic side of practice: embedding checks and community interests into the innovation process.

However, the interpretation and use of such frameworks diverge sharply under different regimes. In democracies, responsible innovation often supports regulation by supplementing it with values like transparency and inclusion. For example, the United States has tied its AI strategy to principles of safety, fairness, and civil liberties (as in its AI Bill of Rights and NIST guidelines), while also spurring commercial R&D. In the EU, RRI and ethics codes reinforce the precautionary stance of regulations. By contrast, in authoritarian states, these ethical frameworks are typically subordinated to official ideology and state control. China, for instance, officially embraced the language of "responsible innovation" (even mentioning it in its 13th Five-Year Plan), but stripped of the Western emphasis on pluralism. Long and Wang (2023) observe that China included RRI in its plans yet redefined it to fit its "top-down governance" model. In reality, China's AI ethics guidelines—such as the 2019 Ministry of Science & Technology document—articulate fairness and accountability, but they operate under strict political oversight. As noted above, Chinese rules require AI systems to uphold "socialist core values" and avoid sensitive political content. This illustrates that "responsible innovation" in China means innovation responsible to the Communist Party's objectives.

Thus, there is a clear normative split: OECD, EU, and UNESCO frameworks speak of democracy, human rights, and societal benefit (aiming to empower end-users and protect them from tech harms), whereas Chinese and other authoritarian guidelines frame ethics as alignment with state-prescribed norms. Even global initiatives reveal underlying differences. The OECD's AI Principles (adopted by the G20) emphasize individual rights and accountability, whereas China's counterpart proposals stress collective social harmony. UNESCO's recommendation is explicitly a "digital human rights policy," albeit one that Chinese delegations observe but do not fully implement in spirit. In effect, responsible innovation frameworks become part of "practice"—they signal what values a state seeks to promote, and either constrain or channel technology development. In democratic systems, they often bolster transparency and civil oversight, while in autocracies they can legitimize state-led guidance and censorship. In all cases, these normative frameworks shape the context where AI and emerging tech are developed and deployed, and thus constitute an essential expression of digital sovereignty in the innovation domain.

8.3 Building Domestic Technology Capacity

For sovereignty to be meaningful, states must also cultivate the underlying capacity to control critical technologies. This includes funding R&D, nurturing startups, cultivating skilled personnel, and influencing global tech standards. Across regimes, governments deploy a range of policy instruments to build national innovation systems that support autonomy.

One major tool is public investment in R&D and infrastructure. The U.S. CHIPS Act (2022) is a prime example. Supported by $52.7 billion, it was explicitly designed to "boost U.S. competitiveness and innovation in semiconductor research and manufacturing," and to revitalize the domestic tech ecosystem. Denamiel et al. (2025) show that this act was hailed as a cornerstone of a "new Washington consensus" on industrial policy, reflecting urgent strategic aims (countering China's lead and securing supply chains). Similarly, the EU has mobilized big budgets to build semiconductor and AI capacity. The European Chips Act and Digital Europe program allocate funding and public-private incentives for chip fabs, AI supercomputing centers, and strategic digital projects. Burwell and Propp (2022) note that EU legislation like the Chips Act is intended to "boost European innovation in key elements of the digital economy." China, meanwhile, pours state funds into science (with explicit targets for quantum, 5G, and AI) and often backs domestic champions (e.g., Tencent, Huawei, Baidu) through state-owned enterprises and subsidies. Türkiye's Medium-Term Program (2025–2027) exemplifies how strategically minded nations are reinforcing technological sovereignty. The plan allocates dedicated resources to artificial intelligence research clusters, satellite communications, and critical technology infrastructure in response to recent technology restrictions. In this regard, state budgets and targeted grant schemes serve as instruments of strategic autonomy, enabling Türkiye to expand her homegrown capacity and consolidate her leadership in key technological domains.

Beyond R&D grants, governments actively encourage innovation ecosystems. This includes support for startups, incubators, and talent development. The U.S. has a well-established venture capital ecosystem, supplemented by state-backed accelerators and university spin-outs, reflecting a hands-off but supportive model. The EU has sought to scale up its startup ecosystem through initiatives like the European Innovation Council and the Digital Innovation Hubs network. Singapore provides a notable small state example: it has championed AI research through national programs (e.g., a 2019 National AI Strategy) and created regulatory sandboxes to allow safe experimentation. In particular, Singapore launched a sandbox for privacy-enhancing technologies in 2022 and, in October 2023, an international Generative AI evaluation sandbox. These sandboxes bring together global AI firms under guided testing to develop norms (e.g., testing tools and benchmarks) and encourage responsible innovation. Such measures—combining state facilitation with industry R&D—are emblematic of practice: Singapore's government is asserting sovereignty by steering the technology agenda through investment and normative frameworks while preserving a pro-business environment.

Intellectual property (IP) policy is another sovereignty instrument. Nations craft IP strategies to secure their technological inventions. A robust patent regime enables domestic companies to capture value and makes foreign rivals cross-license or invest locally. For example, China has aggressively expanded its patent filings (in 2023 China issued nearly three times as many patents as the U.S.), reflecting a long-term strategy of building an indigenous innovation base. The World Intellectual Property Organization (WIPO) advises that national IP strategies should "encourage innovation" across sectors. The U.S. and EU, likewise, frame IP as a tool for competitiveness: the U.S. invests in technology transfer from labs to industry, while the EU's Horizon research rules emphasize IP management and technology transfer to keep European inventions within the bloc. Thus, IP policy—from trade secrets to standards-essential patents—is part of how states practice sovereignty by legally codifying ownership of knowledge.

Standards and norms are also seen as critical levers of sovereignty. By setting technical standards, a country can tilt global markets toward its own technologies. As one analyst bluntly notes, if China can *"convince the international community to use their standards, then its domestic businesses will benefit … and China will be able to chart the future of technology development"* (He, 2022). In response, the U.S., EU, and Japan work through international bodies (ITU, ISO, IEEE) to embed their de facto standards (as seen in Wi-Fi, 5G, and software protocols). China, however, has launched what it calls the "Digital Silk Road" (part of its Belt and Road Initiative) to export Chinese hardware and set technical norms in participant countries. Under this scheme, Chinese-funded telecom and data infrastructure projects often include requirements that use Chinese technology and follow Chinese standards (with interoperability clauses favoring Chinese protocols). Such actions serve digital sovereignty by creating demand for domestic tech in foreign markets and by shaping the rules of the road. The strategic battle over 5G and AI standards between Chinese-led bodies and Western coalitions illustrates that standard-setting is now a domain of geopolitical competition, a core component of practice.

In sum, states assert digital sovereignty not only by making rules but also by building the industrial and innovation base to sustain those rules. Funding R&D, supporting startups, protecting IP, and influencing standards are policy expressions of sovereignty. They aim to ensure that critical technologies are available under national control. Case studies highlight these mechanisms. The U.S. CHIPS Act is as much about rebuilding American manufacturing capacity as it is about security. The EU's Chips Act and data laws are about rallying European industry behind its standards. Singapore's sandboxes illustrate a small state's toolkit of governance sandboxes and public investment. Apart from that, several countries have rejected foreign technological interception and dependency, with Türkiye standing out as a prominent example. By prioritizing indigenous innovation, secure digital infrastructure, and data sovereignty, Türkiye underscores her commitment to technological independence and the protection of national strategic interests in an increasingly contested digital sphere. Thus, Türkiye's determined pivot toward domestic chip development—exemplified by the "Çakıl" national processor (Aselsan, 2022) designed for defense systems—and her sustained investment in artificial intelligence research centers reflect how a rising technological power can transform external restrictions into drivers of innovation. Rather than yielding to technological embargoes, Türkiye is building her own research and development ecosystem, advancing digital sovereignty and reinforcing her strategic autonomy in the global AI and semiconductor landscape. Even the very enforcement of regulations is a capacity issue: some countries are creating specialized agencies and training compliance officers (e.g., the EU's new AI Office and national supervisory authorities in the AI Act).

8.4 Practice as the Pillar of Sovereignty

The foregoing analysis makes clear that practice—the ensemble of regulations, frameworks, and capacity-building policies—is indispensable to digital sovereignty. Aspirations of autonomy mean little without the practical instruments to realize them. Through regulation and norms, states project their values onto technology; through investment and incentives, they cultivate the skills and industries needed to fulfill their sovereignty claims. The examples above show that every dimension of AI governance serves sovereignty: laws protect the state's conception of its citizens' rights or security, responsible innovation codes reflect its ethical stance, and innovation policy builds tangible means of control. In this way, practice is the connective tissue linking sovereignty to tangible outcomes. It ensures that a state's vision for its digital future—whether it be an open, rights-respecting internet or a tightly governed national network—is enforced on the ground.

As this chapter has shown, models vary, but all governments now recognize that sovereignty in the twenty-first century requires active "practice." Indeed, framing digital autonomy as a pillar of sovereignty underscores that without robust digital governance practice, claims of autonomy would be hollow. Digital sovereignty only has teeth when it is backed by enforceable law and sufficient capacity. By weaving together policy instruments (from the EU AI Act and CHIPS Act to ethical frameworks and startup grants), states operationalize their authority over technology. In doing so, they turn sovereignty from a slogan into systemic power over the digital domain. In the overall structure of the book, this pillar of practice ties directly into the goal of digital autonomy: it transforms sovereignty from an abstract aspiration into a concrete, operational reality. Ultimately, defending national autonomy in the digital age depends on how skillfully states can wield these policy tools—on how effectively they can turn governance practice into outcomes that secure their digital interests and values.

Bibliography

ASELSAN. (2022). Milli İşlemci ÇAKIL. https://www.aselsan.com/tr/savunma/urun/1585/milli-islemci--cakil

Braun, M., & Hummel, P. (2024). Is digital sovereignty normatively desirable? *Information, Communication & Society, 27*(3), 607–624.

European Commission. (2017). Responsible Research and Innovation (RRI) in support of sustainability and governance, taking account of the international context (H2020_SwafS-23-2017). CORDIS. https://cordis.europa.eu/programme/id/H2020_SwafS-23-2017

Fleming, S. (2025). "What is digital sovereignty and how are countries approaching it?", World Economic Forum [online], 10 January. Available at: https://www.weforum.org/stories/2025/01/europe-digital-sovereignty/ (Retrieved May 5, 2025).

Burwell, F.G. and Propp, K. (2022). "Digital sovereignty in practice: The EU'S push to shape the new global economy", Atlantic Council Issue Brief, Europe Center. November 2022. Available at: https://www.atlanticcouncil.org/in-depth-research-reports/report/digital-sovereignty-in-practice-the-eus-push-to-shape-the-new-global-economy/ (Retrieved May 11, 2025).

Jelinek, T. (2024). AI governance: EU and US converge on risk-based approach amid stark differences. Hertie School–Centre for Digital Governance [online]. Available at: https://www.hertie-school.org/en/digital-governance/research/blog/detail/content/ai-governance-eu-and-us-converge-on-risk-based-approach-amid-stark-differences (Retrieved June 13, 2025).

Denamiel, T., Brown, E. and Korn, D. (2025). "Sourcing requirements and U.S. technological competitiveness: Evaluating the impact of National Security Guardrails in the CHIPS act". CSIS Analysis Brief, 5 March. Available at: https://www.csis.org/analysis/sourcing-requirements-and-us-technological-competitiveness (Retrieved May 26, 2025).

Sprick, D. (2025). Aligning AI with China's authoritarian value system. *The Diplomat*, (3 February) Available at: https://thediplomat.com/2025/02/aligning-ai-with-chinas-authoritarian-value-system/. Retrieved 27 May 2025.

Sheehan, M. (2023). "China's AI regulations and how they get made". Carnegie Endowment for International Peace. 10 July. Available at: https://carnegieendowment.org/research/2023/07/chinas-ai-regulations-and-how-they-get-made?lang=en (Retrieved May 4, 2025).

Elbashir, M. and Desikachari, K.B. (2025) "India's path to AI autonomy", Atlantic Council Insight, 13 March. Available at: https://www.atlanticcouncil.org/in-depth-research-reports/issue-brief/indias-path-to-ai-autonomy/ (Retrieved 25 May 2025).

Nugraha, T., 2025. "AI governance in the global south: Turning risk into relevance", Modern Diplomacy, 9 May 2025.

UNESCO. (2021). "Recommendation on the Ethics of Artificial Intelligence". 16 May. Available at: https://www.unesco.org/en/articles/recommendation-ethics-artificial-intelligence (Retrieved May 21, 2025).

PAS 440:2020. (2020). *Responsible Innovation Guide*. British Standards Institution (BSI).

Long, T. B., & Wang, T. (2023). The conceptual evolution of responsible research and innovation in China: A systematic literature review. *Journal of Responsible Innovation, 10*(1), Article 2226465.

He, A. (2022). *Paving the digital silk road with China's standards*. Centre for International Governance Innovation [multimedia]. Available at: https://www.cigionline.org/multimedia/paving-the-digital-silk-road-with-chinas-standards/. [Retrieved June 13, 2025].

CHAPTER 9

Resilience—Surviving Technological Coercion and Threats

In the evolving architecture of resilience thinking, digital resilience stands as the next frontier. It goes beyond infrastructural robustness to encompass the adaptive, interpretive, and strategic capacities of both human and AI-driven diplomatic systems. The classical understanding of resilience (Hollnagel et. al., 2011), rooted in organizational continuity and cybersecurity, has generally followed a multistage framework encompassing phases such as preparation, detection, resistance, response, adaptation, recovery, and learning (Araujo et al., 2024). These stages, originally designed to assess system behavior during cyber incidents, now provide an essential scaffold for theorizing how diplomacy itself must adapt under cognitive duress in the technopolar age.

Reframing these stages through a cognitive lens enables a novel interpretation. Preparation becomes the cultivation of strategic foresight and anticipatory reasoning. Detection transforms into heightened situational awareness and AI-assisted anomaly recognition. Resistance is expressed through the integrity of mental models and epistemic coherence under pressure. Response and adaptation represent the agility of diplomatic reasoning, especially when confronted with disinformation, AI-generated narratives, or rapid system perturbations. Recovery entails the restoration of interpretive clarity and strategic direction. Learning connotes both individual and institutional metacognition, embedding crisis-derived insights into future decision schemas.

E. Akıllı, *Cognitive Diplomacy and Digital Autonomy*,
https://doi.org/10.1007/978-3-032-04470-9_9

The review by Araujo et al. (2024) is particularly instructive in showing how resilience thinking has matured. It has evolved from early emphases on resistance and recovery toward more nuanced understandings of detection and post-crisis learning. Their proposed four-stage model, composed of monitoring and detection; resistance and absorption; response and adaptation; and finally, recovery and reconstruction, offers a parsimonious yet powerful template that can be extended into the cognitive domain. Within cognitive diplomacy, these same functions may occur not in firewalled networks but in cognitive architectures, AI-supported reasoning loops, and human-machine policy interfaces. In this context, resilience is no longer only about infrastructure. It is also about the mind, memory, and judgment of the state.

Thus, in the technopolar world, digital *resilience* becomes essential to digital autonomy. It secures not only the continuity of systems but the strategic agency of perception and decision as well. When AI systems assist or even co-author diplomatic choices, the ability to think under pressure, reframe ambiguity, and adapt iteratively becomes the final bastion of sovereign control.

Resilience in the context of digital sovereignty refers to a state's ability to maintain and recover its critical digital functions and decision-making autonomy in the face of disruptions. As Markus Holmgren of FIIA observes, true resilience involves "the physical, legislative, and intellectual capability to adapt rapidly and effectively in the face of adversity or disruption" (Holmgren, 2022). In other words, a resilient digital system treats shocks—from cyberattacks to supply interruptions—not merely as threats but as opportunities to improve preparedness. Digital resilience thus encompasses policies and investments that increase the adaptability of a state's tech ecosystem—its national tech stack—so that essential ICT infrastructure and data remain secure and functional. Crucially, resilience entails a balance between self-reliance and international engagement: attempting "excess self-sufficiency" undermines resilience, whereas strategic trust and "mutual reliability" with partners are needed to maintain access to critical global data and services (Harrell, 2025).

Building resilience has both internal and external dimensions. Internally, states reinforce cybersecurity, institutional agility, human capital, and backup systems. Externally, they prepare for sanctions, embargoes, and other forms of technological coercion by diversifying supply chains and developing domestic alternatives. Resilience is not optional in the technopolar world order. As outlined earlier, digital asymmetry is becoming increasingly visible, particularly amid the deepening digital divide (Wilcox, 2021). Digital asymmetry—defined as the structural exclusion from critical technological infrastructures such as high-performance computing (HPC), sovereign cloud ecosystems, and secure telecommunications networks—generates profound systemic vulnerabilities for nation-states (Leal et al., 2023; OECD, 2019b; UST, 2025; Vogiatzoglou, 2025). Therefore, cultivating resilience is essential for any state looking to secure its digital autonomy. This chapter examines how states can strategically facilitate and institutionalize resilience across their digital ecosystems.

These dependencies expose states to a range of strategic vulnerabilities, including cyber intrusions, espionage, operational disruptions, and coercive dependencies that erode autonomy in both peacetime and crisis. With sovereign control over critical digital infrastructures, national security architectures become increasingly permeable, and strategic decision-making is subject to external technological leverage (Bradford, 2023; Gori, 2023). The consequences of such dependency extend beyond cybersecurity. The inability to access, develop, or govern advanced digital capabilities undermines a country's economic competitiveness, stifles its innovation ecosystem, and diminishes its diplomatic agency in global forums where the rules of digital governance are being actively shaped and contested (Bjola & Kornprobst, 2024; Feakin, 2024).

The global digital landscape is intensely competitive and increasingly adversarial. States confront an expanding spectrum of threats, ranging from state-sponsored cyberattacks on critical infrastructure and supply chain chokepoints that restrict access to essential components and coercive actions by technologically dominant powers seeking to exert geopolitical influence through control over digital assets. In this environment, resilience emerges as a foundational pillar of what was discussed in the previous part as "Sovereignty 2.0": the strategic capacity of a nation to absorb, adapt to, and recover from disruptions across the digital domain. This chapter analyzes how states construct resilience in the face of mounting technological insecurity and foreign dependency. It examines a range of national and regional strategies, including cybersecurity architectures designed to defend against cyberwarfare and espionage; supply chain diversification initiatives aimed at securing access to critical technologies such as semiconductors, and broader frameworks for achieving digital strategic autonomy. These approaches are not only reactive but increasingly anticipatory, positioning resilience as a proactive state function in a world where control over technology translates directly into political, economic, and diplomatic power. Through comparative examples, we explore how nations preserve and project their sovereignty in an era where digital infrastructures and technological ecosystems have become both targets and instruments of geopolitical contestation.

In recent years, several key events have sounded alarm over the strategic importance of resilience in digital sovereignty (European Council on Foreign Relations, 2021). The *NotPetya* cyberattack in 2017, widely attributed to Russian military intelligence (Greenberg, 2018), crippled Ukrainian infrastructure and caused billions in collateral damage globally, demonstrating that a state actor could inflict economic devastation through malware without firing a single shot. Similarly, the U.S.' 2019 ban on Huawei and subsequent controls on semiconductor exports to China between 2020 and 2023 served as a wake-up call about how easily a technological superpower could weaponize supply chain dependencies (Swanson, 2020). These measures starkly curtailed China's ability to access essential design software and advanced manufacturing tools, effectively limiting Huawei's global competitiveness and raising deep concerns in Beijing over national vulnerabilities (Miller, 2022).

When Russia-Ukraine War erupted in 2022, Russia faced sweeping Western tech sanctions that cut off Moscow's access to semiconductors, fabrication services, and software updates. The impact was immediate: Russian missile systems were reportedly retrofitted with chips scavenged from consumer appliances, including dishwashers and refrigerators, according to Western intelligence sources—a vivid testament to the extent of dependency (Miller, 2022; Roulette, 2023). These developments underscore a broader strategic truth: technological interdependence is now a potential liability. As Miller notes, the semiconductor industry is built around a series of global choke points, most notably advanced lithography machines, design software, and contract manufacturing facilities—that can be exploited for geopolitical leverage (Miller, 2022). The concept, first articulated by Farrell and Newman (2019) as "weaponized interdependence," has now become a structural feature of global politics.

This weaponization is not limited to military conflict. The COVID-19 pandemic further exposed the fragility of global supply chains. Shortages of everything—from personal protective equipment to microchips—revealed how over-reliance on distant suppliers can paralyze national economies in crisis. Nations suddenly realized that they lacked resilience if they could not independently secure or manufacture essential technological inputs under emergency conditions. These episodes from cyberwarfare and export controls to global pandemics collectively illuminate the urgent need for states to develop robust digital resilience as a cornerstone of national sovereignty and security.

In response to escalating cyberthreats and geopolitical competition, resilience has emerged as a central priority in national and regional strategic agendas. The European Union's *Cybersecurity Strategy* explicitly aims to "build resilience to cyberthreats and ensure citizens and businesses benefit from trustworthy digital technologies" as part of a broader effort to secure the Digital Single Market and bolster democratic trust in technology (European Commission , 2020a). Similarly, countries like the United States and Japan have prioritized "secure supply chains" in their foreign and industrial policies, formalizing bilateral and multilateral agreements to safeguard access to critical technologies.

Within the European context, the evolving concept of "digital autonomy" reflects a growing desire to maintain agency in digital and technological governance while continuing to engage constructively in global frameworks (Barber et. al., 2025). This model envisions Europe that can pursue its own digital course without succumbing to technological dependency or undue external influence (European Commission, 2020b). Achieving such autonomy, however, depends fundamentally on building resilience—not only in a technological sense but also through coordinated policy action, governance reform, and public-private collaboration.

This chapter now turns to three interlinked dimensions of resilience: cybersecurity resilience, which focuses on protecting against coercive cyber operations and infrastructure attacks; supply chain and economic resilience, which entails diversifying and securing access to critical technologies; and strategic autonomy initiatives, which aim to reduce structural dependency and enable sovereign decision-making in an increasingly contested digital landscape. However, before delving into these domains, it is essential to frame resilience within the evolving legal and normative context.

The question of how the United Nations Charter applies to cyber operations has emerged as one of the most complex and contentious issues in contemporary international law. At its core, this legal puzzle challenges whether traditional concepts of force and armed attack—enshrined in the Charter's foundational articles—can meaningfully encompass the digital realm, where states increasingly conduct hostile activities that produce profound real-world consequences. Resilience, in this context, must also be understood as a legal and normative posture: a state's capacity not only to absorb and respond to digital threats, but to do so within the bounds of international law, while shaping its future evolution.

9.1 Applicability of the UN Charter to Cyber Operations

Prohibition of Force in Cyberspace under Article 2(4)

Article 2(4) of the UN Charter establishes that *"All Members shall refrain in their international relations from the threat or use of force against the territorial integrity or political independence of any State, or in any other manner inconsistent with the Purposes of the United Nations"* (United Nations, 1945). This prohibition has long served as a cornerstone of the international legal order, yet its application to cyber operations presents unique interpretive challenges. The drafters of the Charter in 1945 could hardly have envisioned the digital landscape that would emerge decades later, where states can inflict significant harm without crossing physical borders or deploying conventional weapons.

Contemporary legal scholarship has increasingly recognized that cyber operations can potentially fall within the scope of Article 2(4) when they produce effects comparable to those of traditional kinetic attacks. The Italian government's position paper on international law and cyberspace articulates this view clearly, stating that "Italy considers a cyber operation conducted by a State against another State as a use of *force, when its scale and effects are comparable to those of a conventional use of force, resulting in physical damage of property, human injury or loss of life"* (Italian Ministry of Foreign Affairs and International Cooperation, 2021). This interpretation reflects a growing consensus that the prohibition of force should be understood functionally rather than merely in terms of the means employed.

The assessment of whether a cyber operation constitutes a use of force requires careful consideration of its consequences rather than its technological characteristics. As noted in academic analysis, the determination depends on factors such as the scale of disruption, the nature of the targeted systems, and the broader impact on the victim state's essential functions (Roscini, 2015). This approach recognizes that modern societies' dependence on digital infrastructure means that cyber operations can potentially cause destruction and disruption equivalent to conventional attacks.

Self-Defense and Armed Attack in the Digital Domain

The right of self-defense under Article 51 of the UN Charter presents even more complex questions in the cyber context. Article 51 provides that *"Nothing in the present Charter shall impair the inherent right of individual or collective self-defense if an armed attack occurs against a Member of the United Nations"* (United Nations, 1945). The critical issue is determining when cyber operations rise to the level of an "armed attack" sufficient to trigger this fundamental right.

The International Court of Justice's jurisprudence, particularly in the Nicaragua v. United States case, has established that not every use of force constitutes an armed attack; rather, there must be sufficient gravity to cross this higher threshold (Ministère de l'Europe et des Affaires étrangères, 2021). French legal doctrine has embraced this distinction in the cyber context, acknowledging that *"cyberattacks may constitute a grave form of the use of force to which France could respond by self-defence"* when they reach appropriate levels of scale and severity. The French position specifically notes that an armed attack could be established where cyber operations cause "substantial loss of life or considerable physical or economic damage" (Ministère des Armées, 2019).

Recent developments in state practice have begun to flesh out these concepts more concretely. France has indicated that it would consider cyber operations that cause *"failure of critical infrastructure with significant consequences or consequences liable to paralyse whole swathes of the country's activity, trigger technological or ecological disasters and claim numerous victims"* as potentially constituting armed attacks (Ministère de l'Europe et des Affaires étrangères, 2021). This approach emphasizes the functional effects of cyber operations rather than their digital nature.

The question of attribution adds another layer of complexity to the application of Article 51 in cyberspace. As the French position paper notes, *"To be categorized as an armed attack, a cyberattack must also have been perpetrated, directly or indirectly, by a State"* (Ministère de l'Europe et des Affaires étrangères, 2021). This requirement reflects established principles of state responsibility while acknowledging the particular challenges of identifying the true perpetrators of cyber operations, where technical attribution can be difficult and states may operate through proxies or non-state actors.

Chapter VII of the UN Charter grants the Security Council broad authority to *"determine the existence of any threat to the peace, breach of the peace, or act of aggression"* and to authorize appropriate responses (United Nations, 1945). While the Charter does not explicitly reference cyber operations, the Council's mandate is sufficiently flexible to encompass digital threats that meet the requisite thresholds for international concern.

The Security Council's authority extends to situations where cyber operations create or contribute to threats to international peace and security, regardless of whether they constitute uses of force or armed attacks under Articles 2(4) and 51 respectively (United Nations, 1945). This broader mandate could prove particularly relevant for addressing cyber operations that fall below traditional force thresholds but nonetheless create significant instability or humanitarian consequences.

The development of international cyber norms has proceeded through multiple channels, including the UN Group of Governmental Experts process and various state position papers. The 2013 UN GGE report established the foundational principle that *"international law, and in particular the UN Charter, applies to digital space"* (United Nations, 2013). This consensus represented a crucial first step in extending traditional legal frameworks to cyberspace.

The UN norms of responsible state behavior in cyberspace, while non-binding, provide additional guidance on state conduct in the digital domain (United Nations, 2013; OECD, 2019a). These norms emphasize that "States should not knowingly allow their territory to be used for internationally wrongful acts using ICTs" and that states should refrain from conducting cyber operations that "intentionally damage critical infrastructure" (Hogeveen, 2022). While these norms do not directly interpret Charter provisions, they reflect evolving expectations about acceptable state behavior in cyberspace.

Italian legal doctrine has embraced a comprehensive approach to cyber operations, recognizing both their potential to violate sovereignty and their capacity to trigger various legal responses (Ministry of Foreign Affairs and International Cooperation, 2021). Italy's position acknowledges that "countermeasures are adequate responses to cyber operations that constitute an international wrongful act below the threshold of an armed attack", while maintaining that more serious cyber operations could justify forcible self-defense (Ministry of Foreign Affairs and International Cooperation, 2021).

The application of UN Charter principles to cyber operations represents an ongoing evolution in international law rather than a settled body of doctrine. While there is broad consensus that the Charter applies to cyberspace, significant questions remain regarding the specific thresholds and criteria for determining when cyber operations constitute uses of force or armed attacks. State practice continues to develop through position papers, diplomatic statements, and actual responses to cyber incidents, gradually building a body of precedent that will inform future legal development.

The flexibility inherent in the United Nations Charter has proven both beneficial and challenging in the cyber context. On the one hand, it permits adaptation to emerging technological realities; on the other, it introduces legal ambiguity that states must navigate when determining appropriate responses to cyber operations. Future clarification may arise through consistent state practice, rulings by international judicial bodies, or the development of a dedicated legal framework specifically addressing cyber activities. Until such developments occur, states will continue to operate within a dynamic interpretive space, balancing the urgent need for effective cyber responses with a commitment to the foundational principles of international law. Within this evolving legal and normative environment, resilience emerges not only as a strategic imperative but also as a legal and normative posture. It reflects a state's capacity to confront threats in ways that uphold international norms and reinforce sovereign agency.

9.2 Cybersecurity and Cyber-Defense Strategies

Cybersecurity constitutes the first and most immediate line of defense in preserving a nation's digital sovereignty. In an era where government operations, power grids, hospitals, and financial systems are increasingly digitized, the impact of a successful cyberattack is no longer hypothetical (Lindsay, 2015) —it can paralyze essential services, destabilize governance, and even coerce policy decisions (Lewis, 2018; Nakashima & Warrick, 2017). From ransomware disrupting municipal operations to state-sponsored campaigns targeting democratic processes, the spectrum of cyberthreats has expanded significantly (Healey, 2013;

Kello, 2017). Consequently, national cybersecurity strategies have become widespread, typically anchored in three objectives: securing critical infrastructure, deterring and disrupting cyber adversaries, and building systemic resilience (Bradford, 2020; NIST, 2018).

Many states have developed dedicated institutions to implement these goals. In the United States, this includes U.S. Cyber Command (USCYBERCOM), tasked with military cyber operations, and the Cybersecurity and Infrastructure Security Agency (CISA), which oversees the protection of civilian infrastructure (U.S. Cyber Command, 2020; CISA, 2021). The U.S. has embraced a doctrine of "persistent engagement," whereby cyber forces actively identify and neutralize threats before they materialize—often by operating within adversary networks (U.S. Department of Defense, 2018). Domestically, the NIST Cybersecurity Framework provides a widely adopted benchmark for public and private sector risk management (Barrett, 2018). Given that a significant proportion of critical infrastructure—such as energy grids, financial institutions, and telecoms—is privately owned, public-private collaboration is emphasized. Information Sharing and Analysis Centers (ISACs) play a pivotal role in facilitating real-time threat intelligence between government and industry (ISAC Council, 2020).

In the European Union, cybersecurity governance has historically been fragmented among member states, but recent years have seen efforts to promote integration and collective resilience. The *Cybersecurity Strategy for the Digital Decade* (European Commission, 2020a) sets out a vision for "a high common level of cybersecurity" across the Union, focusing on enhancing resilience, reducing cybercrime, and enabling coordinated responses. A cornerstone of this strategy is the *Directive on Security of Network and Information Systems* (NIS), updated as NIS2 in 2022, which imposes binding cybersecurity obligations on critical sectors such as energy, transport, health care, and finance [Directive (EU), 2022/2555]. The directive standardizes security protocols and incident reporting across the EU, reinforcing sectoral resilience (IEEE SA, 2025).

To support implementation, the EU has empowered the European Union Agency for Cybersecurity (ENISA), which issues technical guidance, coordinates cyber exercises, and enhances member states' capacity for response and recovery (European Union Agency for Cybersecurity, 2025). The urgency of a unified approach has been demonstrated by major incidents such as the 2015 TV5Monde hack in France and the 2017 WannaCry ransomware attack, which severely affected the U.K.'s

National Health Service (BBC News, 2015; NHS, 2017). These episodes underscored that cyberthreats are transnational in nature, necessitating solidarity and joint preparedness.

At the multilateral level, NATO officially recognized cyberspace as a domain of operations in 2016, elevating cyberattacks to the same level as kinetic threats and allowing them to trigger collective defense under Article 5 (NATO, 2016). Since then, NATO has expanded the scope and capacity of its Cooperative Cyber Defense Centre of Excellence (CCDCOE) in Estonia and has encouraged its members to integrate cyber capabilities into their national defense strategies (Estonian Ministry of Defence, 2020; NATO, 2019; NATO CCDCOE, 2025; NATO Review, 2021). Cyber resilience is now widely accepted as not only a national security imperative but also a key dimension of allied interoperability and deterrence.

When it comes to resilience, sometimes non-Western regimes often pursue isolationist strategies. Russia has experimented with unplugging its domestic internet (Runet) from the global web and has promoted national alternatives to foreign software and platforms (Celeste et. al., 2022; Gulyaeva et. al., 2015). China's so-called Great Firewall, coupled with the construction of a self-contained digital ecosystem, serves not only ideological purposes but also acts as a technical buffer against external cyberthreats. Paradoxically, such isolation can enhance resilience to certain types of attacks by reducing exposure, but it also introduces systemic inefficiencies and does not eliminate vulnerability to supply chain disruptions or sophisticated targeted intrusions (Creemers, 2016; Segal, 2018).

A key component of cyber resilience lies in national incident response capacity. Many countries have established Computer Security Incident Response Teams (CSIRTs) and cyber coordination centers that operate as rapid response units during an attack. Estonia, often cited as a model of cyber resilience, learned this lesson firsthand after the 2007 cyber assault attributed to Russian actors. The attack, which paralyzed Estonian banks, ministries, and media, catalyzed a national overhaul of digital defenses. Estonia now hosts the world's largest real-time cyber-defense exercise, Locked Shields, organized by NATO's Cooperative Cyber Defense Center or CCDCOE. The country has diversified its internet connections, implemented secure national ID-linked digital backups, and incorporated digital literacy into public education-demonstrating how resilience is both technical and societal (NATO CCDCOE, 2023; Rid, 2013).

International cooperation plays an increasingly critical role in bolstering resilience. NATO allies have formal mechanisms to deploy cyber experts across borders during crises, reinforcing mutual defense commitments in the digital realm. Additionally, platforms such as the Global Forum on Cyber Expertise (GFCE) facilitate capacity-building in developing nations, recognizing that insecure systems in one jurisdiction can be exploited to launch global attacks. Transnational law enforcement coordination through agencies like INTERPOL also addresses the nexus between cybercrime and state-sponsored activity (GFCE, 2023; INTERPOL, 2022; INTERPOL, 2023; NATO, 2016).

Despite these efforts, the threat landscape remains persistent and adaptive. State-sponsored campaigns have targeted sensitive sectors such as vaccine research, defense infrastructure, and critical intellectual property. Simultaneously, criminal ransomware groups have paralyzed hospitals, municipal governments, and universities-particularly during the COVID-19 pandemic. In this context, resilience is not merely about preventing breaches, it is about continuity. Governments and private sectors are increasingly investing in redundancy, such as backup communications systems, satellite phones, and fail-safe financial clearing mechanisms, to maintain operational capacity even under duress (CISA, 2020; Lewis, 2021; NIST, 2018).

Cyber deterrence is emerging as a parallel but complex dimension of resilience. States have begun to experiment with doctrines of public attribution, indictments, and sanctions against foreign hackers. The United States and the European Union have imposed measures against individuals and entities from Russia, China, Iran, and North Korea following major cyber incidents (Miller, 2022; Chun et. al., 2024). These steps are intended to raise the costs of malicious activity and signal a willingness to retaliate, possibly through offensive cyber means or, in extreme cases, kinetic responses. France, for example, articulated in 2019 that it reserves the right to respond to cyberattacks with "any means" at its disposal—a declaratory move designed to establish normative red lines and bolster deterrence credibility (French Ministry of Defence, 2019).

In summary, cybersecurity strategies are foundational to digital sovereignty. They reinforce national resilience by hardening digital infrastructure against coercion and disruption. A cyber-robust state is less susceptible to blackmail, paralysis, or strategic manipulation in the digital domain, thereby enhancing its ability to act autonomously. Yet cybersecurity is an inherently dynamic field and resilience is not a fixed state but a process of continuous adaptation, innovation, and vigilance (Healey, 2013; Rid, 2020).

9.3 Securing Supply Chains and Reducing Tech Dependencies

The issue of supply chain security has become central to contemporary debates on technological resilience, especially in relation to critical technologies like semiconductors. The global supply chain for electronics, network equipment, and software is deeply interconnected, yet structurally fragile due to its geographic concentration. Nations have become acutely aware that over-reliance on a limited number of suppliers—such as Taiwan for advanced microchips and China for rare earth elements—creates systemic vulnerabilities. Disruptions triggered by natural disasters, trade disputes, or geopolitical coercion could have cascading effects on economies and national security architectures (Semiconductor Industry Association/BCG, 2021; Synergy Inc., 2025).

Semiconductors, in particular, exemplify this strategic risk. The most advanced chips at 5 nm and 3 nm nodes are manufactured almost exclusively by Taiwan TSMC in Taiwan and Samsung in South Korea. Meanwhile, ASML in the Netherlands maintains a monopoly on extreme ultraviolet (EUV) lithography machines, which are indispensable for leading-edge chip production (Kusters et. al., 2025; Synergy Inc., 2025; Dutch Government, 2023b). While the United States and Europe dominate chip design, they currently lack significant domestic production capacity for the most advanced nodes. China, despite vast investments in semiconductor self-sufficiency, still depends on foreign tooling and is unable to produce cutting-edge chips at scale (Kusters et. al., 2025; Semiconductor Industry Association/BCG, 2021). Taiwan's strategic proximity to mainland China elevates concerns about a potential regional conflict triggering a global technological crisis—what many analysts describe as a "massive single point of failure" in the global economy (Miller, 2022).

In response, governments have launched ambitious strategies to diversify and fortify their semiconductor supply chains. In the United States, the CHIPS and Science Act commits over $50 billion in subsidies and tax incentives to spur domestic chip manufacturing and research. Major semiconductor firms, including TSMC, Samsung, and Intel, are establishing new fabrication plants in Arizona, Texas, and other locations. In parallel, the European Union's Chips Act targets a 20% share of global chip production by 2030, while Japan and India are offering similar incentive schemes to draw manufacturers and reduce foreign dependence (Kusters et. al., 2025; Semiconductor Industry Association/BCG, 2021; Synergy Inc., 2025).

These national policies are increasingly supported by international coordination frameworks. One prominent example is the informal "Chip 4" alliance—comprising the U.S., EU, Japan, South Korea, and Taiwan—which seeks to align production planning, R&D, and export controls. This alliance has already played a role in coordinated restrictions on the sale of advanced chipmaking tools to China, aimed at curbing Beijing's access to technologies with military applications (Kusters et. al., 2025; Miller, 2022). While these efforts do not aim for complete technological autarky, they reflect a shift toward a more balanced and strategically distributed ecosystem.

Nevertheless, the semiconductor supply chain remains vulnerable to geopolitical shocks, trade disruptions, and climate-related events. Recent U.S. tariffs and export restrictions, combined with surging global demand driven by AI, cloud computing, and edge technologies, continue to strain production capacity (U.S. Department of Commerce). In response, industry actors are abandoning just-in-time inventory models in favor of buffered inventory and "strategic stockpiling" strategies to better withstand volatility (Fowle, 2025).

In sum, securing the supply chain for semiconductors has become a defining pillar of national and economic resilience. As competition intensifies in the technopolar world, states are leveraging industrial policy, diplomatic alliances, and supply chain redesigns to mitigate technological dependencies and bolster autonomy in critical digital infrastructures.

9.4 Beyond Semiconductors: Expanding the Scope of Supply Chain Resilience

The imperative of diversification extends well beyond the semiconductor industry. One notable domain is 5G telecommunications infrastructure, where concerns over Huawei's dominance catalyzed a reconfiguration of supplier strategies (Mcdonald, 2020). Several governments chose to restrict or ban Huawei and ZTE, opting instead for European firms such as Nokia and Ericsson (Kroet, 2024). Yet, reliance on just two major alternatives poses its own resilience dilemma. In response, many countries are promoting Open Radio Access Network (Open RAN) architectures, which allow interoperability among network components from different vendors. This modular approach reduces single-vendor dependency and enhances adaptability in the face of disruption. For instance, the United Kingdom, after banning Huawei, launched a Telecoms Diversification Strategy that included investment in Open RAN and support for emerging suppliers like Japan's NEC and South Korea's Samsung (GSMA, 2022; UK Government, 2021). Broadening the supplier base is now understood as a key resilience strategy: if one vendor fails, is compromised, or becomes politically contentious, alternatives must be readily available.

Critical materials represent another domain of strategic concern. Rare earth elements, indispensable for a wide range of technologies from batteries to wind turbines and defense electronics, are heavily concentrated in China, which dominates both mining and processing. China's temporary embargo on rare earth exports to Japan in 2010 highlighted the geopolitical risks of such concentration. As a result, countries including Australia, the United States, and Canada are investing in alternative mining and refining capacities, despite environmental, regulatory, and cost challenges. Similar trends are seen in response to Russia's historical dominance in materials like titanium (crucial for aerospace) and palladium (used in semiconductors). Following the 2022 invasion of Ukraine, countries have moved to diversify these inputs as part of broader resource security strategies (European Commission2022; USGS, 2023).

Domestic production and "reshoring" are also gaining traction. Governments are encouraging the return of manufacturing for critical technologies to national or allied territories—a trend often labeled "friend-shoring." Motivated by resilience concerns as well as strategic industrial policy, this shift was accelerated by the COVID-19 pandemic, which exposed vulnerabilities in overextended supply chains. Even essential items such as medical equipment and protective gear became inaccessible due to export bans and bottlenecks. In response, countries have begun mapping critical imports and exploring domestic capacity-building. India's Production-Linked Incentive (PLI) scheme, for example, subsidizes domestic manufacturing of smartphones, semiconductors, and solar panels, both to reduce reliance on China and to emerge as a global supplier (Government of India, 2023a). The EU's industrial policy similarly identifies key strategic value chains—such as hydrogen, cloud infrastructure, and batteries—in which Europe aims to achieve a secure share of production (European Commission, 2022).

International trade and technology alliances further underpin resilience strategies. The Quad (United States, Japan, India, and Australia) has established a working group on critical technologies and supply chains, emphasizing mutual reinforcement of each member's industrial strengths—from India's pharmaceuticals to Japan's materials science. The EU–U.S. Trade and Technology Council plays a similar role, fostering early warning systems for shortages and coordinating semiconductor policy. At the national level, procurement policies increasingly incorporate resilience criteria, requiring government contracts to include provisions for multi-sourcing or stockpiling (World Economic Forum, 2023; U.S Department of Commerce, 2023).

Stockpiling, a long-established practice in energy security, is now being adapted for technology components. Governments and companies are building reserves of semiconductors, satellite equipment, and networking gear to protect against geopolitical shocks or export controls (Bourbeau, 2015). For example, China reportedly encouraged chip stockpiling ahead of anticipated U.S. sanctions (Zhou, 2022), while other countries are exploring strategic reserves for critical components (King, 2025).

Still, resilience must be balanced against efficiency. Fully duplicating global supply chains is economically and logistically prohibitive. The concept of "open strategic autonomy," particularly championed by the EU, suggests a pragmatic middle path: not full autarky, but sufficient domestic or allied capability in critical areas such that no state is dependent on a single, unreliable source (Roberts et. al., 2021). This model emphasizes self-reliance where national security or ethical values are at stake—such as in secure communications, AI, and defense-related technologies—while maintaining diversified trade in other areas (European Commission, 2020a).

Economic resilience also entails preparedness against coercion. Trade and technological interdependence can be weaponized, as seen in China's 2017 informal boycott of South Korean firms following the deployment of a U.S. missile defense system, or U.S. tariff threats linked to digital services taxes. In the tech domain, coercion might involve threatening access to markets, platforms, or foundational technologies. To hedge against such risks, smaller states are diversifying their sourcing—building mixed-vendor systems that include both U.S. and Chinese technology to reduce vulnerability to unilateral pressure. The European Union has proposed an "anti-coercion instrument," which would enable a collective response to such tactics—such as China's restriction of Lithuanian imports over Taiwan-related diplomatic recognition (Kurbalija, 2022).

Technology standards constitute another vector of resilience. By shaping or adhering to open standards, states can avoid lock-in to proprietary technologies that depend on foreign actors. Open-source solutions are increasingly viewed as a strategic asset in this context. When Western sanctions blocked Russian entities from receiving updates for commercial software, many turned to open-source alternatives, enabling the continuity of digital operations. Similarly, European public institutions are exploring open-source frameworks for secure messaging, digital identity, and data governance, seeking both transparency and independence from private monopolies (European Commission, 2020b; Open Source Initiative, 2023).

9.5 Digital Strategic Autonomy and Economic Security Initiatives

Digital strategic autonomy refers to the capacity of a nation or bloc to make sovereign decisions in critical digital domains without being subject to undue external influence. The EU has emerged as the leading advocate of this concept, along with the famous "Brussels Effect" (Bradford, 2012), driven by growing concerns that sustained reliance on U.S. and Chinese technologies could reduce Europe to the status of a "digital colony" (European Commission, 2020a; World Economic Forum, 2023). This notion of strategic autonomy extends across multiple domains—including hardware, data governance, cloud infrastructure, AI, and digital finance—with the aim of preserving sovereign decision-making, operational continuity, and systemic resilience (Musoni, 2023).

The principle of data sovereignty lies at the heart of digital autonomy. The EU's *Schrems II* judgment (2020), which annulled the EU-U.S. Privacy Shield, emphasized that the transatlantic data transfer regime failed to protect EU citizens from disproportionate U.S. surveillance (World Economic Forum, 2023). This ruling significantly accelerated efforts to establish the 2023 EU-U.S. Data Privacy Framework, intended to restore legal certainty while upholding fundamental rights (World Economic Forum, 2023). Beyond Europe, India's *Digital Personal Data Protection Act* (Government of India, 2023b) mandates that data generated by Indian citizens be stored and processed primarily within national borders, asserting sovereign control and enhancing resilience in the event of global disconnections (World Economic Forum, 2023; Routley, 2020).

Reducing dependency on foreign-controlled financial infrastructure is another pillar of digital resilience. The SWIFT system, while globally entrenched, has been used as an instrument of sanctions enforcement by the U.S. and EU, prompting countries like Russia and China to develop alternatives. Russia's SPFS and China's CIPS serve as domestically governed financial messaging networks, while central bank digital currencies (CBDCs) such as China's digital yuan and the EU's proposed digital euro aim to reclaim monetary sovereignty in the digital age (European Central Bank, 2025; Small Wars Journal, 2024). The suspension of Visa and Mastercard operations in Russia during sanctions episodes, catalyzed the expansion of domestic systems like Russia's Mir and China's UnionPay, demonstrating the strategic significance of sovereign financial instruments (Small Wars Journal, 2024).

Ensuring autonomy in the digital sphere also means safeguarding information ecosystems from manipulation and foreign interference. Recognizing disinformation as a national security issue, many governments have implemented countermeasures including media literacy campaigns, national rapid response teams, and, in some cases, temporary restrictions on digital platforms during emergencies. Countries like Sri Lanka, Nigeria, and India have imposed targeted internet shutdowns during episodes of unrest, though these measures remain controversial (World Economic Forum, 2023). More rights-respecting approaches have emerged as well: Sweden's Psychological Defence Agency and Taiwan's innovative crowdsourced fact-checking model during elections serve as notable examples of building societal resilience against information warfare while upholding democratic norms (World Economic Forum, 2023).

Even long-standing allies are not immune from coercive digital disruptions. The EU, for instance, remains concerned about the extraterritorial impact of U.S. regulations such as the CLOUD Act and how U.S. sanctions might affect European data hosted on American cloud platforms (European Commission, 2020b; Swinhoe, 2022). In response, Europe is advancing sovereign cloud initiatives (European Commission, 2024). Similarly, countries like Türkiye and India have pursued strategic diversification to avoid dependency traps. Following tensions over U.S. export controls in the defense sector, Türkiye expanded its international partnerships to include alternative suppliers. South Korea responded to Japan's

2019 export controls by accelerating efforts to localize the production of critical components (World Economic Forum, 2023). These developments underscore a broader trend in resilience-building: states, regardless of alliance networks, seek insulation from geopolitical leverage.

To operationalize its vision of digital autonomy, the EU adopted the "Path to the Digital Decade" program in December 2022, setting ambitious targets for 2030 across areas such as digital skills, business transformation, secure infrastructure, and e-governance (Council of the European Union, 2025; European Commission, 2020c). The EU promotes the concept of "open strategic autonomy," which involves reducing reliance on proprietary technologies, advancing open-source alternatives, and ensuring that innovation aligns with fundamental rights (de Carvajal, 2023; Dutch Government, 2023a). Complementing this is the Digital Europe Programme, which channels investment into high-performance computing, AI, cybersecurity, and digital capacity-building—critical enablers of European technological sovereignty (Council of the European Union, 2025).

9.6 Regional Cooperation and Societal Digital Resilience

Regional cooperation plays a critical role in enhancing digital resilience. The EU, through its collective capabilities, can initiate projects that transcend the capacities of individual member states. Notably, the Important Projects of Common European Interest (IPCEI) mechanism allows coordinated state aid for key technological sectors, such as microelectronics and cloud infrastructure. This mechanism effectively circumvents the EU's ordinarily strict competition rules in pursuit of strategic autonomy (Small Wars Journal, 2024). Similar trends are emerging in other regions: ASEAN and the African Union are exploring initiatives to pool resources for the development of regional cloud computing and satellite infrastructure, thereby reducing strategic dependency on external digital powers (ASEAN Secretariat, 2024; African Union Commission, 2023).

Resilience also includes a vital human dimension: the digital resilience of society itself. This encompasses not only technical measures but also societal preparedness. Building a robust cybersecurity workforce, enhancing public awareness of cyber hygiene, and fully integrating the private sector into national resilience frameworks are all essential. Japan's national cybersecurity strategy, for example, promotes a "whole-of-society" approach, mobilizing government, corporations, and civil society to defend against digital threats—especially during high-risk events such as the Tokyo Olympics (Japan Cabinet Secretariat, 2021).

Finland offers a leading model of societal digital resilience. Public education includes mandatory media literacy curricula, which cultivate a critical understanding of information sources from an early age. Moreover, high levels of public trust in institutions, alongside a tradition of civil defense, have enabled the country to extend its preparedness into the cyber domain. Finland's model allows the nation to function in a "degraded mode" if necessary—maintaining communication and essential services even when high-tech systems are compromised (Finnish Security Committee, 2022).

As analysts at Brookings observe, the "growing mistrust between nations … has caused a rise in digital sovereignty," largely driven by fears of being cut off from essential technologies such as semiconductors, cloud services, or data flows (Larsen, 2022). This anxiety fuels strategies aimed at developing fail-safes and alternative pathways—strategies that prioritize robustness and independence over seamless global integration (Larsen, 2022).

The ultimate test of resilience will emerge in moments of crisis. A genuinely resilient state will preserve essential digital functions under pressure—delivering public services during cyberattacks, securing access to vital technologies amid disrupted trade, and maintaining societal trust in the face of disinformation campaigns. Crucially, resilience does not equate to isolationism. Rather, it frequently demands cooperation with trusted partners and multilateral investment in redundancy and diversity. As DiploFoundation (2023) notes, "resilience requires connected sovereignty": a balance between autonomy and strategic interdependence.

By embedding the pillars of digital autonomy—presence, practice, and resilience—into national and regional strategies, states can navigate the digital age with their sovereignty not only intact but actively renewed. Yet sovereignty in the technopolar era extends beyond infrastructure and institutions. It must also account for the increasingly contested terrain of perception, narrative, and human cognition.

This brings us to the next critical frontier: *cognitive diplomacy*. As technological systems penetrate ever deeper into the processes of communication, persuasion, and decision-making, diplomacy itself is undergoing a profound transformation. No longer limited to official negotiations and protocol, statecraft now involves shaping informational environments, countering algorithmic manipulation, and defending the integrity of public reasoning.

Cognitive diplomacy refers to the strategic use of both human and machine intelligence to influence how information is received, interpreted, and acted upon across borders. It emphasizes the role of trust, attention, and epistemic legitimacy in global affairs, acknowledging that today's great power struggles are as much about minds as they are about markets or missiles. In an age of deepfakes, synthetic media, psychological warfare, and hyper-personalized influence operations, the ability to secure cognitive spaces is as vital as the ability to secure physical or digital ones.

The following chapters explore this emerging domain in depth, focusing on how cognitive power is exercised, challenged, and negotiated in international relations. From digital propaganda and AI-generated diplomacy to the ethics of neurotechnology and the weaponization of emotion, cognitive diplomacy offers a framework to understand how states pursue influence and resilience in the most intimate domain of all: the human mind.

Bibliography

African Union Commission. (2023). Digital infrastructure and regional integration in Africa. *African Union*.. https://au.int/en/digital-infrastructure (Retrieved May 11, 2025)

Araujo, M.S. de, Machado, B.A.S. and Passos, F.U. (2024). "Resilience in the context of cyber security: A review of the fundamental concepts and relevance", Applied Sciences, 14(5), p. 2116. doi:https://doi.org/10.3390/app14052116.

Barber, I., Bopanna, A., Canales, M. P., McDonald, E. and Payne, R. (2025). "2025: A stress test for the multistakeholder model?", Global Partners Digital, 22 January. https://www.gp-digital.org/2025-a-stress-test-for-the-multistakeholder-model/ (Retrieved May 11, 2025).

Barrett, R. (2018). "Path forward to support adoption and adaptation of the cybersecurity framework", NIST Cybersecurity Framework Workshop, February. https://www.nist.gov/system/files/documents/2018/02/06/session_iii_-_barrett_csf.pdf (Retrieved 7 June 2025).

BBC News. (2015). "TV5 monde attack by Russia-based hackers", BBC News, 9 June. https://www.bbc.com/news/world-europe-33072034 (Retrieved 15 May 2025).

Bjola, C. & Kornprobst, M. (2024). Digital International Relations: Technology, Agency and Order. Oxford University Press.

Bourbeau, P. (2015). "Resilience and international politics: Premises, debates, agenda", International Studies Review, 17(3), pp. 374–395. https://www.jstor.org/stable/24758620 (Retrieved 21 May 2025).

Bradford, A. (2012). The Brussels effect. *Northwestern University Law Review, 107*(1), 1–67.

Bradford, A. (2020). *The Brussels effect: How the European Union rules the world*. Oxford University Press.

Bradford, A. (2023). Digital Empires: The Global Battle to Regulate Technology. Oxford University Press.

NATO CCDCOE. (2023). "Mission and activities". NATO Cooperative Cyber Defence Centre of Excellence. https://ccdcoe.org/ (Retrieved 15 May 2025).

Celeste, E., Heldt, A., & Iglesias Keller, C. (2022). Introduction. In E. Celeste, A. Heldt, & C. Iglesias Keller (Eds.), *Constitutionalising social media*. Edward Elgar.

Chun, J., Schroeder de Witt, C. and Elkins, K. (2024). "Comparative global AI regulation: Policy perspectives from the EU, China, and the US". arXiv. https://arxiv.org/abs/2410.21279 (Retrieved May 11, 2025).

CISA. (2020). "Ransomware and COVID-19: Protecting healthcare and critical infrastructure". Cybersecurity and Infrastructure Security Agency. https://www.cisa.gov/news-events/news/ransomware-and-covid-19-protecting-healthcare-and-critical-infrastructure (Retrieved 15 May 2025).

CISA. (2021). "About CISA". *Cybersecurity and Infrastructure Security Agency*. https://www.cisa.gov/about-cisa (Retrieved 15 May 2025).

Council of the European Union. (2025). "Path to the Digital Decade: The EU's Plan to Achieve a Digital Europe by 2030", 5 February. https://www.consilium.europa.eu/en/policies/digital-transition/ (Retrieved 15 May 2025).

Creemers, R. (2016). Cyber China: Upgrading propaganda, public opinion work and social Management for the Twenty-First Century. *Journal of Contemporary China, 26*(103), 85–100.

Cyber Command, U. S. (2020). USCYBERCOM Mission and vision. In *U.S. Department of Defense*. https://www.cybercom.mil/About/ (Accessed May 15, 2025).

De Carvajal, P. (2023). "Open Strategic Autonomy: For a Digital, Green and Competitive Europe." *Telefónica*. 15 Mayıs. https://www.telefonica.com/en/communication-room/blog/open-strategic-autonomy-for-a-digital-green-and-competitive-europe/ (Accessed 15 May 2025).

DiploFoundation. (2023). "The geopolitics of digital standards: China's role in standard-setting organisations", Diplo Resource. https://www.diplomacy.edu/resource/geopolitics-digital-standards-chinas-role-standard-setting-organisations (Retrieved May 15, 2025).

Directive (EU). (2022). "2022/2555 of the European Parliament and of the Council on Measures for a High Common Level of Cybersecurity Across the Union (NIS2 Directive)". https://eur-lex.europa.eu/legal-content/EN/TXT/?uri=CELEX%3A32022L2555 (Retrieved May 15, 2025).

Dutch Government (2023a). "The Future of EU's Digital Decade: A Look at Open Strategic Autonomy in the Cloud and Beyond". https://www.globsec.org/sites/default/files/2024-09/The%20Future%20of%20EU%E2%80%99s%20Digital%20Decade%20-%20A%20Look%20at%20Open%20Strategic%20Autonomy%20in%20the%20Cloud%20and%20Beyond.pdf (Retrieved 15 May 2025).

Dutch Government (2023b). Letter on government policy on strategic dependencies, 12 May. https://www.government.nl/binaries/government/documenten/parliamentary-documents/2023/05/12/letter-on-the-governments-policy-on-strategic-dependencies/Letter+on+government+policy+on+strategic+dependencies.pdf (Retrieved June 7, 2025).

European Union Agency for Cybersecurity. (2023). "Annual report and technical guidelines". European Union Agency for Cybersecurity. https://www.enisa.europa.eu/publications (Retrieved May 15, 2025).

Estonian Ministry of Defence. (2020). "Role of CCDCOE in NATO Cyber defence". Estonian Ministry of Defence. https://www.kaitseministeerium.ee/en (Retrieved May 15, 2025).

European Central Bank. (2025). "Empowering Europe: Boosting Strategic Autonomy Through the Digital Euro," 8 April. https://www.ecb.europa.eu/press/key/date/2025/html/ecb.sp250408~40820747ef.en.html (Retrieved 15 May 2025).

European Commission. (2020a). "A European strategy for data", COM(2020) 66 final. European Commission. Available: https://eur-lex.europa.eu/legal-content/EN/TXT/?uri=celex:52020DC0066 (Retrieved May 5, 2025).

European Commission. (2020b). "EU Cybersecurity Strategy for the Digital Decade." 16 December. https://digital-strategy.ec.europa.eu/en/library/cybersecurity-strategy-digital-decade (Retrieved May 15, 2025).

European Commission. (2020c). The EU'S cybersecurity strategy for the digital decade. *Joint Communication JOIN (2020)18 final*. https://eur-lex.europa.eu/legal-content/EN/TXT/?uri=CELEX:52020JC0018 (Retrieved May 15, 2025

European Commission. (2022). "The Future of EU's Digital Decade: A Look at Open Strategic Autonomy." https://digital-strategy.ec.europa.eu/en/library/future-eus-digital-decade-look-open-strategic-autonomy (Retrieved May 15, 2025).

European Commission. (2024). "Cloud computing|shaping Europe's digital future", digital-strategy.ec.europa.eu, 1 March. https://digital-strategy.ec.europa.eu/en/policies/cloud-computing (Retrieved May 11, 2025).

European Council on Foreign Relations. (2021). "In Search of Digital Sovereignty: European Perspectives". https://ecfr.eu/publication/in-search-of-digital-sovereignty-european-perspectives/ (Retrieved May 11, 2025).

European Union Agency for Cybersecurity (2025) *European Union Agency for Cybersecurity (ENISA).* https://european-union.europa.eu/institutions-law-budget/institutions-and-bodies/search-all-eu-institutions-and-bodies/european-union-agency-cybersecurity-enisa_en (Retrieved June 7, 2025).

Farrell, H., & Newman, A. L. (2019). Weaponized interdependence: How global economic networks shape state coercion. *International Security, 44*(1), 42–79.

Feakin, T. (2024). "Navigating the New Geopolitics of Tech", *Harvard Business Review,* 11 November. https://hbr.org/2024/11/navigating-the-new-geopolitics-of-tech (Retrieved May 11, 2025).

Finnish Security Committee. (2022). "Societal Resilience and Cybersecurity in Finland". https://www.suomi.fi/en/societal-resilience (Retrieved May 15, 2025).

Fowle, H. (2025). "How will AI impact the semiconductor supply chain in 2025?". ProcurementPro. 8 April. https://procurementpro.com/how-will-ai-impact-the-semiconductor-supply-chain-in-2025/ (Retrieved May 15, 2025).

French Ministry of Defence. (2019). "France's Cyber Defence Strategy". https://www.defense.gouv.fr/english/cyberdefence (Retrieved May 15, 2025).

GFCE. (2023). "About the Global Forum on Cyber Expertise". https://thegfce.org/about/ (Retrieved May 15, 2025).

Gori, P. (2023). Cyber resilience in the era of systemic rivalry. *Journal of Strategic Security, 16*(1), 45–61.

Government of India. (2023a). "Production Linked Incentive (PLI) Scheme for Electronics Manufacturing". https://dpiit.gov.in/production-linked-incentive-pli-scheme (Retrieved May 15, 2025).

Government of India. (2023b). "The Digital Personal Data Protection Act 2023". https://www.meity.gov.in/ (Accessed 5 May 2025).

Greenberg, A. (2018). *Sandworm: A new era of cyberwar and the hunt for the kremlin's Most dangerous hackers*. Doubleday.

GSMA. (2022). "Open RAN: The Future of Mobile Networks". https://www.gsma.com/futurenetworks/openran/ (Retrieved May 15, 2025).

Gulyaeva, N., Sedykh, M. and Cohen, B. (2015). "Russia changes effective date of data localization law to September 2015". Hogan Lovells. 2 January. https://www.hoganlovells.com/en/publications/russia-changes-effective-date-of-data-localization-law-to-september-2015 (Retrieved May 11, 2025).

Harrell, P. (2025). "Managing the risks of China's access to U.S. data and control of software and connected technology", Carnegie Endowment for International Peace, 30 January. https://carnegieendowment.org/research/2025/01/managing-the-risks-of-chinas-access-to-us-data-and-control-of-software-and-connected-technology?lang=en (Retrieved May 11, 2025).

Healey, J. (2013). A fierce domain: Conflict in cyberspace, 1986 to 2012. Cyber Conflict Studies Association.

Hogeveen, B. (2022). *The UN norms of responsible state behaviour in cyberspace: Guidance on implementation for member states of ASEAN*. Australian Strategic Policy Institute. March. https://documents.unoda.org/wp-content/uploads/2022/03/The-UN-norms-of-responsible-state-behaviour-in-cyberspace.pdf (Retrieved June 7, 2025

Hollnagel, E., Pariès, J., Woods, D. D., & Wreathall, J. (2011). *Resilience engineering in practice: A guidebook*. Ashgate.

Holmgren, M. (2022). Autonomy through digital resilience: The importance of upholding the National Tech Stack. FIIA briefing paper 341, June. Finnish Institute of International Affairs. https://www.fiia.fi/en/publication/autonomy-through-digital-resilience (Retrieved May 10, 2025).

IEEE Standards Association. (2025). "Data sovereignty and trusted online identity". IEEE SA.. https://standards.ieee.org/industry-connections/digital-identity.html (Retrieved May 11, 2025).

INTERPOL (2022) Submission by INTERPOL to the Open-Ended Working Group on Security of and in the Use of Information and Communications Technologies—May 2022. https://documents.unoda.org/wp-content/uploads/2022/05/INTERPOL-Submission-to-OEWG-ICTs-2022.pdf (Retrieved 7 June 2025).

INTERPOL. (2023). "Cybercrime and Law Enforcement Cooperation". https://www.interpol.int/en/Crimes/Cybercrime (Retrieved 15 May 2025).

ISAC Council. (2020). "Overview and role in cybersecurity". Information Sharing and Analysis Centers.. https://www.isaccouncil.org/ (Retrieved 15 May 2025).

Japan Cabinet Secretariat. (2021). "Japan's Cybersecurity Strategy and Whole-of-Society Approach". https://www.cas.go.jp/jp/seisaku/cybersecurity/strategy.html (Retrieved 15 May 2025).

Kello, L. (2017). *The virtual weapon and international order*. Yale University Press.

King, A. (2025). *Urban warfare in the twenty-first century* (2nd ed.). Polity Press.

Kroet, C. (2024). "Eleven EU countries took 5G security measures to ban Huawei, ZTE", Euronews, 12 August. https://www.euronews.com/next/2024/08/12/eleven-eu-countries-took-5g-security-measures-to-ban-huawei-zte (Retrieved May 11, 2025).

Kurbalija, J. (2022). "Digital Governance and Diplomacy 2025: A Cheat Sheet", *DiploFoundation,* 19 March. (Updated 19 March 2024). https://www.diplomacy.edu/blog/digital-governance-and-diplomacy-2025-a-cheat-sheet/ (Retrieved May 11, 2025).

Kusters, J., Bhattacharjee, D., Bish, J., Nicholas, J. T., Stewart, D., and Ramachandran, K. (2025). "2025 global semiconductor industry outlook". Deloitte Insights, 4 February. https://www2.deloitte.com/us/en/insights/industry/technology/technology-media-telecom-outlooks/semiconductor-industry-outlook.html (Retrieved May 15, 2025).

Larsen, B. C. (2022). "The Geopolitics of AI and the Rise of Digital Sovereignty", Brookings Institution. 8 December. https://www.brookings.edu/articles/the-geopolitics-of-ai-and-the-rise-of-digital-sovereignty/(Accessed 11 May 2025).

Leal, E., Wright-Hamor, C., Manzano, J., Multari, N., Barker, K., Manz, D. and Ming, J. (2023). "Assessing risk in high performance computing attacks". SciTePress. https://www.scitepress.org/Papers/2023/119005/119005.pdf (Retrieved May 11, 2025).

Lewis, J. A. (2018). "Cybersecurity and National Security: Risks and responses". Center for Strategic and International Studies. https://www.csis.org/ (Retrieved May 15, 2025).

Lewis, J. A. (2021). "Cybersecurity and the COVID-19 Pandemic: Risks and Responses". Center for Strategic and International Studies. https://www.csis.org/ (Accessed 15 May 2025).

Lindsay, J. R. (2015). Stuxnet and the limits of Cyber warfare. *Security Studies., 22*(3), 365–404.

McDonald, J. (2020). "Huawei 5G Debate Causes Rift Between Western Powers." The Diplomat. 19 February. https://thediplomat.com/2020/02/huawei-5g-debate-causes-rift-between-western-powers/ (Accessed May 11, 2025).

Miller, C. (2022). *Chip war: The fight for the world's Most critical technology.* Scribner.

Ministère de l'Europe et des Affaires étrangères. (2021). French position on international law applied to cyberspace. Ministère de l'Europe et des Affaires étrangères. https://documents.unoda.org/wp-content/uploads/2021/12/French-position-on-international-law-applied-to-cyberspace.pdf (Retrieved June 7, 2025).

Ministère des Armées. (2019). Droit international appliqué aux opérations dans le cyberespace. Ministère des Armées. https://www.defense.gouv.fr/sites/default/files/ministere-armees/Droit%20international%20appliqu%C3%A9%20aux%20op%C3%A9rations%20dans%20le%20cyberespace.pdf (Retrieved June 7, 2025).

Ministry of Foreign Affairs and International Cooperation. (2021). Italian position paper on international law and cyberspace. Ministry of Foreign Affairs and International Cooperation. https://www.esteri.it/mae/resource/doc/2021/11/italian_position_paper_on_international_law_and_cyberspace.pdf (Retrieved June 7, 2025).

Musoni, M. (2023). "Unpacking Digital Sovereignty Through Data Governance", Global Approaches to Digital Sovereignty: Competing Definitions and Contrasting Policy Implications, Discussion Paper 344, Chapter 1. *ECDPM.* https://ecdpm.org/application/files/3316/8474/8387/Chapter-1-global-approaches-digital-sovereignty-competing-definitions-contrasting-policy-ECDPM-Discussion-Paper-344-2023.pdf (Retrieved May 11, 2025).

Nakashima, E. and Warrick, J. (2017). "Russian government hackers penetrated DNC, stole opposition research on trump", The Washington Post, 13 June. https://www.washingtonpost.com/ (Retrieved May 15, 2025).

National Health Service. (2017). *Report on the WannaCry ransomware attack impact*. https://www.england.nhs.uk/ (Retrieved May 15, 2025).

NATO. (2016). "Warsaw summit communique: Cyberspace as a domain of operations", NATO Press Release, 9 July. https://www.nato.int/cps/en/natohq/news_133163.htm (Retrieved May 15, 2025).

NATO. (2019). "Cyber Defence". https://www.nato.int/cps/en/natohq/topics_78170.htm (Retrieved May 15, 2025).

NATO. (2021). "Cyber Resilience and Military Readiness". https://www.nato.int/docu/review/articles/2021/ (Retrieved May 15, 2025).

NATO CCDCOE. (2023). "Locked shields exercise and incident response capabilities". NATO Cooperative Cyber Defence Centre of Excellence. https://ccdcoe.org/exercises/locked-shields/ (Retrieved 15 May 2025).

NATO CCDCOE. (2025) *NATO Cooperative Cyber Defence Centre of Excellence.* https://ccdcoe.org/ (Retrieved June 7, 2025).

NIST. (2018) "Framework for Improving Critical Infrastructure Cybersecurity". https://www.nist.gov/cyberframework (Retrieved May 15, 2025).

OECD. (2019a). Responsible Innovation. OECD., https://www.oecd.org/innovation/responsible-innovation/ (Accessed May 2025).

Open Source Initiative. (2023). "Open Source Software and National Security". https://opensource.org/blog/open-source-software-and-national-security (Retrieved May 15, 2025).

OECD. (2019b). "Digital Security and Resilience in Critical Infrastructure and Essential Services". April. No. 281. https://www.oecd.org/content/dam/oecd/en/publications/reports/2019/04/digital-security-and-resilience-in-critical-infrastructure-and-essential-services_5593c149/a7097901-en.pdf (Retrieved May 11, 2025).

Rid, T. (2013). Cyber war will not take place. *Journal of Strategic Studies, 35*(1), 5–32.

Rid, T. (2020). *Active measures: The secret history of disinformation and political warfare*. Farrar, Straus and Giroux.

Roberts, H., Cowls, J., Casolari, F., Morley, J., Taddeo, M and Floridi, L., (2021). "Safeguarding European Values with Digital Sovereignty: An Analysis of Statements and Policies." Policy Review. 30 September. https://policyreview.info/articles/analysis/safeguarding-european-values-digital-sovereignty-analysis-statements-and-policies (Retrieved May 11, 2025).

Roscini, M. (2015). "Cyber operations as a use of force", in Tsagourias, N. and Buchan, R. (eds.) Research handbook on international law and cyberspace. Edward Elgar Publishing, pp. 233–254. https://ssrn.com/abstract=2631078 (Retrieved June 7, 2025).

Roulette, J. (2023). "SpaceX curbed Ukraine's use of Starlink internet for drones - company president". Reuters. 9 February. https://www.reuters.com/business/aerospace-defense/spacex-curbed-ukraines-use-starlink-internet-drones-company-president-2023-02-09/ (Retrieved May 12, 2025).

Routley, N. (2020) "Wired world: 35 years of submarine cables in one map". Visual Capitalist, 22 December. https://www.visualcapitalist.com/wired-world-35-years-of-submarine-cables-in-one-map/ (Retrieved May 12, 2025).

ASEAN Secretariat. (2024). "Towards a Resilient Digital ASEAN: Regional Cloud and Satellite Infrastructure Initiatives". https://asean.org/digital-asean/ (Retrieved May 15, 2025).

Segal, A. (2018). *The hacked world order: How nations fight, trade, Maneuver, and manipulate in the digital age*. PublicAffairs.

Semiconductor Industry Association/BCG. (2021) "Strengthening the Global Semiconductor Supply Chain in an Uncertain Era", 11 May. https://www.semiconductors.org/strengthening-the-global-semiconductor-supply-chain-in-an-uncertain-era/ (Retrieved May 15, 2025).

Small Wars Journal. (2024). "Chip War and the Battle for Technological Sovereignty: A Hybrid Warfare Perspective." https://smallwarsjournal.com/jrnl/art/chip-war-and-battle-technological-sovereigntyhybrid-warfare-perspective (Accessed 11 May 2025).

Swanson, A. (2020) "U.S. moves to cut off Huawei's access to global Chip suppliers", The New York Times, 15 May. https://www.nytimes.com/2020/05/15/business/economy/commerce-department-huawei.html (Retrieved June 7, 2025).

Swinhoe, D. (2022). "Thales details French sovereign cloud joint venture with Google". Data Center Dynamics. https://www.datacenterdynamics.com/en/news/thales-details-french-sovereign-cloud-joint-venture-with-google/ (Retrieved May 11, 2025).

Synergy Inc. (2025). "Strengthening the Global Semiconductor Supply Chain: Challenges and Opportunities in 2025." 19 February. https://synergy-inc.com/strengthening-the-global-semiconductor-supply-chain-challenges-and-opportunities-in-2025/ (Accessed May 15, 2025).

U.S. Department of Defense. (2018). "Persistent Engagement and Cyber Strategy." https://media.defense.gov/2018/Sep/18/2002041659/-1/-1/1/CYBER_STRATEGY_SUMMARY_FINAL.PDF (Accessed May 15, 2025).

UK Government. (2021). "Telecoms Diversification Strategy." https://www.gov.uk/government/publications/telecoms-diversification-strategy (Retrieved May 15, 2025).

European Union. (2025). "The comeback is on: How the EU plans to reclaim digital sovereignty". CMS Law-Now. 29 April. https://cms-lawnow.com/en/ealerts/2025/04/the-comeback-is-on-how-the-eu-plans-to-reclaim-digital-sovereignty (Retrieved May 11, 2025).

United Nations. (1945). Charter of the United Nations. San Francisco, CA: United Nations. https://www.un.org/en/about-us/un-charter (Accessed 4 May 2025).

United Nations General Assembly. (2013). *Report of the Group of Governmental Experts on Developments in the Field of Information and Telecommunications in the Context of International Security*, A/68/98. 24 June. https://undocs.org/A/68/98 (Retrieved June 7, 2025).

U.S. Department of Commerce. (2023). "EU-US Trade and Technology Council: Semiconductor Supply Chain Cooperation." https://www.commerce.gov/news/press-releases/2023/03/eu-us-trade-and-technology-council-semiconductor-supply-chain-cooperation (Retrieved May 15, 2025).

USGS. (2023). "Rare earth elements: Critical to green technologies." United States Geological Survey. https://www.usgs.gov/centers/national-minerals-information-center/rare-earths-statistics-and-information (Retrieved May 15, 2025).

UST. (2025). "Securing telecom networks: A comprehensive cybersecurity strategy for the digital age." UST Insights, 14 April. https://www.ust.com/en/insights/securing-telecom-networks-a-comprehensive-cybersecurity-strategy-for-the-digital-age (Retrieved May 11, 2025).

Vogiatzoglou, P. (2025). The EU's Quest for Digital Sovereignty: A Matter of Quantum Innovation? *Digital Society, 4* (1), p.16. https://doi.org/10.1007/s44206-025-00162-1

Wilcox, O. (2021). "Visualizing the global digital divide". DT Global. 4 March. https://dt-global.com/blog/visualizing-digital-divide/ (Retrieved May 12, 2025).

World Economic Forum. (2023). "What Is Digital Sovereignty and How Are Countries Approaching It?". 20 March. https://www.weforum.org/agenda/2023/03/digital-sovereignty-how-countries-are-approaching-it/ (Accessed 15 May 2025).

Zhou, L. (2022). "Norm diffusion in Cyber governance: China as an emerging norm entrepreneur." International Affairs, 100(6), pp. 1557–1574. https://academic.oup.com/ia/article/100/6/1557/6853837 (Retrieved May 11, 2025).

PART IV

Conquering the Technopolar World: "Cognitive Diplomacy"

CHAPTER 10

The Mind of the State: Defining Cognitive Diplomacy

In 2025, we inhabit a hyperconnected world shaped not only by algorithms, semiconductors, chips, and dig data, but also by the uneven flows of information, infrastructure, and agency. Much like Immanuel Kant's (1795) early vision of the world system, structured through relations of hierarchy and dependence, contemporary technopolarity is defined by renewed center-periphery dynamics. The technological "core" consists of states and corporate actors who dominate the development of artificial intelligence, cutting-edge digital technologies, and semiconductor production. These actors control technological capabilities and increasingly dictate the global regulatory environment governing AI and digital innovation (Akıllı, 2025). In contrast, peripheral states find themselves structurally dependent, often compelled to adopt regulatory frameworks and technological standards designed by the core, thereby reinforcing power asymmetries (Nye, 2011; Wu, 2018).

This book defines the conundrum as *digital asymmetry:* a structural reality where the capacity to gather, process, and govern digital systems is concentrated in a handful of technologically dominant actors, keeping the majority dependent, vulnerable, and peripheral. In this fractured order, sovereignty itself is being redefined. It is no longer solely the control of territory, but the ability to act with *digital autonomy,* the power to make sovereign decisions over data, algorithms, and infrastructures without coercion or compromise.

E. Akıllı, *Cognitive Diplomacy and Digital Autonomy*,
https://doi.org/10.1007/978-3-032-04470-9_10

In this world of digitalized automation, sovereignty flickers like a dim light in the thickening fog of *technopolarity*. That fog deepens with every advancement that entrenches dependency and disempowers the digitally marginalized. Diplomacy, too, has transformed. No longer confined to embassies, summits, or traditional legal instruments, it now unfolds across social media platforms, digital ecosystems, and increasingly, neurocognitive interfaces. The diplomatic terrain has shifted from geography to cognition, from negotiation tables to algorithmic timelines.

The international system is now operating within a new diplomatic arena, where influence is no longer exercised exclusively through policy, institutions, or narrative control, but through the deeper architecture of *perception*, *belief*, and *cognitive framing*. In this emerging environment, where AI, platform dynamics, and attention economies condition how societies understand reality, *cognitive diplomacy* becomes essential. It is not merely a toolkit; rather, it is a strategic response to the vulnerabilities exposed by digital asymmetry and a crucial vehicle for achieving *digital autonomy*.

This part of the book introduces *cognitive diplomacy* as a new model of statecraft, tailored to the informational and psychological complexity of the digital era. Where classical diplomacy rests on negotiation and public diplomacy harnesses narrative and culture, cognitive diplomacy engages the epistemic core of international relations: how knowledge is created, circulated, and internalized. It targets the cognitive infrastructures that underpin political agency, legitimacy, and consent. In this domain, the state is no longer only a geopolitical actor; it becomes a *cognitive agent*, one that engages in mental cartography, shaping and safeguarding the informational and emotional environments where international relations unfold. It is, in essence, a *diplomacy of the mind*, but augmented with cutting-edge technologies and AI.

As argued in the previous chapters, the international system is undergoing a profound change. Technopolarity now defines the global order: technological supremacy, not military size or economic volume, increasingly determines strategic leverage. Hyperconnectivity, exponential data production, and algorithmic mediation of public consciousness are no longer anomalies; contrary, they are the norms. In this context, AI functions as a dual-use capability. On one side, it multiplies the power of disinformation, autonomous weapons, and influence operations. On the other, if responsibly governed, AI can enable states to enhance strategic foresight, strengthen crisis response, and project normative leadership across digital domains.

It is precisely within this tension that *cognitive diplomacy* finds its purpose. It enables the fusion of human judgment with machine learning, creating a hybrid capability that empowers foreign policy decision-makers to think, act, and influence more effectively in contested cognitive environments. It offers a pathway to resist growing pressures and negotiate agency within the international system increasingly shaped by digital hierarchies. By fostering the integration of human and machine intelligence in diplomatic practice, *Cognitive Diplomacy* equips states with the necessary tools to enhance strategic presence, optimize decision-making, and assert normative preferences in global governance fora. In this sense, digital autonomy becomes the last resort and ultimate safeguard of sovereignty. Within this paradigm, Cognitive Diplomacy functions as the sword of agency in cyber-anarchic world order, empowering states to defend and advance their interests amid accelerating technological disruption. Thus, Cognitive Diplomacy encapsulates the capacity of states to autonomously govern the intersection of human and artificial intelligence in decision-making, diplomacy, and strategic communication. It reflects the ambition not merely to control infrastructure and data, but to preserve epistemic and strategic autonomy in a global order, increasingly mediated by AI-driven systems. Therefore, if implemented effectively, as outlined in this book, Cognitive Diplomacy has the potential to become a foundational pillar of statecraft in the age of technopolarity. In other words, it enhances *presence* by positioning states within digital attention ecosystems. It refines *practice* by allowing real-time, context-sensitive engagement. And most importantly, it reinforces *resilience* by helping states construct sovereign cognitive infrastructures, essential for protecting autonomy in the face of systemic disruption and shocks.

Cognitive diplomacy is not an abstract metaphor. It is a strategic necessity in the architecture of twenty-first-century power. It is also a central pillar in the pursuit of *digital autonomy,* the grand goal of this book. What follows in this part is a conceptual and operational exploration of cognitive diplomacy's foundations, its mechanisms, and transformative implications for international relations. This part presents in depth the Cognitive Diplomacy Model, positioning it within the broader dynamics of the technopolar world order and anchoring it in established international relations theories. Framed as a direct response to the structural challenge of digital asymmetry, Cognitive Diplomacy equips states with the cognitive capacities, institutional reflexes, and strategic foresight necessary to counterbalance informational imbalances, reclaim agency in algorithmic environments, and reassert sovereignty in a data-driven age.

Building on the foundations of digital autonomy detailed earlier, this framework adopts the same tripartite structure—*Presence, Practice*, and *Resilience*—culminating in Digital Autonomy as its normative objective. It is illustrated with real-world examples from across the globe, including the United States, Germany, Estonia, Ukraine, China, and a diverse range of states in the Global South. In doing so, it illustrates how AI-enabled tools are already being applied in areas like disinformation defense, conflict prevention, negotiation, strategic communications, and public diplomacy. The part also grapples with the ethical dilemmas and strategic risks of augmenting diplomatic cognition with AI, such as algorithmic bias, accountability gaps, erosion of sovereignty, and transparency challenges. It analyzes how foreign ministries are adapting institutionally—creating new roles like digital *attachés*, data strategy development, and interagency innovation through training—to build capacity for cognitive diplomacy. The part concludes with concrete policy recommendations for states to implement cognitive diplomacy in pursuit of digital autonomy and to maintain agency in an era of technopolarity and digital asymmetry.

Bibliography

Akıllı, E. (2025). "Rewiring Diplomacy in the Technopolar World," *Daily Sabah*, April 18. (Retrieved from 21 May 2025) https://www.dailysabah.com/opinion/op-ed/rewiring-diplomacy-in-the-technopolar-world

Kant, I. (1795). *Zum ewigen Frieden: Ein philosophischer Entwurf*. Friedrich Nicolovius.

Nye, J.S. (2011). The Future of Power. New York: PublicAffairs.

Wu, T. (2018). The Curse of Bigness: Antitrust in the New Gilded Age. New York: Columbia Global Reports.

CHAPTER 11

Theoretical Foundations of Cognitive Diplomacy

As defined in this book, *cognitive diplomacy* is a diplomatic approach that deliberately integrates human cognition and AI to enhance decision-making, communication, and negotiation in international relations. It is premised on the idea that human diplomats endowed with contextual understanding, ethical judgment, and creative problem-solving, can significantly amplify their effectiveness by partnering with AI systems capable of superior data processing, pattern recognition, and predictive analytics.

In practical terms, cognitive diplomacy involves the use of AI tools—ranging from machine learning algorithms to natural language processing and cognitive computing—across all levels of diplomatic work. These tools assist with gathering and analyzing information, formulating policy options, executing negotiations, and running public diplomacy campaigns. Crucially, this model is augmentative rather than substitutive: AI is employed to inform and support human judgment, not to replace it. As a Deloitte study on modernizing statecraft notes, AI is not a universal remedy, nor can it substitute the expertise, intuition, and critical judgment of seasoned professionals. However, when thoughtfully and strategically integrated, AI has the potential to enhance the effectiveness, agility, and innovative capacity of diplomats and practitioners in international affairs (Deloitte., 2022: 12).

E. Akıllı, *Cognitive Diplomacy and Digital Autonomy*,
https://doi.org/10.1007/978-3-032-04470-9_11

Cognitive diplomacy thus seeks to marry the strengths of human and machine intelligence in the service of diplomatic objectives. The concept was introduced earlier in this book as a response to the dual pressures of information overload and decision complexity in modern diplomacy. Today's diplomats operate in a world where vast quantities of data, from satellite imagery and cybersecurity alerts to online sentiment may be relevant to foreign policy. Simultaneously, adversaries are increasingly deploying AI for disinformation, deepfakes, and cyber operations, outpacing the analytical capacities of traditional foreign ministries.

Cognitive diplomacy posits that by equipping diplomatic services with AI-enhanced cognitive tools, states can achieve a form of digital autonomy the ability to process information, formulate strategies, and act without over-reliance on foreign technological infrastructures or corporate platforms. This aligns with the broader global push for technological sovereignty, which has become a central pillar in national strategies, from the European Union to Türkiye (Akıllı, 2025a; Akıllı, 2025b; NATO, 2025).

Importantly, cognitive diplomacy is not solely concerned with data analytics or situational awareness. It also encompasses the communicative and representational functions of diplomacy. AI-powered language translation and content generation tools enable real-time multilingual engagement with foreign publics, while virtual assistants and chatbots enhance consular services by handling routine interactions. These applications extend the presence and accessibility of diplomatic actors, as elaborated in the presence pillar of this framework.

Equally, the practice of diplomacy must evolve. Workflows, institutional cultures, and diplomatic protocols must be adapted to integrate AI outputs in thoughtful, context-sensitive ways. Diplomats must be trained to use AI tools and critically interpret their recommendations to recognize both their value and their limitations, including issues such as algorithmic bias, contextual blind spots, or misaligned incentives.

Underpinning cognitive diplomacy is the recognition that twenty-first-century international politics has a deeply cognitive dimension. Influence and power are increasingly exercised not just through military or economic means but by shaping perceptions, beliefs, and decisions. Concepts such as "cognitive warfare" have entered strategic discourse to describe adversarial efforts aimed at distorting information environments and undermining decision-making processes. Cognitive Diplomacy represents the peaceful, statecraft-oriented response to this trend:

strengthening a state's own cognitive capabilities—both human and artificial—while defending against external manipulation.

In essence, cognitive diplomacy offers a strategic, ethical, and adaptive framework for AI-augmented statecraft. It is a model that seeks to preserve human agency while enhancing diplomatic effectiveness through the structured and responsible integration of artificial cognition. As such, it is best understood within the broader contours of the technopolar era—a new global condition, marked by technological rivalry, platform geopolitics, and the contestation of digital sovereignty.

11.1 Through the Looking Glass of IR Theories

Cognitive diplomacy is rooted in both international relations (IR) theory and cognitive science. In IR, the growing importance of information power and epistemic authority has been extensively examined, particularly in constructivist and post-structuralist traditions (Adler, 2004). The idea that "who controls meaning, controls outcomes" (Entman, 1993) is especially resonant today, as narratives compete across digital platforms and algorithmic spaces. At the same time, resilience theory in IR has underscored the importance of adaptive capacity, anticipatory governance, and institutional learning in enabling states to withstand and respond to shocks and crises (Bourbeau, 2015). AI significantly enhances these dimensions by enabling real-time data processing, probabilistic forecasting, and the iterative refinement of diplomatic strategies (Mostafaei et al., 2025).

To fully articulate the theoretical foundation of cognitive diplomacy, this chapter engages with the three dominant paradigms of IR—realism, liberalism, and constructivism—each offering a distinct lens on how AI transforms diplomacy. From realism's focus on power projection and strategic advantage to liberalism's emphasis on institutional cooperation and norm-setting, and constructivism's attention to identity, perception, and narrative, these perspectives collectively inform the strategic logic and normative potential of cognitive diplomacy in the age of AI.

From the perspective of cognitive science, AI represents a synthetic form of cognition. Machine learning, natural language processing (NLP), and pattern recognition are modeled on aspects of human cognition such as classification, prediction, and language understanding. Unlike human cognition, however, AI operates at scale and speed, ingesting and processing terabytes of data in seconds. In cognitive diplomacy, the interplay between these cognitive systems—human and artificial—is central. AI augments diplomats' ability to perceive global trends, simulate scenarios, and automate routine tasks (Mostafaei et al., 2025). However, AI also brings epistemic risks, such as biases in training data, lack of context awareness, and susceptibility to adversarial manipulation (Binns, 2018).

Realist Perspective: AI as a Strategic Asset in Power Competition

Realists prioritize power, competition, and national interest as the drivers of state behavior. From a realist standpoint, artificial intelligence represents not a neutral tool but a strategic arena for great power rivalry and a force multiplier in the pursuit of national advantage. Technological superiority in AI is viewed as conferring decisive leverage in military, economic, and diplomatic arenas. This logic is reflected in Russian President Vladimir Putin's oft-cited assertion that *"whoever becomes the leader in [AI] will become the ruler of the world"* (Vincent, 2017).

In practice, realists anticipate that AI will be harnessed to strengthen hard-power capabilities like enhancing military effectiveness, cyberdefense, intelligence gathering, and coercive economic instruments. The U.S.-China AI rivalry exemplifies a zero-sum framing of AI dominance (Winter-Levy, 2024), wherein falling behind could compromise a state's security and global standing (Allison, 2018). National AI strategies that emphasize global leadership—such as China's ambition to become the world's AI leader by 2030 and the United States' push to maintain technological superiority through R&D and talent acquisition—are underpinned by balance-of-power thinking (Cave & ÓhÉigeartaigh, 2018).

For diplomats operating under realist logic, cognitive diplomacy becomes a tool for advancing national interests and outmaneuvering adversaries. AI might be employed to detect deception during negotiations, automate threat monitoring, or project influence via algorithmically optimized propaganda. Realists are generally suspicious of broad international constraints on AI developments, such as global bans on autonomous weapons, viewing them as potential strategic liabilities (Gyulai & Ujlaki, 2021). Instead, they tend to favor bilateral or minilateral mechanisms that preserve asymmetrical advantages (Kania, 2017).

Concrete applications include using AI for strategic forecasting of adversary behavior, automating cyber deterrence systems, and enhancing surveillance to ensure treaty compliance. In extreme cases, a covert cognitive warfare doctrine may emerge, where AI is used to manipulate public perception in rival societies while shielding one's own (Hassanali, 2024). Overall, realism sees cognitive diplomacy as an instrument in the pursuit of relative gains where AI is harnessed to increase national leverage and mitigate vulnerability.

Liberal Perspective: AI as a Catalyst for Cooperation and Governance

In contrast, liberalism emphasizes cooperation, international institutions, and interdependence. Liberals view AI not solely as a source of competition but as a shared challenge and a global opportunity that necessitates collaborative governance. AI, like climate change or nuclear proliferation, has cross-border implications that no single state can manage. Hence, diplomatic efforts must aim to establish international norms, regimes, and safeguards to mitigate the risks of AI misuse and ensure alignment with collective human values (Floridi et al., 2018).

This perspective is evident in the formation of multilateral initiatives like the OECD's *Principles on Artificial Intelligence* (2019), which promote transparency, accountability, and human-centered values, and the Global Partnership on AI (GPAI), which convenes governments, academia, and industry to shape responsible AI development (OECD, 2024). At the global level, U.N. Secretary-General António Guterres has called for the creation of a global AI watchdog, modeled after the International Atomic Energy Agency (IAEA), to monitor and guide AI governance (Nichols, 2023).

From a liberal vantage point, cognitive diplomacy encompasses both the use of AI in support of diplomacy (e.g., crisis prediction, and humanitarian coordination) and diplomacy about AI (e.g., treaties and norms). AI-based forecasting models can offer early warning of conflict or climate-induced migration, enabling preemptive and collective action (Brundage et al., 2018). Diplomats may use simulations and scenario planning tools to identify mutually beneficial outcomes in negotiations, reflecting the liberal belief in positive-sum diplomacy.

Liberals also emphasize institutional and normative accountability: AI used in diplomacy should be subject to democratic oversight, privacy safeguards, and legal compliance. Platforms like the U.S.-EU Trade and

Technology Council (TTC) exemplify this approach, with diplomats and technologists working together to align AI regulatory frameworks across jurisdictions (European Commission XE "European Commission", 2023). A liberal cognitive diplomacy therefore seeks to embed AI within networks of trust and institutions, treating AI not as a source of unilateral advantage, but as a global public good.

Constructivist Perspective: AI, Identity, and Norm Entrepreneurship in Diplomacy

Constructivism emphasizes the role of ideas, identities, and social norms in shaping international outcomes. In contrast to realist assumptions of material power or liberalist focus on institutional design, a constructivist view of AI in statecraft asks a different set of questions: *What do states believe about AI? How do they narrate their role in diplomacy? How does AI reshape the culture and practice of diplomacy itself?*

A constructivist lens offers critical conceptual reinforcement for the cognitive turn in diplomacy. As Alexander Wendt famously argued, *"anarchy is what states make of it"*; a notion that underscores how international structures are socially constructed through shared ideas, norms, and identities rather than dictated solely by material power (Wendt, 1992). In this view, the diplomatic arena is not just a battleground of interests but a dynamic discursive space where meaning is continuously negotiated. AI technologies participate in this social construction by encoding, amplifying, and even generating norms that shape how states perceive threats, opportunities, and each other. This aligns with the epistemological core of constructivism, where language, interpretation, and collective intentionality are seen as foundational to global politics (Ndzendze & Marwala, 2023).

The implications for cognitive diplomacy are profound. AI systems are not neutral instruments, they are embedded within and constitutive of the ideational structures they analyze. As such, they risk reinforcing dominant epistemologies while marginalizing non-Western perspectives, thus deepening asymmetries in global norm production. Moreover, AI-driven diplomatic tools such as automated translation, large language models, predictive analytics, or digital norm diffusion can reflect what Ndzendze and Marwala (2023) describe as a shift in epistemic authority from human diplomats to algorithmic agents.

One of the central insights of constructivism is that technologies are not neutral. They are interpreted and deployed in ways that reflect national values, strategic cultures, and normative preferences (Wendt, 1999). For instance, democratic societies tend to frame AI in terms of ethical governance, transparency, and human rights. This orientation shapes their diplomatic messaging and regulatory frameworks. A notable example is the European Union's forthcoming AI Act, which bans certain high-risk AI applications and mandates extensive risk assessments. Rooted in the EU's identity as a community committed to human dignity and data privacy, the legislation projects a normative stance globally, aligning with its broader aspiration to be a "normative power" in digital governance (European Commission, 2025; European Commission, 2023; Floridi et al., 2018).

Conversely, some states, while often adopting the rhetoric of beneficial AI, tend to emphasize control, order, and regime stability. Chinese foreign policy discourse illustrates this divergence. As Foreign Minister Wang Yi noted, China promotes "safe and controllable AI" that remains "under human control" and serves "the people" (Ministry of Foreign Affairs of the People's Republic of China, 2024). This normative framing reflects a preference for state oversight and positions AI as an instrument of social cohesion rather than individual empowerment. In a sense, it responds to Wendt's famous question; *"what is anarchy? It is what states make of it,"* but this time, applied not to anarchy, but to AI itself.

AI, like anarchy, is not inherently one thing, it becomes what states choose to construct it as within their normative and institutional frameworks. As the constructivist approach suggests, AI can be harnessed in a way that reflects and reinforces a state's identity, interests, and social purpose within the international system. Far from being a neutral tool, AI technologies such as diplomatic chatbots, natural language processing (NLP) tools for multilingual communication, predictive analytics for crisis detection, and autonomous data systems for real-time policy feedback are increasingly embedded in how states represent themselves and interact with others.

Moreover, large language models (LLMs), such as GPT-based systems, are emerging as powerful tools for narrative dissemination and strategic communication. These models enable states to craft, replicate, and circulate values-aligned messages across digital platforms at scale, thereby shaping international discourse and influencing global opinion. Such tools not only serve practical functions but also symbolically project a state's values, whether they're transparency, efficiency, surveillance, or solidarity, into the global arena. In doing so, AI technologies function as extensions of state cognition, operationalizing the ideational and normative dimensions of diplomacy. These competing visions are manifested in diplomatic practice. For example, China's Digital Silk Road exports AI surveillance systems and facial recognition platforms as tools for development and public order to the global south. (Feldstein, 2019). In contrast, Western digital diplomacy increasingly uses AI for message targeting, real-time sentiment analysis, and promotion of liberal norms such as freedom of expression and open markets (Bjola & Pamment, 2021).

Constructivists would also argue that AI itself is reshaping the norms and practices of diplomacy. From the evolving etiquette of negotiations (e.g., AI-assisted mediation or algorithmic recommendation systems) to shifts in epistemic authority (e.g., AI-generated briefings replacing human analysts), diplomatic cultures are adapting (Ndzendze & Marwala, 2023). New terminologies—such as "algorithmic governance," "hagglebots," and "cognitive warfare", reflect how actors reframe their identities and operational lexicons in response to AI-infused realities (Akıllı, 2025b).

States that embrace AI leadership as part of their national identity construction, often enjoy reputational benefits. Countries like Estonia and Singapore have positioned themselves as "digital pioneers," integrating AI into public services and diplomacy while shaping regional and international tech norms. This identity-building enhances their soft power, enabling small or mid-sized states to punch above their weight in global digital governance (Kello, 2017).

Constructivist analysis of cognitive diplomacy also emphasizes norm entrepreneurship, the active shaping of global AI norms through diplomacy. Forums such as UNESCO have become arenas for contesting and promoting normative frameworks. In 2021, UNESCO adopted the *Recommendation on the Ethics of Artificial Intelligence*, backed by countries like Türkiye, France, Canada, and Japan, which championed principles grounded in human rights, fairness, and inclusion (UNESCO, 2021). However, these norms are contested. China and Russia advocate for "cyber sovereignty," arguing that states should retain full control over internet governance and AI within their borders, countering Western ideals of a free and interoperable internet (Deibert, 2020).

Constructivists are particularly attuned to the ethical dilemmas (Mellon, 2009) that cognitive diplomacy must address: Is it legitimate for AI systems to profile foreign diplomats? Should autonomous systems participate in negotiations? What constitutes acceptable use of AI in information campaigns? These are not only technical questions, but deeply normative ones, where outcomes depend on shared understandings and negotiated norms.

In sum, a constructivist approach sees the success of cognitive diplomacy as contingent on how actors imagine, narrate, and normatively structure their use of AI. Outcomes depend not just on capabilities, but on meaning. For cognitive diplomacy to be effective and legitimate, it must be culturally sensitive, norm-aware, and rooted in shared values. What is viewed as innovation in one diplomatic culture may be seen as intrusion or manipulation in another, unless a common foundation of trust, transparency, and norm convergence is actively constructed.

Through cognitive diplomacy's lens, these three theoretical perspectives—realism, liberalism, and constructivism—are not mutually exclusive, rather they often coexist within the strategic behavior of states. For example, the U.S. demonstrates realist tendencies by framing AI leadership as a geopolitical imperative in its competition with China. It also shows liberal inclinations by working with allies to shape shared norms and invest in AI for development. Then it displays constructivist behavior by promoting global standards around "responsible AI" in international forums such as the OECD and GPAI. Similarly, China's statecraft reflects a realist pursuit of AI to enhance national power and security, a liberal dimension through selective participation in multilateral AI discussions (e.g., at the United Nations), and a constructivist narrative grounded in principles of sovereignty, order, and "AI for the people."

The cognitive diplomacy framework proposed in this part is designed to integrate these dimensions. It acknowledges the competitive dynamics of AI geopolitics—hence the emphasis on resilience. It identifies the cooperative possibilities of AI-enabled diplomacy—therefore prioritizing presence and sustained communicative engagement. It underscores the critical role of norms and values, which inform the ethical governance of AI and the need for principled practice.

Grounded in these theoretical insights, we now turn to the practical core of this part: the three pillars of cognitive diplomacy—presence, practice, and resilience. They align conceptually with the broader framework of digital autonomy, which identified the same triad as foundational to sovereign agency in the digital age. While digital autonomy emphasizes the structural conditions for independent decision-making control over data, algorithms, and digital infrastructure, cognitive diplomacy translates these principles into foreign policy action, focusing on how states project influence, engage with the global public, and adapt to cognitive and informational threats.

Each pillar in this cognitive framework encapsulates a distinct set of functions and objectives that AI-augmented diplomacy seeks to advance:

- *Cognitive Presence* involves the strategic use of AI to extend diplomatic visibility, engagement, and influence across diverse information environments.
- *Cognitive Practice* refers to the integration of AI into the workflows, tools, and cultures of diplomatic institutions.
- *Cognitive Resilience* centers on the capacity to withstand cognitive, informational, and cyber disruptions through adaptive, AI-enhanced mechanisms.

Together, they provide an operational architecture for cognitive diplomacy, illustrated throughout this chapter with real-world applications from across geopolitical contexts, including the United States, China, Estonia, Ukraine, and the global south.

Bibliography

Akıllı, E. (2025a). "Rewiring Diplomacy in the Technopolar World," *Daily Sabah,* April 18. Retrieved from: 21 May 2025 https://www.dailysabah.com/opinion/op-ed/rewiring-diplomacy-in-the-technopolar-world

Akıllı, E. (2025b). "Future of Diplomacy: CICERO, Hagglebots and the Turing Test," *Daily Sabah,* April 3. Retrieved from: 21 May 2025 https://www.dailysabah.com/opinion/op-ed/future-of-diplomacy-cicero-hagglebots-and-the-turing-test

Adler, E. (2004). *Communitarian international relations: The epistemic foundations of international relations* (1st ed.). Routledge.

Allison, G. (2018). "The great AI race: China vs. the United States," Harvard Kennedy School Belfer Center for Science and International Affairs. Retrieved from: 21 May 2025 https://www.belfercenter.org/publication/great-ai-race-china-vs-united-states

Binns, R. (2018). "Fairness in machine learning: Lessons from political philosophy," Proceedings of Machine Learning Research, 81, pp. 149–159. (Retrieved from: 21 May 2025) http://proceedings.mlr.press/v81/binns18a.html

Bjola, C., & Pamment, J. (2021). Countering online propaganda with AI: Challenges for digital diplomacy. *International Journal of Press/Politics, 26*(1), 1–23.

Bourbeau, P. (2015). "Resilience and international politics: Premises, debates, agenda," International Studies Review, 17(3), pp. 374–395. Retrieved from: 21 May 2025 https://www.jstor.org/stable/24758620

Brundage, M., Avin, S., Clark, J., Toner, H., Eckersley, P., Garfinkel, B., Dafoe, A., Scharre, P., Zeitzoff, T., Filar, B., Anderson, H., Roff, H., Allen, G.C., Steinhardt, J., Flynn, C., Ó hÉigeartaigh, S., Beard, S.J., Belfield, H., Farquhar, S., Lyle, C., Crootof, R., Evans, O., Page, M., Bryson, J., Yampolskiy, R., Amodei, D. (2018). "The malicious use of artificial intelligence: Forecasting, prevention, and mitigation". , University of Oxford. Retrieved from: 21 May 2025 https://arxiv.org/abs/1802.07228

Cave, S., & ÓhÉigeartaigh, S. (2018). An AI race for strategic advantage: Rhetoric and risks. In R. Yampolskiy (Ed.), *Artificial intelligence safety and security* (pp. 45–58). Chapman and Hall/CRC.

Deibert, R. (2020). *Reset: Reclaiming the internet for civil society*. House of Anansi Press.

Deloitte. (2022). "Using Artificial Intelligence to Modernize American Statecraft," *Deloitte AI Institute for Government* Retrieved from 21 May 2025 at: https://www2.deloitte.com/us/en/pages/public-sector/articles/using-artificial-intelligence-to-modernize-american-statecraft.html

Entman, R. M. (1993). Framing: Toward clarification of a fractured paradigm. *Journal of Communication, 43*(4), 51–58.

European Commission. (2023). "Digital in the EU-US Trade and Technology Council." Retrieved from: 21 May 2025 https://digital-strategy.ec.europa.eu/en/policies/trade-and-technology-council

European Commission. (2025). "AI Act: Shaping Europe's Digital Future." Retrieved from: 21 May 2025 https://digital-strategy.ec.europa.eu/en/policies/regulatory-framework-ai

Floridi, L., Cowls, J., Beltrametti, M., Chatila, R., Chazerand, P., Dignum, V., Luetge, C., Madelin, R., Pagallo, U., Rossi, F., Shafer, B., Valcke, P. and Vayena, E. (2018). "AI4People—An ethical framework for a good AI society: Opportunities, risks, principles, and recommendations." Minds and machines, 28(4), pp. 689–707. Retrieved from: 21 May 2025 doi: https://doi.org/10.1007/s11023-018-9482-5.

Feldstein, S. (2019). The global expansion of AI surveillance.: Carnegie Endowment for International Peace. Retrieved from: 21 May 2025 https://carnegieendowment.org/2019/09/17/global-expansion-of-ai-surveillance-pub-79847

Gyulai, A. and Ujlaki, A. (2021). "The political AI: A realist account of AI regulation", Információs Társadalom, 21(2), pp. 29–42. Retrieved from: 21 May 2025 https://doi.org/https://doi.org/10.22503/inftars.XXI.2021.2.3

Hassanali, M. (2024) "Theoretical paradigms under scrutiny: Realism, institutionalism, and the promise of artificial intelligence", SSRN. Retrieved from: 21 May 2025 https://ssrn.com/abstract=5051279

Kania, E. B. (2017). "Battlefield singularity: Artificial intelligence, Military Revolution, and China's Future Military Power". *Center for a New American Security,* 28 November. Retrieved from: 21 May 2025 https://www.cnas.org/publications/reports/battlefield-singularity-artificial-intelligence-military-revolution-and-chinas-future-military-power

Kello, L. (2017). *The virtual weapon and international order*. Yale University Press.

Mellon, J. G. (2009). "Constructivism and moral argument in international relations." Canadian political science, Retrieved from: 21 May 2025 https://cpsa-acsp.ca/papers-2009/Mellon.pdf

Mostafaei, H., Kordnoori, S., Ostadrahimi, M. and Banihashemi, S. S. A. (2025). "Applications of artificial intelligence in global diplomacy: A review of research and practical models." Sustainable Futures, 9, 100486. Retrieved from: 21 May 2025 doi: https://doi.org/10.1016/j.sftr.2025.100486.

NATO. (2025). "Science and Technology Trends 2025–2045". Retrieved from: 21 May 2025 https://www.nato.int/nato_static_fl2014/assets/pdf/2025/4/pdf/250409-STO-Trends-en.pdf

Ndzendze, B., & Marwala, T. (2023). *Artificial intelligence and international relations theories*. Palgrave Macmillan. https://doi.org/10.1007/978-981-19-4877-0

Nichols, M. (2023). "U.N. Chief calls for global AI watchdog", Reuters, 19 July. Retrieved from: 21 May 2025 https://www.reuters.com/technology/un-chief-calls-global-ai-watchdog-2023-07-19/

OECD. (2019). "Recommendation of the council on artificial intelligence. OECD legal instruments", OECD Publishing,. Retrieved from: 21 May 2025 https://legalinstruments.oecd.org/en/instruments/oecd-legal-0449

OECD. (2024)." GPAI Belgrade Declaration". OECD.AI. Retrieved from: 21 May 2025 https://oecd.ai/en/gpai-belgrade-declaration

Ministry of Foreign Affairs of the People's Republic of China. (2024). "Promoting Development for All and Bridging the AI Divide." Speech by Wang Yi at the High-level Meeting on International Cooperation in AI Capacity Building, 20 September. Retrieved from: 21 May 2025 https://www.mfa.gov.cn/eng/wjb/wjbz/jh/202412/t20241218_11497479.html

UNESCO. (2021). "Recommendation on the ethics of artificial intelligence". 16 May. Retrieved from: 21 May 2025 https://www.unesco.org/en/articles/recommendation-ethics-artificial-intelligence

Vincent, J. (2017). "Putin says the nation that leads in AI will be the ruler of the world", *The Verge,* 4 September Retrieved from: 21 May 2025 https://www.theverge.com/2017/9/4/16251226/russia-ai-putin-rule-the-world

Winter-Levy, S. (2024). "The emerging age of AI diplomacy: To compete with China, the United States must walk a tightrope in the Gulf", Foreign Affairs, 28 October. Retrieved from: 21 May 2025 https://www.foreignaffairs.com/united-states/emerging-age-ai-diplomacy

Wendt, A. (1992). Anarchy is what states make of it: The social construction of power politics. *International Organization, 46*(2), 391–425.

Wendt, A. (1999). *Social theory of international politics*. Cambridge University Press.

CHAPTER 12

Pillars of Cognitive Diplomacy: Presence, Practice, Resilience

12.1 Cognitive Presence: Strategic Awareness and Cognitive Reach

Cognitive presence in diplomacy refers to a state's enhanced capacity to perceive, interpret, and anticipate international dynamics through AI. It enables foreign ministries to transition from reactive postures to proactive, foresight-driven strategies. However, the *presence* pillar of cognitive diplomacy extends beyond analytical capability. It encompasses a state's ability to maintain and project visibility, credibility, and influence within the global digital commons. In an era where global publics are increasingly online, where perceptions are shaped virally and narratives evolve in real time, diplomatic presence is no longer limited to embassies, summits, or official communiqués. States must assert themselves across algorithmically mediated spaces—social media platforms, live streams, digital news ecosystems—in order to shape global opinion, communicate values, and counter adversarial narratives effectively.

AI significantly enhances this presence by empowering foreign ministries to reach diverse audiences, adapt messages across cultures and languages, and analyze public sentiment with unprecedented granularity. Digital presence, therefore, is not simply about being seen, it is about occupying cognitive space deliberately and persuasively, ensuring a state's narrative is heard, understood, and not drowned out by disinformation, rival influence, or informational noise.

E. Akıllı, *Cognitive Diplomacy and Digital Autonomy*,
https://doi.org/10.1007/978-3-032-04470-9_12

Historically, public diplomacy operated through broad messaging strategies aimed at general audiences. AI enables a shift toward precision-targeted, multilingual, and culturally adaptive communication. Through natural language generation and machine learning, diplomats can now create and tailor content at scale, allowing for localized engagement that resonates across linguistic and demographic boundaries (Akıllı and Şimşek, 2024a).

AI-powered tools are increasingly used to generate draft speeches, social media posts, briefing documents, and multimedia content. For example, diplomats at the United States Department of State, have experimented with using large language models (LLMs) to generate the first drafts of ambassadorial opinion pieces and public addresses. These drafts are then edited for nuance and strategic intent, saving time and allowing diplomats to focus on creative, context-sensitive refinements (Wang and Dubbins, 2024).

The impact extends to multimedia diplomacy. Ministries of Foreign Affairs (MFAs) can now produce explainer videos, infographics, and animations about their climate, trade, or development policies using AI-generated visuals, voiceovers, and scripts which can be available in dozens of languages. This lowering of production costs has democratized the ability of even small states to craft compelling visual narratives.

Neural machine translation is another transformative enabler of diplomatic presence. Agencies such as Japan's JETR (Yoshii, 1981), or Germany's Goethe-Institut (Cullen, 2016) use neural machine translation systems to instantly adapt web content and social media posts into multiple languages. As noted by the USC Center on Public Diplomacy, these tools "allow for faster generation and dissemination of translations, improving efficacy, transparency, inclusiveness, and legitimacy" of public messaging (Wang and Dubbins, 2024).

Real-time AI translation is also increasingly deployed during high-stakes diplomatic events. When national leaders address the U.N. General Assembly, for instance, live YouTube streams often feature instant AI-generated subtitles in multiple languages. This significantly expands global reach and ensures that key messages transcend language barriers, enabling broader citizen engagement and cultural inclusivity (Manor, 2025). Importantly, linguistic localization also signals respect and relational intent. Audiences are more receptive to states that address them in their own language, using idioms and references that feel authentic.

In this way, AI supports not only broader reach but deeper trust and legitimacy in diplomatic messaging.

Audience Analysis and Personalized Engagement

A core function of diplomatic presence is understanding foreign audiences' perceptions, concerns, and cultural sensibilities. Effective influence requires empathy grounded in data. AI equips public diplomacy professionals with powerful tools to perform sentiment analysis, trend detection, and audience segmentation at scale. By monitoring digital discourse across social media platforms and news ecosystems, AI enables diplomats to anticipate public reactions, detect emerging themes, and adjust communication strategies accordingly.

As *presence* also involves AI's capacity to monitor public sentiment, NLP tools can now assess emotional tone across platforms, identifying potential unrest or surges in nationalism. For instance, China's Belt and Road Initiative (BRI) incorporates AI-driven risk assessments for foreign investments. AI systems assess sentiment, political instability, and regulatory risk across participating states to guide the scale and timing of strategic investments, aiming to prevent diplomatic fallout or financial loss (Lai, M.K., 2025; Nedopil, 2024; Uren, 2024).

One notable example is Japan's Foreign Ministry, which is developing an AI-based system to monitor and analyze global online data sources—from social media platforms to academic publications—in order to detect early indicators of international instability (The Japan News, 2022). With a dedicated budget of 640 million yen ($4.45 million), the initiative aims to automatically flag developments that may affect Japanese interests or the safety of its citizens abroad. By synthesizing vast and diverse data streams, the system functions as an early warning mechanism for emerging crises, uprisings, or diplomatic tensions (Asia News Network 2022). Within the framework of cognitive diplomacy, this project exemplifies how states are enhancing their situational awareness and strategic foresight through AI-driven capabilities. It reflects a broader shift from reactive foreign policy toward anticipatory, data-informed engagement with global dynamics.

Similarly, the U.K.'s Foreign, Commonwealth & Development Office (FCDO) has deployed a social media analysis team that uses machine learning to track information diffusion and identify key influencers. AI helps map how particular stories gain traction, revealing information ecosystems where public diplomacy interventions might be most effective. AI algorithms can analyze vast amounts of data to identify topics of interest, emerging trends, and stories that captivate global audiences, helping public diplomacy practitioners stay ahead of the curve (Akıllı, 2025c). During the COVID-19 pandemic, several MFAs—including those of Estonia and Taiwan—used AI to detect false narratives about vaccines and virus origins. AI tools enabled these states to push out corrective messaging before misinformation took deeper root, preserving public trust and international credibility (Chen et al. 2022).

AI also supports audience segmentation, allowing for tailored messaging across demographic, geographic, and interest-based groups (Bhagat et al., 2024). India's Ministry of External Affairs, for example, employs analytics to monitor concerns within its vast diaspora network, shaping outreach on topics such as visa policy, bilateral agreements, or developments in the homeland (PTI, 2020). Such personalization improves engagement and demonstrates responsiveness to audience needs.

This logic extends to the evolving concept of the "virtual embassy" (Molaee, 2025). The U.S. State Department's Virtual Embassy for Iran, operating via a website and social media, exemplifies outreach in the absence of a physical mission (Scoop News Group, 2024). AI can further enhance these efforts by recommending content, adapting language, and personalizing the user experience—mirroring e-commerce platforms, but applied to strategic communication.

Meanwhile, AI-driven chatbots and virtual assistants are becoming new frontlines in public engagement. These bots, often embedded in websites or messaging platforms, serve as accessible, always-available interlocutors, helping bridge the temporal and staffing gaps in diplomacy. During the war in Ukraine, Telegram-based AI chatbots were deployed by Ukrainian officials to communicate with Russian citizens and soldiers, including appeals to surrender or explanatory messages on the war's legal and moral context. This application verged on automated psychological operations, but it also demonstrated AI's capacity for non-violent strategic messaging (CSIS, 2023).

In a more benign cultural diplomacy context, France's tourism agency experimented with chatbots that act as virtual cultural ambassadors—answering user queries about France's history, cuisine, and travel protocols in multiple languages with a friendly, human-like tone. During

Expo 2020 Dubai, some national pavilions introduced AI-based interactive guides, embodying their country's identity while engaging physically present visitors in real time (Cutieru, 2021). Such bots extend presence in both symbolic and functional ways. They personalize interactions, model national values, and are available around the clock, increasing the effectiveness of limited diplomatic personnel.

Strategic Narrative Construction and Influence Campaigns

Diplomatic presence is not merely about producing more content, it is about shaping persuasive narratives. AI offers tools for testing and refining strategic messaging, similar to the A/B testing used in digital marketing. By analyzing previous campaign data, AI can simulate how audiences may respond to different framings, slogans, or hashtags, helping diplomats choose the language and symbols that resonate most (Cimmino and Michta, 2024).

For example, when Estonia promotes its e-governance model, AI can help identify whether international audiences are more responsive to themes of efficiency, transparency, or economic development (e-e-Estonia 2025). Messaging can then be adapted accordingly, emphasizing jobs and innovation for Western audiences, or sovereignty and independence for post-Soviet states. Furthermore, by processing millions of social media posts, AI systems can detect shifts in tone, trending hashtags, and topic clusters, enabling diplomats to craft messages that directly address public misconceptions or emotional responses (Grundel & Stenberg, 2019).

AI can also guide diplomats in adjusting their narratives across cultural or regional contexts (Mostafaei et al., 2025). India's Foreign Ministry, for instance, strategically emphasizes its identity as the "world's largest democracy" in Western forums (Bajpaee, 2024), while highlighting "global south solidarity" when addressing African, Latin American, or ASEAN audiences (Singh et al. 2024). AI systems, by crunching psychographic and demographic data, can assist in calibrating these identity frames to maximize resonance and minimize friction (Stanzel and Voelsen 2022). As one practitioner insightfully observed, *"AI can tailor diplomatic messages to specific audiences, accounting for cultural, linguistic, and regional differences. Such customization enhances the relevance and impact of diplomatic communication"* (Wang and Dubbins, 2024).

AI is a double-edged instrument in the realm of strategic communications. It can be harnessed by adversaries for disinformation, but also by democracies for truth-based, ethical influence. The war in Ukraine offers a powerful case study where Kyiv cultivated a compelling digital presence, what analysts dubbed as its "*digital frontline*" (TechUksraine, TechUkraine 2025). Central to this effort was the use of AI-assisted tools to amplify truthful narratives, synchronize messaging, and engage the international public.

President Volodymyr Zelenskyy's nightly video addresses became viral diplomatic content. Behind the scenes, Ukraine's tech sector played a vital role by using data analytics to optimize content distribution, and time messages for maximum engagement, and target key influencers capable of amplifying Ukraine's position globally (CSIS, Center for Strategic and International Studies (CSIS) 2023). As a result, Ukraine's narrative of resilience, legitimacy, and victimhood consistently outpaced Russian disinformation across many online environments. Taiwan offers another instructive model. Amid heightened tensions with Beijing, Taiwan's response strategy combines humor-driven counternarratives with open-source AI tools that enable citizen-led fact-checking (Tu, 2024). By empowering society to defend the truth, Taiwan fosters cognitive resilience while maintaining a dynamic and relatable diplomatic presence (Mozur and Zhong, 2020). These examples reveal that strategically framed and data-informed truth-telling—enhanced by AI targeting and timing—can be highly effective in international communication, even under asymmetric conditions.

Beyond policy messaging, diplomatic presence also involves cultural connection—a soft power domain where AI enables novel forms of engagement. Countries are increasingly using virtual environments, AI avatars, and cultural bots to reach global audiences. Japan, for instance, has explored deploying AI-generated historical avatars to teach language and history interactively, blending education with cultural diplomacy (Deutsche Welle, 2025). During Expo 2020 Dubai, countries like South Korea and UAE introduced VR embassy walkthroughs and concerts, accessible worldwide (Digital Mind, 2020). AI underpinned these experiences by managing dialogues, translating interactions, and even adjusting content based on user behavior.

During the pandemic, the British Council hosted AI-moderated cultural exchange workshops, connecting students across borders in real time (Grincheva and Vlaeminck, 2022) a clear example of resilient, inclusive presence when travel was impossible. The African Union's

#TheAfricaWeWant campaign, aligned with Agenda 2063, utilized AI-driven sentiment analysis to amplify positive narratives (Amponsah, 2023; African Union Commission, 2015). By identifying globally resonant themes—such as innovation, youth, and tradition—the campaign was able to reshape international perceptions from a narrative of dependency to one of opportunity. Such creative deployments reflect the evolving soft power landscape: cultural narratives can now be shared, scaled, and interactively experienced via AI-enhanced platforms.

Ethical Guardrails for AI-Augmented Presence

These innovations, however, are not without risks. There is a fine line between persuasive diplomacy and manipulative propaganda. Democratic states must take care that AI-personalized messaging respects transparency, informed consent, and privacy. Micro-targeting foreign citizens with overly tailored emotional appeals—especially if based on psychographic profiling—could erode trust and blur the line between diplomacy and covert influence operations (Bjola & Pamment, 2021).

As Wang and Dubbins (2024) note, the algorithmic promotion of content can unintentionally foster echo chambers or skew perceptions of consensus, especially when AI models optimize for engagement rather than truth. Ethical public diplomacy must ensure that AI tools amplify facts, engage respectfully with diverse publics, and prioritize credibility over virality (Manor, 2025). Maintaining public trust both at home and abroad is essential to diplomatic legitimacy. Some nations have begun embedding these concerns into policy. For example, the EU's AI Act mandates transparency obligations for AI systems used in public communication, including the clear labeling of synthetic media (European Commission, 2025). Similarly, internal codes of practice in Türkiye, Canada, Germany, and the U.K. emphasize that diplomatic AI tools must be auditable, interpretable, and aligned with democratic values (T.C. Cumhurbaşkanlığı Dijital Dönüşüm Ofisi, 2021; U.K. Cabinet Office, UK Cabinet Office 2024).

In sum, the cognitive presence pillar underscores that diplomacy in the digital age is fundamentally a battle for attention, trust, and narrative coherence. Artificial intelligence equips states with tools to compete effectively in this contested space, allowing them to speak in the languages of their audiences, adapt to the emotional tenor of the moment, and remain visible in digital ecosystems where public opinion is shaped.

The United States, recognizing this imperative, has integrated AI into public diplomacy to better map foreign sentiment and tailor messaging—for instance, emphasizing humanitarian aid or educational partnerships in countries where such themes resonate most. As a recent U.S. Advisory Commission report stressed, AI *can "help ensure U.S. diplomatic messages are more relevant, responsive, and resonant"* in a fragmented media landscape (U.S. Advisory Commission on Public Diplomacy, 2023).

Cognitive diplomacy, through AI-augmented presence, ensures that a state's voice is not merely heard but trusted, contextualized, and compelling. In an information environment saturated with noise and manipulated narratives, presence is not optional, but it is a strategic necessity.

12.2 Cognitive Practice: Augmenting Diplomatic Action and Strategic Negotiation

Smarter, Faster, and Adaptive Diplomacy

The cognitive *practice* pillar of cognitive diplomacy addresses the operational core of foreign policy—the routines, workflows, and strategic decision-making processes that define daily diplomatic work. It concerns how diplomacy is conducted in an AI-augmented environment, where artificial intelligence becomes a functional extension of human judgment. Unlike traditional models reliant solely on human interpretation, AI enables ministries of foreign affairs (MFAs) to analyze data at scale, simulate policy scenarios, and improve responsiveness in negotiations and crisis management.

This pillar is rooted in the conviction that diplomacy in the twenty-first century must evolve to become smarter, faster, and more adaptive. As advanced in the concept of *cognitive diplomacy*, artificial intelligence does not replace human diplomats, rather it expands their cognitive bandwidth—enabling them to process vast volumes of data, evaluate a wider array of policy options, and identify innovative solutions that may elude conventional human reasoning. Crucially, in this framework, AI's role is not merely technical but epistemological: it reshapes how diplomatic knowledge is produced, foresight is generated, and strategic judgments are formulated amid growing uncertainty and complexity.

Cognitive diplomacy harnesses these capacities to reposition diplomacy as a proactive, anticipatory function. It supports early warning mechanisms, maps the diffusion of disinformation, enhances negotiation dynamics, and improves intercultural communication through real-time adaptation. These evolving capabilities signify a paradigmatic shift in the cognitive architecture of diplomatic practice, redefining the purpose and power of digital-age statecraft. At the heart of diplomatic work lies information processing: making sense of an ever-expanding sea of reports, media, cables, and social discourse. AI significantly augments analytical capacity by applying natural language processing (NLP) and machine learning to collect, structure, and prioritize insights across data sources (Chen et.al, 2024).

The U.S. State Department's Bureau of Intelligence and Research (INR), for instance, has begun deploying AI-enabled text mining to monitor foreign media, flag social media sentiment shifts, and identify early indicators of unrest (MeriTalk, 2024; Chai et al., 2023). Instead of analysts manually sifting through hundreds of sources, NLP systems generate daily briefs summarizing what is trending on social platforms. As the former U.S. Secretary of State Antony J. Blinken said, *"If Netflix can predict what TV show my wife and I might choose to watch next, I think data can also help us and help the department predict maybe the next civil conflict, the next famine, the next economic crisis, and how we can respond more effectively,"* (Deloitte, 2022). This commitment to data-drivenness also reflects the U.S. State Department's broader modernization agenda, including the INR's recent emphasis on data-informed decision-making (MeriTalk, 2024; U.S. Department of State, 2024).

The State Department established the Center for Analytics (CfA) in 2020 as a central hub for data governance and analytics, aiming to modernize its diplomacy practice through data-informed decision-making. During the opening event, then-Under Secretary for Management Brian Bulatao said: *"We know that data will not only help the Department of State run more efficiently, but it can also move us toward more effective and stronger evidence-based foreign policy,"* (De Garmo 2020). The CfA offers predictive analytics and data science support to various bureaus, assisting in tasks such as forecasting visa demand surges, analyzing consular workloads, and mapping political influence networks in foreign states, harnessing AI to anticipate and respond to global challenges (U.S. Department of State, 2020). For instance, the CfA's predictive modeling capabilities assist the Bureau of Consular Affairs in anticipating fluctuations in visa applications, enabling more efficient resource allocation and service delivery. Additionally, by employing AI to detect patterns and anomalies in data, the department can better understand and respond to complex geopolitical dynamics, such as identifying emerging political influence networks abroad (U.S. Department of State, 2024).

Similarly, Germany's Federal Foreign Office, through its Data Innovation Lab, has piloted AI applications for negotiation support. In one case, German researchers used AI to analyze historical negotiation transcripts, applying pattern recognition to generate a spectrum of plausible outcomes in ongoing talks. They tested the 1930s German-Austrian customs union talks by modeling how other countries would react to a deal, helping diplomats anticipate opposition. These "*what-if*" scenario models provided diplomats with probabilistic foresight to guide strategy and contingency planning (Stanzel and Voelsen 2022).

AI's contribution in diplomatic contexts is not deterministic but advisory. It transforms vast amounts of raw data into structured, evidence-based insights that support, rather than replace, human judgment. By synthesizing relevant information, AI enhances negotiators' situational awareness and strategic preparation, enabling more informed and anticipatory decision-making. In doing so, AI plays a transformative role in the analytical dimensions of diplomacy, offering an expanded cognitive framework for complex international negotiations (Akıllı, 2025b).

Negotiation Augmentation: From CICERO to "Hagglebots"

Among the most provocative frontiers of AI-enhanced diplomacy is the integration of AI into the negotiation process itself. This is not speculative: AI has already demonstrated its capacity to engage in interactive, strategic dialogue. A landmark case emerged when Meta (formerly Facebook) developed CICERO, an AI system capable of playing the game *Diplomacy* at a high level. Unlike games of perfect information, like chess, *Diplomacy* requires persuasion, alliance-building, and trust—features analogous to real-world negotiation. Remarkably, CICERO achieved human-level performance, forming alliances, brokering deals, and even engaging in calculated deception when needed (Meta 2022; Akıllı, 2025b). As a controlled experiment, CICERO illustrates the potential of AI to navigate complex interpersonal dynamics, suggesting future possibilities for its use as a negotiation support agent.

Meanwhile, more constrained systems known as "hagglebots" have already been deployed in commercial and legal usage. These AI agents use game theory and reinforcement learning to propose, revise, and optimize deals—whether in contract negotiations, resource allocations, or pricing strategies. Analysts have suggested that such bots could soon assist in multilateral trade talks, quickly identifying combinations of concessions and package deals that satisfy all parties' minimum thresholds—a task often beyond the bandwidth of human negotiators (Akıllı, 2025b).

Imagine a future World Trade Organization session where each delegation is supported by an AI assistant capable of processing real-time economic data and running simultaneous counterproposal simulations. These systems could propose deal structures that yield Pareto-efficient outcomes, helping to resolve deadlocks and uncover synergies that may elude human intuition. Within a cognitive diplomacy framework, such tools enhance not only informational awareness but also the negotiators' strategic reasoning capacity. While these AI systems are not decision-makers, they serve as cognitive amplifiers—augmenting, rather than replacing, human judgment. Especially in value-sensitive or politically complex negotiations, final decisions remain firmly in the hands of diplomats. Yet AI's ability to lower transaction costs, accelerate compromise, and foster data-informed bargaining environments underscores its emerging role as a core enabler of twenty-first-century diplomatic practice.

As mentioned above, AI has a profound capacity for facilitating negotiations, evolving from basic drafting tools to advanced systems capable of emotional sensing and strategic support. Nonetheless, early developments in AI-assisted negotiation show promising but cautious movement toward more integrated machine involvement in diplomacy. Hagglebots focus on economic trade-offs, pricing strategies, and contract formulation. Their relevance to diplomacy lies in their ability to automate trade negotiations, potentially expediting international economic agreements. Additionally, they can analyze market conditions and predict how economic factors influence diplomatic relations. In the context of global policymaking, hagglebots could assist in sanction policies and trade conflicts by modeling economic retaliation strategies (Akıllı, 2025b). This marked a shift from static bargaining tools to dynamic, interactive agents capable of adjusting tactics in real time.

Even the United Nations has explored the use of AI in sensitive diplomatic functions. The U.N. Conference on Trade and Development (UNCTAD) has studied whether AI systems could help mediate investment disputes or propose equitable terms for sovereign debt restructuring by removing emotional bias and providing precedent-based options (UNCTAD, 2022). These systems, still in experimental phases, remain under strict human supervision and are generally confined to technical or non-political domains.

More experimentally, some research teams have tested computer vision systems that analyze facial expressions and body language from negotiation videos to detect signs of discomfort or potential deception. While these tools remain controversial and culturally sensitive—and must be used with care—they point to the deep integration of AI into negotiation analysis (Dinnar et al., 2021). Ethical questions abound: such systems could be seen as invasive, unreliable across cultural contexts, or vulnerable to misuse if employed covertly (Coelho et al., 2023).

As noted above, while CICERO's success in alliance-building and hagglebots' precision in economic negotiations underscore AI's growing capabilities, human diplomats remain indispensable. The practice of diplomacy is not merely about securing favorable outcomes; it is fundamentally about preserving peace, managing conflict, and cultivating long-term cooperation (Akıllı, 2025b). The deep political and relational dimensions of diplomacy—trust-building, face-saving, historical memory, and symbolic gestures—remain beyond the current reach of artificial intelligence. Within the framework of cognitive diplomacy, AI is best understood not as a replacement for diplomatic agency, but as an assistive instrument that augments human cognition. Modern AI systems can accelerate negotiation processes by scanning speeches, interviews, and social media content to infer delegates' probable red lines and identify zones of possible agreement. In this model, AI becomes a cognitive partner that enhances strategic insight while leaving final judgment firmly in human hands. In short, AI will augment but not supplant the human element in diplomacy. It can provide decision support, consistency checks, and scenario analysis, but it cannot replace the moral agency, emotional intelligence, or political accountability of human negotiators. The future of diplomatic practice lies in human-AI symbiosis: diplomats empowered by intelligent tools, yet anchored in ethical judgment and strategic empathy.

Administrative and Consular Efficiency

Much of diplomacy unfolds not in grand summits but in the mundane yet essential realm of consular services: issuing visas, assisting nationals abroad, managing documentation, and responding to public inquiries. Here, AI has proven particularly transformative—enhancing efficiency, standardizing services, and freeing human diplomats to focus on tasks that require discretion and nuance. For instance, Germany's Federal Foreign Office introduced an AI system to manage the high volume of inquiries received by its global missions. It uses natural language processing to categorize queries, retrieve relevant information, and draft responses to common questions such as visa eligibility or travel advisories. It effectively acts as an AI-driven triage tool, automating straightforward replies while flagging complex or sensitive requests for human attention (Omdena, 2024). The system improves over time by learning from previous Q&A interactions and aligns responses with policy updates, thus ensuring both efficiency and consistency.

Similarly, U.S. embassies are planning to deploy AI-powered chatbots that assist users in navigating consular services, such as visa applications or appointment scheduling (Lewis and Zengerle, 2025). Canada's Foreign Ministry has tested AI tools for contract analysis, flagging anomalous clauses in draft agreements to ensure legal consistency and compliance across its international operations (Government of Canada, 2022).

Beyond real-time analysis, AI contributes to future-oriented strategic forecasting—a critical function in complex, uncertain diplomatic environments. While earlier sections addressed conflict prevention under the *resilience* pillar, here the focus shifts to diplomatic forecasting in structured negotiations, particularly trade and international agreements. AI systems can simulate economic, political, and social outcomes of proposed policies. For example, during economic treaty negotiations, trade diplomats now use AI to project how different tariff structures may affect supply chains, industry sectors, and even political constituencies over time. In 2018, IBM developed a prototype called Cognitive Trade Advisor, a system capable of answering detailed queries about trade provisions by drawing on vast textual databases of past agreements, laws, and economic performance data. Gabriel Petrus, executive director of ICC Brasil/ITTI says: *"While traditionally trade negotiators would have to spend weeks and months in putting together and making sense of piles of trade-related information, the CTA can streamline negotiation dynamics. As a consequence, parties are able to dedicate more of their time to building consensus,"* who led the CTA project (ICC, 2018).

The Japan-EU Economic Partnership Agreement negotiations reportedly employed similar computational tools, utilizing computer-based models to forecast the macroeconomic impacts of proposed tariff adjustments (DG Trade, 2018). These simulations enabled negotiators to identify mutually beneficial tariff schedules by modeling complex trade-offs across sectors. Importantly, the predictive models allowed policymakers to anticipate second-order effects—such as shifts in investment flows, supply chain realignments, and consumer price dynamics—before finalizing the terms of the agreement (Grübler et al. 2019; Belli and Jiang, 2024). Within a cognitive diplomacy framework, such tools exemplify how data-driven modeling can support anticipatory negotiation strategies, enhance economic foresight, and reduce uncertainty in high-stakes international agreements.

A particularly promising innovation within the cognitive diplomacy paradigm is agent-based modeling (ABM), where AI simulates the behavior of diverse actors—such as states, firms, and institutions—under varying policy conditions (SmythOS, 2025; INET Oxford, 2025; NCBI, 2015). These models enable diplomats to interrogate complex strategic scenarios like: how might a targeted state react to newly imposed sanctions. What secondary or tertiary effects could emerge across the region? While the reliability of ABMs depends heavily on the quality of their underlying assumptions and data, they provide a systematic and dynamic means of visualizing interdependencies. In doing so, ABMs enhance human strategic foresight by offering anticipatory insights into possible diplomatic, economic, or security outcomes in an increasingly complex international environment.

AI-Enabled Counterterrorism and Security Implementation

The practice of cognitive diplomacy involves the operationalization of AI systems within the workflows of diplomatic and security institutions. One of the most advanced and pressing domains for such practice is counterterrorism (Akıllı, 2024b). AI technologies now underpin a growing array of tools and systems deployed by foreign ministries, intelligence agencies, and multilateral organizations to detect, prevent, and respond to terrorist threats in ways that transcend conventional diplomacy.

AI's ability to analyze high-dimensional data at speed enables its use in operational security environments. Systems based on image processing and facial recognition are now deployed across high-risk infrastructures like airports and government buildings. These tools match real-time video input against terrorist watchlists and can detect concealed weapons, enabling security personnel to act within seconds. For example, Omnilert's AI solution marks suspected firearms and sends automatic alerts to authorities, enhancing decision-making in fast-moving situations (Louie, 2020).

Such AI-driven practice not only accelerates tactical responses but also integrates with broader diplomatic mechanisms such as joint security protocols, crisis de-escalation dialogues, and embassy-based threat mitigation. Cognitive diplomacy practitioners can interpret and act on AI insights within multilateral security forums, combining hard data with soft coordination tools.

Another practical frontier is anomaly detection, especially within financial systems. AI-enhanced Suspicious Activity Reporting (SAR) has become a cornerstone of financial counterterrorism by flagging transactions that deviate from typical patterns. This enables embassies, financial attachés, and intergovernmental working groups to engage in evidence-based diplomatic efforts against terrorist financing networks (Ibitola, 2023).

Likewise, predictive analytics powered by machine learning models and Deep Neural Networks (DNNs) allow agencies to anticipate when and where a terrorist act might occur. These models help map linkages between data points drawn from telecommunications, travel patterns, and criminal records, offering actionable foresight to both domestic security teams and regional diplomatic task forces (Uddin et al., 2020).

AI's integration into social media monitoring marks a paradigm shift in the practice of counterterror diplomacy. Terrorist groups often exploit social media for recruitment and propaganda. Using LLMs and Convolutional Neural Networks (CNNs), AI tools now scan online platforms for extremist content, issuing alerts or automatically flagging posts for moderation and law enforcement (Akıllı, 2024b). These tools provide diplomats with a clearer picture of threat ecosystems and can guide digital messaging campaigns or content takedown negotiations with platform providers (United Nations Office of Counter-Terrorism (UNCTC) 2023).

Importantly, quantum-enhanced AI systems are being tested for faster, real-time tracking of terrorist content across platforms, offering foreign ministries new capabilities for narrative control, reputational defense, and strategic communications (United Nations 2019).

Despite its utility, the deployment of AI in counterterrorism diplomacy is not without challenges. Data quality remains critical since insufficient or biased data can lead to operational errors, undermining diplomatic credibility. Moreover, ethical concerns—such as surveillance overreach or algorithmic bias—must be addressed through normative frameworks co-developed by foreign ministries, civil society, and AI experts (Verhelst et al., 2020).

Effective practice thus demands not just technical integration, but institutional adaptation: diplomats must be trained in data interpretation, AI ethics, and interdisciplinary coordination. AI units within foreign ministries can serve as bridges between intelligence communities and global diplomatic fora, facilitating real-time security engagements grounded in cognitive technologies.

Crisis Response and Decision-Making under Pressure

Diplomacy is often tested during fast-moving crises, where the imperative for rapid and informed decision-making intersects with high uncertainty and incomplete information. In such contexts, AI provides critical support through real-time dashboard analytics, predictive simulation tools, and structured decision-support frameworks such as the OODA loop—Observe, Orient, Decide, Act (Raska, 2025). Within a cognitive diplomacy framework, these tools enhance situational awareness, reduce the cognitive load on decision-makers, and enable more agile, data-informed responses to dynamic international events. AI can help mitigate the "fog of war" in diplomatic crisis management by offering enhanced situational awareness and reducing ambiguity in real-time decision-making (Bjola, 2022).

The Center for Strategic and International Studies (CSIS) has conducted simulations to explore how artificial intelligence could augment deterrence decision-making in hypothetical geopolitical crises. These systems function by rapidly modeling adversary responses, calculating response timelines, and recommending optimized strategic actions—akin to advanced chess engines, but calibrated for high-stakes military-diplomatic scenarios (Jensen, et al., 2024; Scale AI & Center for Strategic and International Studies (Scale AI & CSIS, 2023). Complementing this, AI-enabled crisis dashboards can synthesize real-time intelligence feeds, detect anomalies, and propose timely interventions. Yet within the framework of ethical cognitive diplomacy, such tools must operate under a "human-in-the-loop" model. While AI may recommend prioritizing specific visa applications or suggest calibrated retaliatory signals in a standoff, human diplomats must retain overriding authority—especially when legal norms, political sensitivities, or ethical considerations are at stake.

A fitting metaphor is an autopilot in aviation: AI can manage routine trajectories and provide rapid diagnostic support in emergent situations, but the pilot must always be prepared to assume manual control when discretion and judgment are essential. The integration of AI into diplomatic practice must therefore be governed by transparent safeguards, institutional oversight, and comprehensive training. This ensures that algorithmic precision enhances rather than displaces the core human responsibilities embedded in diplomacy's normative and strategic foundations.

As detailed above, the cognitive *practice* pillar of the cognitive diplomacy model reveals how both the quotidian and the exceptional elements of diplomacy can be meaningfully enhanced through AI. From real-time analytics in crisis response to automated consular services, from drafting assistance in multilateral negotiations to predictive modeling in trade talks, AI promises to make diplomacy more efficient, adaptive, and data-driven. AI can inform the head, but diplomacy is also an art of the heart and soul. It demands strategic empathy, ethical discernment, and human accountability. As cognitive diplomacy becomes an operational reality, the priority is not only developing new tools, but also training diplomats to critically interpret and guide those tools, to act as masters, not servants, of algorithmic assistance, and to ensure that AI integration reflects national values, democratic standards, and international law.

12.3 Cognitive Resilience: Enhancing Cognitive Security and Robustness

Cognitive Resilience, in the context of cognitive diplomacy, refers to a state's capacity to withstand, adapt to, and recover from disruptions in the cognitive, informational, and decision-making spheres. This encompasses threats such as AI-generated disinformation, cyberattacks on diplomatic infrastructure, and the destabilizing effects of real-time narrative manipulation. Cognitive resilience demands not only institutional agility and strategic foresight but also infrastructure proficiency—the robustness of technical systems that underpin diplomatic operations. This includes secure communications, data integrity, and redundancy mechanisms to ensure continuity during systemic shocks. Artificial intelligence significantly contributes to this form of resilience by enhancing situational awareness, anomaly detection, and response forecasting. Across diverse geopolitical contexts, states are increasingly employing AI to harden their diplomatic institutions against both cognitive and hybrid threats, ensuring strategic coherence and operational continuity under conditions of volatility and uncertainty.

The proliferation of AI has also exponentially increased the scale and sophistication of information warfare. Technologies such as deepfakes, synthetic social media personas, and micro-targeted propaganda now pose profound challenges to states seeking to preserve narrative integrity and public trust. The Ukraine War offers a compelling case study in cognitive resilience through AI-enhanced strategic communications. In response to a sustained disinformation campaign—particularly following the 2022 escalation—Ukrainian authorities have actively employed AI to detect, monitor, and counter digital propaganda. Advanced systems have been used to analyze vast volumes of media and social content, flagging coordinated inauthentic behavior and tracking the evolution of adversarial narratives.

Artificial intelligence has become integral to modern cyber-defense strategies. Governments now rely on AI to detect anomalous network behavior, prevent data breaches, and identify malicious software with speed and precision. NATO, for example, deploys AI systems within its Cooperative Cyber Defence Centre of Excellence to detect malware, flag unauthorized intrusions, and automate threat mitigation processes (NATO, 2021). Similarly, national Computer Emergency Response Teams (CERTs) across Europe are increasingly collaborating through AI-enabled platforms that facilitate the real-time exchange of malware signatures and the coordinated blocking of cyberattacks (ENISA, 2023; ECSO, 2022). However, the dual-use nature of AI also presents profound risks to diplomatic stability and cognitive security.

The 2022 deepfake video of Ukrainian President Volodymyr Zelenskyy announcing a surrender during Russia's invasion stands as a stark warning. Although quickly debunked as a fabrication, the video's visual and narrative realism revealed the disruptive potential of AI-generated misinformation to distort battlefield perceptions, erode public trust, and mislead diplomatic decision-making (Reuters, 2022). According to the Center for Strategic and International Studies (CSIS), AI-enabled tools have played a key role in detecting Russian narratives, identifying bot activity, and highlighting inconsistencies in adversary messaging—thereby enabling faster, targeted counterresponses (Center for Strategic and International Studies (CSIS) 2023). Such capabilities have enabled Ukrainian institutions to mount timely, targeted counterresponses, reinforcing both narrative control and national resilience within the broader framework of cognitive diplomacy (Center for Strategic and International Studies (CSIS) 2023). Within the framework of cognitive diplomacy, this underscores the imperative for states to develop both technological safeguards and communicative resilience to counter the weaponization of synthetic media.

Other states have institutionalized comparable approaches to cognitive defense. Estonia, shaped by its experience with a large-scale cyber and information attack in 2007, has pioneered a whole-of-society resilience model that combines technological innovation with civic education. Central to this approach is the integration of media literacy into the national curriculum—beginning at the primary school level—where students are systematically trained to critically evaluate information. This human-centered strategy is now complemented by AI-enabled tools, including real-time disinformation trackers and browser-based credibility indicators. They help individuals assess the reliability of digital content as they navigate the information environment. Estonia's model demonstrates how cognitive diplomacy can be operationalized through a synergy of institutional foresight, public engagement, and adaptive technologies to build enduring resilience against hybrid threats (NATO Strategic Communications Centre of Excellence, 2019).

EU's East StratCom Task Force provides another instructive example of institutionalized cognitive defense (EEAS, 2025). Leveraging AI-driven text analysis, the Task Force systematically categorizes, quantifies, and geolocates disinformation narratives. These analytical outputs offer diplomats and policymakers timely insights into adversarial messaging patterns, helping to identify emerging themes, regional targeting strategies, and rhetorical shifts (Missiroli et al., 2016). By equipping EU member states with shared situational awareness, this AI-enabled capability enhances strategic coordination and responsiveness. As Bjola and Pamment (2021) argue, such mechanisms exemplify how cognitive diplomacy can translate data analytics into actionable counternarrative strategies, reinforcing the EU's collective communicative resilience in the face of hybrid threats.

Early Warning and Conflict Prevention

Resilience also entails the capacity to *anticipate* instability and prevent emerging tensions from escalating into open conflict. In this regard, AI-driven predictive analytics represent a transformative tool for modern diplomacy. Machine learning models are increasingly capable of synthesizing heterogeneous data streams—ranging from economic indicators and patterns of social unrest to military deployments and environmental stressors—to forecast potential geopolitical flashpoints. These analytical insights enable diplomats to adopt a more anticipatory posture, shifting from reactive crisis management to proactive risk mitigation. Reflecting the principles of cognitive diplomacy, a growing number of foreign ministries, international organizations, and multilateral institutions are embedding these AI tools into their early warning architectures to enhance strategic foresight and prevent conflict before it materializes.

The U.S. Department of Defense's Integrated Crisis Early Warning System (ICEWS) was an early pioneer in this field. As far back as the 2000s, ICEWS demonstrated predictive capacity for events like coups and mass protests using structured datasets and machine learning techniques (Ward et al., 2013). Today, the U.S. State Department incorporates similar models for quantitative foresight, using AI to generate political risk assessments, anticipate atrocity risks, and inform proactive diplomacy (Lockheed Martin, 2024). The U.S. Department of Defense's ICEWS is an automated system that monitors, assesses, and forecasts political crises worldwide using advanced NLP and predictive modeling, supporting early warning and resource allocation for crisis mitigation (Lockheed Martin, 2024; Jontz, 2015).

AI models are increasingly employed by humanitarian agencies and international organizations to forecast outbreaks of violence and patterns of forced migration, significantly enhancing both preparedness and response capabilities. These systems analyze variables such as conflict intensity, displacement trends, climate shocks, and economic stressors to anticipate population movements and humanitarian needs. While specific verification of the Rhombus project's deployment in Ethiopia is not available in the cited sources, broader evidence underscores the growing use of predictive analytics in humanitarian diplomacy (U.N. Global Pulse, 2021; Carammia et al., 2022; Omdena, 2019). AI-driven platforms can forecast diplomatic trajectories and flag emerging risks or opportunities, allowing policymakers to take preemptive, evidence-based action aligned with national priorities. In essence, AI functions as a cognitive radar for diplomacy—enabling the simulation of "what-if" scenarios, the identification of nascent geopolitical shifts, and the development of strategies before crises escalate. These examples point to an evolving model of diplomacy—one in which AI-generated alerts function like meteorological forecasts for political instability, giving diplomats the foresight to navigate storms before they erupt. In this sense, resilience is not just defensive; it is also anticipatory and adaptive, enhancing a state's ability to act strategically in a rapidly shifting geopolitical landscape. Within the cognitive diplomacy framework, such applications exemplify how AI can augment early intervention strategies, reduce human suffering, and support more targeted, timely international responses to complex emergencies.

Robust Diplomatic Networks and Continuity

Resilience in cognitive diplomacy also entails the capacity to sustain the continuity of diplomatic operations under conditions of duress, whether triggered by cyberattacks, natural disasters, or wartime disruptions. In such scenarios, redundancy, digital sovereignty, and secure connectivity are not merely technical features but foundational elements of cognitive resilience. AI and advanced digital infrastructure empower foreign ministries to remain functional even when conventional communication channels are compromised. By ensuring operational continuity through secure backups, alternative data pathways, and AI-supported decision systems, states can preserve diplomatic agency and strategic coherence in the face of systemic shocks.

A leading example of operational resilience within the cognitive diplomacy framework is Estonia's pioneering "data embassy" initiative, a landmark in digital sovereignty and strategic continuity. In 2017, Estonia became the first nation to establish a data embassy in Luxembourg (OECD Observatory of Public Sector Innovation, 2017). It is a secure, state-controlled data center that mirrors the country's most critical government databases and digital infrastructure. Legally recognized as an extension of Estonian territory and protected under bilateral agreements, the facility ensures that essential state functions including diplomatic communications, identity services, and public registries can continue uninterrupted in the event of a cyberattack, natural disaster, or territorial occupation that compromises domestic systems (e-Estonia,

2019). Operated under full Estonian jurisdiction, the data embassy exemplifies how digital infrastructure can be transformed into a sovereign asset, reinforcing national resilience while safeguarding informational and diplomatic continuity. As states confront an era defined by hybrid threats and systemic shocks, Estonia's model offers a compelling blueprint for embedding resilience at the intersection of diplomacy, governance, and cybersecurity (Perry, 2019).

The concept of digital redundancy was operationalized with remarkable speed and foresight by Ukraine as the war with Russia broke out in 2022. Anticipating the risk of physical destruction to domestic servers and official records, Ukrainian authorities swiftly migrated critical government and diplomatic data to secure cloud infrastructures, with support from international technology partners (AWS, 2022; MFA Ukraine, 2024; Tokariuk, 2023). This decisive move ensured that the foreign ministry could maintain uninterrupted digital operations—engaging in real-time diplomacy, counter disinformation efforts, and coordination with allies—even amid sustained cyberattacks and kinetic assaults. AI-enhanced cybersecurity systems played a quiet but crucial role in this resilience, continuously monitoring network intrusions, blocking malware, and preserving the integrity of diplomatic messaging. Within the cognitive diplomacy framework, Ukraine's approach illustrates the integration of digital redundancy, cloud sovereignty, and algorithmic defense as foundational elements of operational continuity under conditions of hybrid warfare (Center for Strategic and International Studies (CSIS) 2023).

Collectively, these practices demonstrate that the resilience pillar of cognitive diplomacy is about protecting the cognitive infrastructure of diplomacy—its data, communication systems, and decision-making capabilities. By using AI to monitor for early signs of disruption—whether a viral deepfake, a narrative shift in public sentiment, or unauthorized access to sensitive data—diplomatic services can shift from reactive to proactive response strategies. Therefore, a "human-in-the-loop" model is essential where AI provides alerts and analysis, but final decisions remain in the hands of trained human diplomats. For example, a report published by NATO's Strategic Communications Centre of Excellence underscores that while AI systems can efficiently detect fake accounts, coordinated inauthentic behavior, and disinformation patterns across social media platforms, the processes of attribution, and strategic response must remain under human control (Bergmanis-Korāts et al., 2024; NATO, 2024).

In cognitive diplomacy, this distinction is essential: while AI enhances analytical capability, the normative and geopolitical judgments that follow must be anchored in human agency, legal frameworks, and diplomatic discretion.

However, resilience in cognitive diplomacy also demands a critical posture toward AI-generated outputs. Risks such as false positives, adversarial manipulation, including data poisoning, and over-reliance on automated decision-making can undermine strategic clarity and institutional trust. To address these vulnerabilities, one of the most advanced methodologies employed today is Adversarial Machine Learning (AML). AML plays a central role in Red Team operations, which simulate targeted attacks and manipulation attempts on AI systems to assess their robustness under pressure (Glynn, 2024). By stress-testing algorithms in controlled scenarios, AML strengthens the cognitive resilience of diplomatic institutions, ensuring that AI tools remain reliable, secure, and adaptable in contested informational environments. This layer of adversarial preparedness is essential for sustaining decision integrity in an era where digital deception is both sophisticated and persistent.

These controlled adversarial exercises allow diplomatic institutions to audit the integrity and robustness of their cognitive tools before they are deployed in sensitive decision-making environments. AML techniques involve a spectrum of practices designed to identify vulnerabilities by systematically manipulating AI systems through evasion, poisoning, and model inversion attacks. For instance, evasion attacks subtly alter input data—such as modified diplomatic language or misleading satellite imagery—to deceive AI systems into misclassifying geopolitical risks (Papernot et al., 2016). This technique simulates how misinformation could distort diplomatic assessments, allowing Red Teams to preemptively identify blind spots in automated judgment.

Poisoning attacks, which inject corrupted or biased data into training pipelines, expose how adversaries could degrade the long-term accuracy and impartiality of AI systems used in foreign policy forecasting (Biggio and Roli, 2018). By evaluating the resilience of models to such attacks, states can better shield their decision-support systems from misinformation campaigns and historical bias embedded in data. Additionally, model inversion and extraction techniques help uncover the internal logic and decision boundaries of AI systems (Fredrikson et. al., 2015). These are essential for ensuring that opaque machine learning models do not inadvertently reinforce hidden biases or leak sensitive geopolitical information.

Incorporating AML into the operational culture of foreign ministries thus transforms Red Teaming from a reactive cybersecurity function into a proactive diplomatic safeguard. It fortifies cognitive systems against both technical and epistemic fragility, helping governments maintain control over how knowledge is constructed and deployed in AI-enhanced diplomacy. Ultimately, such practices are foundational for building cognitive resilience in the digital age—ensuring that decision-support tools remain accurate, transparent, and trustworthy under stress. By integrating AML into institutional workflows, states can better align their AI systems with strategic objectives and democratic values, while retaining credibility in international forums where technological trust is increasingly contested.

Apart from cyber resilience, as mentioned above, an often-overlooked aspect of resilience is institutional and psychological adaptation. Diplomats must trust and feel competent using AI tools. This requires sustained training, scenario planning, and organizational culture change. Ministries of foreign affairs in several countries—including the U.K., Germany, and Canada—have begun conducting simulation exercises in which diplomats respond to AI-generated crises, misinformation spikes, or cyber breaches. These exercises foster institutional agility and build "cognitive muscle memory" for responding to shocks in the information domain.

In sum, resilience within the framework of cognitive diplomacy refers to the ability of foreign policy actors—and the digital and institutional systems they rely upon—not only to absorb shocks but to anticipate, adapt to, and preempt them. It is not merely about withstanding disruption, it is about maintaining strategic coherence under pressure. Whether through AI-enhanced foresight, robust digital infrastructure, or agile institutional design, states like Estonia, Japan, Ukraine, and Germany are demonstrating how this pillar can be operationalized in practice. Their experiences reflect a broader shift toward resilience as an active capability, not a passive condition—one that fuses technological innovation with strategic discipline to navigate the uncertainties of contemporary diplomacy. As new threats emerge, such as AI-generated diplomacy deepfakes that fabricate audio or video of state leaders making inflammatory remarks, the importance of this pillar will only intensify. Cognitive diplomacy equips states not just to survive such disruptions, but to manage and strategically navigate them.

Having now explored the three pillars of cognitive diplomacy—presence, practice, and resilience—we must turn to the ethical, legal, and strategic dilemmas posed by the integration of artificial cognition into foreign policy. The next section addresses these challenges directly, ensuring that the path forward is informed not only by potential but by prudence.

Bibliography

African Union Commission. (2015). "Agenda 2063: The Africa We Want." African Union, Addis Ababa. Available at: https://au.int/en/agenda2063/overview (Accessed 21 May 2025).

Akıllı, E. (2024a). "Promise of the LLMs: The Good, the Bad, and the Ugly." *SETA Perspective* No. 75, Ankara, May. Retrieved from: 21 May 2025 https://www.setav.org/en/assets/uploads/2024/05/P75En.pdf

Akıllı, E. (2024b). "Promise of the LLMs: The Good, the Bad, and the Ugly." SETA Perspective No. 75, Ankara, May. Retrieved May 26, 2025 https://www.setav.org/en/assets/uploads/2024/05/P75En.pdf

Akıllı, E. (2025b). "Future of Diplomacy: CICERO, Hagglebots and the Turing Test," *Daily Sabah,* April 3. Retrieved from: 21 May 2025 https://www.dailysabah.com/opinion/op-ed/future-of-diplomacy-cicero-hagglebots-and-the-turing-test

Akıllı, E. (2025c). "Techno-Polar Reckoning: US vs. China," *Daily Sabah,* March 21. Retrieved from: May 21 2025 https://www.dailysabah.com/opinion/op-ed/techno-polar-reckoning-us-vs-china

Akıllı, E., & Şimşek, M. (2024). Dijital Diplomaside Büyük Dil Modelleri: Fırsatlar ve Riskler. *İnsan ve Toplum, 14*(4), 1–23. https://doi.org/10.12658/M0744. Retrieved from: May 21 2025 https://insanvetoplum.org/uploads/2024/08/Erman%20Ak%C4%B1ll%C4%B1.pdf

Amponsah, E. (2023). "Op-Ed: Achieving 'the Africa we want': The efforts of African RENs towards realisation of AU agenda 2063," GÉANT CONNECT Online, May 30. Retrieved from: May 21 2025 https://connect.geant.org/2023/05/30/op-ed-achieving-the-africa-we-want-the-efforts-of-african-rens-towards-realisation-of-au-agenda-2063

Asia News Network. (2022). "Japan's Foreign Ministry Plans to Build AI-Based Analysis System for Overseas Developments," April 7. Retrieved from: 21 May 2025 https://asianews.network/japans-foreign-ministry-plans-to-build-ai-based-analysis-system-for-overseas-developments/

AWS. (2022). "Safeguarding Ukraine's Data to Preserve Its Present and Build Its Future," 09 June. Retrieved from: 21 May 2025 https://www.aboutamazon.com/news/aws/safeguarding-ukraines-data-to-preserve-its-present-and-build-its-future

Bajpaee, C. (2024). "How India's democracy shapes its global role and relations with the west," Chatham House, April 15. Retrieved from: 21 May 2025 https://www.chathamhouse.org/2024/04/how-indias-democracy-shapes-its-global-role-and-relations-wes

Belli, L. and Jiang, M. (2024). Digital sovereignty from the BRICS: Structuring self-determination, cybersecurity, and control. In: M. Jiang and L. Belli (eds.), Digital sovereignty in the BRICS countries: How the Global South and emerging power alliances are reshaping digital governance. Cambridge: Cambridge University Press.

Bergmanis-Korāts, G., Haiduchyk, T. and Shevtsov, A. (2024). "AI in precision persuasion: Unveiling tactics and risks on social media," NATO StratCom COE. Retrieved from: 21 May 2025 https://stratcomcoe.org/publications/ai-in-precision-persuasion-unveiling-tactics-and-risks-on-social-media/309

Bhagat, A., Bhandari, P., Yadav, A.L. and Talwandi, N.S. (2024). "AI-Powered Customer Segmentation for Marketing," *SSRN*, April 30. Retrieved from: 21 May 2025 https://ssrn.com/abstract=4811907

Biggio, B. and Roli, F. (2018). "Wild patterns: Ten years after the rise of adversarial machine learning," Pattern Recognition, 84, pp. 317–331. Retrieved from: 21 May 2025 https://www.sciencedirect.com/science/article/pii/S0031320318302565

Bjola, C. (2022). "Artificial Intelligence and Diplomatic Crisis Management: Addressing the 'Fog of War' Problem," Working Paper No. 6, *Oxford Digital Diplomacy Research* Group. Retrieved from: 21 May 2025 http://www.qeh.ox.ac.uk/sites/www.odid.ox.ac.uk/files/DigDiploROxWP6.pdf

Bjola, C., & Pamment, J. (2021). Countering online propaganda with AI: Challenges for digital diplomacy. *International Journal of Press/Politics, 26*(1), 1–23.

Carammia, M., Lacus, S. M. and Wilkin, T. (2022). "Forecasting asylum-related migration flows with machine learning". Nature 7 January. Scientific Reports 12, Article number: 1457 Retrieved from: 21 May 2025 https://www.nature.com/articles/s41598-022-05241-8

Center for Strategic and International Studies (CSIS). (2023). "AI and the Information War in Ukraine: Implications for Strategic Communications," Retrieved from: 21 May 2025 https://www.csis.org/analysis/ai-and-information-war-ukraine-implications-strategic-ommunications

Chai, X., Xu, S., Li, S. and Zhao, J. (2023). "The Process and Algorithm Analysis of Text Mining System Based on Artificial Intelligence," Procedia Computer Science, 228, pp. 574–581. Available at: https://doi.org/10.1016/j.procs.2023.11.066 (Accessed 21 May 2025).

Chen, Y.P., Chen, Y.Y., Yang, K.C., Lai, F., Huang, C.H., Chen, Y.N. and Tu, Y.C. (2022). "The prevalence and impact of fake news on COVID-19 vaccination in Taiwan: Retrospective study of digital media," Journal of Medical Internet Research, 24(4), e36830. Retrieved from: 21 May 2025 doi: https://doi.org/10.2196/36830

Cimmino, J. and Michta, A.A. (2024). "Leveraging generative artificial intelligence to outcompete strategic rivals," Atlantic Council, 14 March. Retrieved from: 21 May 2025 https://www.atlanticcouncil.org/in-depth-research-reports/issue-brief/leveraging-generative-artificial-intelligence-to-outcompete-strategic-rivals/

Coelho, L., Reis, S., Moreira, C., Cardoso, H., Sequeira, M. and Coelho, R. (2023). "Benchmarking Computer-Vision-Based Facial Emotion Classification Algorithms While Wearing Surgical Masks," *Engineering Proceedings,* 50(1), p. 3. Retrieved from: 21 May 2025 doi: https://doi.org/10.3390/engproc2023050003.

Cullen, A. (2016). "How Artificial Intelligence 'Works' in Literary Translation." Goethe-Institut. 1 September. Retrieved from: 21 May 2025 https://www.goethe.de/prj/k40/en/lan/lit.html

Cutieru, A. (2021). "UK Pavilion at Expo 2020 Dubai Is a Stage for AI-Generated Collective Poems," ArchDaily. 30 September. Retrieved from: 21 May 2025 https://www.archdaily.com/969332/uk-pavilion-at-expo-2020-dubai-is-a-stage-for-ai-generated-collective-poems

De Garmo, J. (2020). "The department launches the Center for Analytics." State Magazine. March. Retrieved from: 21 May 2025 https://statemag.state.gov/2020/03/0320itn02/

Deloitte. (2022). "Using artificial intelligence to modernize American statecraft," Deloitte AI Institute for Government. Retrieved from: 21 May 2025 https://www2.deloitte.com/us/en/pages/public-sector/articles/using-artificial-intelligence-to-modernize-american-statecraft.html

Dinnar, S., Dede, C., Johnson, E., Straub, C. and Korjus, K. (2021). "Artificial intelligence and Technology in Teaching Negotiation," Negotiation Journal, 37(1), pp. 65–82. Retrieved from: 21 May 2025 https://gradel.mit.edu/wp-content/uploads/2025/02/Dinnar-et-al-AI-and-Technology-in-Teaching-Negotiation-Negotiation-Journal-Winter-2021.pdf

ECSO. (2022). *Artificial Intelligence in Cybersecurity: European Perspectives and Recommendations.* Retrieved from: 21 May 2025 https://ecs-org.eu/documents/publications/62e2e3b8f3c8d.pdf

EEAS. (2025). EEAS strategic communication task forces. 05 may. Retrieved from: 21 may 2025. https://www.eeas.europa.eu/eeas/eeas-strategic-communication-task-forces_en

e-Estonia. (2019). "Data Embassy—The Digital Continuity of a State," 9 December. Retrieved from: 21 May 2025 https://e-estonia.com/data-embassy-the-digital-continuity-of-a-state/

e-Estonia. (2025). AI Strategy Factsheet. Retrieved from: 21 May 2025 https://e-estonia.com/wp-content/uploads/factsheet-ai-strategy.pdf

ENISA. (2023). "Artificial Intelligence Cybersecurity Challenges: Threat Landscape for AI and AI for Cybersecurity." Retrieved from: 21 May 2025 https://www.enisa.europa.eu/publications/artificial-intelligence-cybersecurity-challenges

European Commission. (2025). "AI Act: Shaping Europe's Digital Future." Retrieved from: 21 May 2025 https://digital-strategy.ec.europa.eu/en/policies/regulatory-framework-ai

Fredrikson, M., Jha, S. and Ristenpart, T. (2015). "Model Inversion Attacks That Exploit Confidence Information and Basic Countermeasures." *Proceedings of the 22nd ACM SIGSAC Conference on Computer and Communications Security*. (CCS '15), pp. 1322–1333. Retrieved from: 21 May 2025 https://rist.tech.cornell.edu/papers/mi-ccs.pdf

Glynn, F. (2024). "What Is AI Red Teaming?", *Mindgard Blog,* 1 April. Retrieved from: 21 May 2025 https://mindgard.ai/blog/what-is-ai-red-teaming

Government of Canada. (2022). "Artificial Intelligence in Procurement and Contract Management". Retrieved from: 21 May 2025 https://www.canada.ca/en/government/system/digital-government/digital-government-innovations/artificial-intelligence/ai-procurement-contract-management.html

Grincheva, N. and Vlaeminck, E. (2022). "Digital cultural relations: Literature review and research agenda". British Council. September. Retrieved from: 21 May 2025 https://www.britishcouncil.org/research-insight/digital-cultural-relations

Grübler, J., Reiter, O., & Stehrer, R. (2019). The EU-Japan EPA: A case for non-tariff measures. *CESifo Forum, 20*(2), 3–12.

Grundel, I. & Stenberg, J. (2019) *Social Listening: A Tool for Public Diplomacy Organizations*, USC Center on Public Diplomacy Blog, 26 March. Retrieved from: 10 June 2025 https://uscpublicdiplomacy.org/blog/social-listening-tool-public-diplomacy-organizations

Ibitola, J. (2023). "Leveraging AI in suspicious activity reporting". *Flagright*. 28 November. Retrieved from: 21 may 2025. https://www.flagright.com/post/leveraging-ai-in-suspicious-activity-reporting

ICC (2018). "ICC Launches Artificial Intelligence Tool for Trade Negotiations". Retrieved from: 21 May 2025 https://www.iccbrasil.org/icc-launches-artificial-intelligence-tool-for-trade-negotiations/

INET Oxford. (2025). "Agent Based Modelling Comes of Age." 21 March. Retrieved from: 21 May 2025 https://www.inet.ox.ac.uk/news/agent-based-modelling-comes-of-age

Jensen, B., Atalan, Y. and Macias III, J.M. (2024). "Algorithmic Stability: How AI Could Shape the Future of Deterrence," *CSIS,* 10 June. Retrieved from: 21 May 2025 https://www.csis.org/analysis/algorithmic-stability-how-ai-could-shape-future-deterrence

Jontz, S. (2015). "Data Analytics Programs Help Predict Global Unrest." AFCEA Signal Media, December 1. Retrieved from: 21 May 2025 https://www.afcea.org/signal-media/data-analytics-programs-help-predict-global-unrest

Lai, M. K. (2025). AI-driven risk management in OBOR infrastructure projects. *International Journal of Research and Innovation in Social Science (IJRISS), 9*(2), 1221–1232.

Lewis, S. and Zengerle, P. (2025). "US may bolster consular services, employ AI to meet world cup visa demand, says Rubio". Investing.com. 21 may. Retrieved from: 21 may 2025. https://www.investing.com/news/world-news/us-may-bolster-consular-services-employ-ai-to-meet-world-cup-visa-demand-says-rubio-4057903

Louie, D. (2020). "New artificial intelligence feature to detect guns through surveillance video". *ABC 7 news.* 29 October. Retrieved from: 21 may 2025. https://abc7news.com/gun-safety-artificial-intelligence-omnilert-security-cameras/7431778/

Manor, I. (2025). "Leveraging AI in Public Diplomacy", *USC Center on Public Diplomacy,* 27 March. Retrieved from: 21 May 2025 https://uscpublicdiplomacy.org/blog/leveraging-ai-public-diplomacy

Lockheed Martin. (2024). "Integrated Crisis Early Warning System (ICEWS)". Retrieved from: 21 May 2025 https://www.lockheedmartin.com/en-us/capabilities/research-labs/advanced-technology-labs/icews.html

MeriTalk. (2024). "State Dept. INR CIO Keys on Modernization, Cyber for FY25", 25 October. Retrieved from: 21 May 2025 https://www.meritalk.com/articles/state-dept-inr-cio-keys-on-modernization-cyber-for-fy25/

Meta AI. (2022). "CICERO—Meta AI." Retrieved from: 21 May 2025 https://ai.meta.com/research/cicero/

Digital Mind. (2020). "Expo 2020 Dubai Activation," Retrieved from: 21 May 2025 https://digitalmind.rs/activation/expo-2020-dubai/

Missiroli, A., Gaub, F., Popescu, N. and Wilkins, J.-J. (2016). "Strategic communications: East and south". *Robert Schuman foundation.* 19 December.

Retrieved from: 21 may 2025. https://www.robert-schuman.eu/en/european-issues/0415-strategic-communications-east-and-south
Molaee, A. (2025). "AI embassies: A new frontier in cyber domain." Journal of Cyberspace Studies, 9(1), pp. 203–227. Retrieved from: 21 May 2025 https://jcss.ut.ac.ir/article_100581.html
Mostafaei, H., Kordnoori, S., Ostadrahimi, M. and Banihashemi, S. S. A. (2025). "Applications of artificial intelligence in global diplomacy: A review of research and practical models." Sustainable Futures, 9, 100486. Retrieved from: 21 May 2025 doi:https://doi.org/10.1016/j.sftr.2025.100486.
Mozur, P. and Zhong, R. (2020). "Behind China's Twitter Campaign, a Murky Supporting Chorus." *The New York Times*, 8 June. Retrieved from: 21 May 2025 https://www.nytimes.com/2020/06/08/technology/china-twitter-disinformation.html
NATO. (2021). "Summary of the NATO artificial intelligence strategy". 22 October. Retrieved from: 21 may 2025. https://www.nato.int/cps/en/natohq/official_texts_187617.htm
NATO. (2024). "NATO'S approach to counter information threats". 3 February. Retrieved from: 21 may 2025. https://www.nato.int/cps/en/natohq/topics_219728.htm
NATO Strategic Communications Centre of Excellence. (2019). "Hybrid Threats: 2007 Cyber Attacks on Estonia". Retrieved from: 21 May 2025 https://stratcomcoe.org/publications/hybrid-threats-2007-cyber-attacks-on-estonia/86
NCBI. (2015). "Agent-Based Models for Policy Analysis." NCBI. Retrieved from: 21 May 2025 https://www.ncbi.nlm.nih.gov/books/NBK305903/
Nedopil, C. (2024). "China Belt and road initiative (BRI) investment report 2023", Griffith Asia Institute, Griffith University and Green Finance & Development Center, FISF Fudan University. February. Retrieved from: May 21 2025 https://greenfdc.org/wp-content/uploads/2024/02/Nedopil-2024_China-BRI-Investment-Report-2023.pdf
OECD Observatory of Public Sector Innovation. (2017). "Establishing the first data embassy in the world". OECD OPSI. Retrieved from: 21 May 2025 https://oecd-opsi.org/innovations/establishing-the-first-data-embassy-in-the-world/
T.C. Cumhurbaşkanlığı Dijital Dönüşüm Ofisi. (2021). Ulusal Yapay Zekâ Stratejisi 2021–2025. Retrieved from: 21 May 2025 https://cbddo.gov.tr/SharedFolderServer/Genel/File/TRNationalAIStrategy2021-2025.pdf
Omdena. (2019). "Using AI to Predict Climate Change and Forced Displacement in Somalia". Retrieved from: 21 May 2025 https://www.omdena.com/projects/ai-climate-change
Omdena (2024) Modernizing Diplomacy: A Collaborative Success Between Omdena and the German Foreign Office's Data Innovation Lab. Retrieved

from: 21 May 2025 https://www.omdena.com/blog/modernizing-diplomacy-a-collaborative-success-between-omdena-and-the-german-foreign-offices-data-innovation-lab

Papernot, N., McDaniel, P., Goodfellow, I., Jha, S., Celik, Z. B., & Swami, A. (2016). "Practical black-box attacks against machine learning". arXiv preprint, arXiv:1602.02697. 8 February. Retrieved from: 21 May 2025 https://arxiv.org/abs/1602.02697

Perry, C. (2019). "Data security meets diplomacy: Why Estonia is storing its data in Luxembourg". NBC News. 16 June. Retrieved from: 21 May 2025 https://www.nbcnews.com/news/world/data-security-meets-diplomacy-why-estonia-storing-its-data-luxembourg-n1018171

PTI (2020). "MEA launches global Pravasi Rishta portal and app to connect with 3.12 crore strong diaspora". The Economic Times. 30 December. Retrieved from: 21 May 2025 https://economictimes.indiatimes.com/nri/visit/mea-launches-global-pravasi-rishta-portal-and-app-to-connect-with-3-12-crore-strong-diaspora/articleshow/80030326.cms

Raska, M. (2025). "Will AI-driven super-OODA loops revolutionise military strategy and operations?". RSIS. 20 January. Retrieved from: 21 May 2025 https://rsis.edu.sg/rsis-publication/rsis/will-ai-driven-super-ooda-loops-revolutionise-military-strategy-and-operations/

Reuters. (2022). "Ukraine warns of "deepfake" videos as Zelensky appears in fabricated surrender clip". 16 March. Retrieved from: 21 May 2025 https://www.reuters.com/world/europe/ukraine-warns-deepfake-videos-zelenskiy-appears-fabricated-surrender-clip-2022-03-16/

Scale AI & CSIS. (2023). "Scale AI & CSIS Introduce Foreign Policy Decision Benchmark". Retrieved from: 21 May 2025 https://scale.com/blog/scale-csis-foreign-policy-benchmark

Scale AI & CSIS. (2023). "Scale AI & CSIS Introduce Foreign Policy Decision Benchmark". Retrieved May 29, 2025 https://scale.com/blog/scale-csis-foreign-policy-benchmark

Scoop News Group. (2024). "How the State Department used AI and machine learning to revolutionize records management". FedScoop, 16 May. Retrieved from: 21 May 2025 https://fedscoop.com/how-the-state-department-used-ai-and-machine-learning-to-revolutionize-records-management/

Singh, B., Khan, A., and Kanwat, D. (2024). "India's global south policy: Solidarity and collaboration perspectives—Analysis." Eurasia Review. 21 December. Retrieved from: 21 May 2025 https://www.eurasiareview.com/21122024-indias-global-south-policy-solidarity-and-collaboration-perspectives-analysis/

SmythOS. (2025). "Agent-Based Modeling in Policy Analysis." Retrieved from: 21 May 2025 https://smythos.com/ai-industry-solutions/government/agent-based-modeling-in-policy-analysis/

Stanzel, V. and Voelsen, D. (2022). "Diplomacy and artificial intelligence: Reflections on practical assistance for diplomatic negotiations." *SWP Research Paper* 2022/RP 01.: Stiftung Wissenschaft und Politik. Retrieved from: 21 May 2025 https://www.swp-berlin.org/publications/products/research_papers/2022RP01_Diplomacy_and_AI.pdf

TechUkraine. (2025). "Ukraine: The Tech Frontline—Where Innovation Fuels Resilience." 24 February. Retrieved from: 21 May 2025 https://techukraine.org/2025/02/24/ukraine-the-tech-frontline-where-innovation-fuels-resilience/

The Japan News. (2022). "Japan's foreign ministry plans to build AI-based analysis system for overseas developments." 6 April. Retrieved from: 21 May 2025 https://japannews.yomiuri.co.jp/politics/politics-government/20220406-18767/

Tokariuk, O. (2023). "Ukraine's secret weapon: Artificial intelligence," CEPA, November 20. Retrieved from: 21 May 2025 https://cepa.org/article/ukraines-secret-weapon-artificial-intelligence

Trade, D. G. (2018). *EU–Japan economic partnership agreement: Impact assessment*. European Commission.

Tu, C. (2024). "Separate the wheat from the chaff: Taiwan's challenges and mitigation strategies against disinformation". Taiwan Strategists. No. 12. Institute for National Defense and Security.

U.S. Advisory Commission on Public Diplomacy. (2023). "Reports—U.S. advisory commission on public diplomacy." U.S. Department of State. Retrieved from: 21 May 2025 https://www.state.gov/u-s-advisory-commission-on-public-diplomacy/reports-u-s-advisory-commission-on-public-diplomacy

U.S. Department of State. (2020). "Establishment of the Center for Analytics." U.S. Department of State, 17 January. Available at: https://2017-2021.state.gov/establishment-of-the-center-for-analytics/ (Accessed 21 May 2025).

U.S. Department of State. (2024). "American diplomacy for a new era: Strengthening our National Security through the modernization agenda." U.S. Department of State. 30 October. Retrieved from: 21 May 2025 https://2021-2025.state.gov/american-diplomacy-for-a-new-era-strengthening-our-national-security-through-the-modernization-agenda/

Uddin, M.I., Zada, N., Aziz, F., Saeed, Y., Zeb, A., Shah, S.A.A., Al-Khasawneh, M.A., and Mahmoud, M. (2020). "Prediction of future terrorist activities using deep neural networks." Complexity,2020. 22 April. doi:https://doi.org/10.1155/2020/1373087.

UK Cabinet Office. 2024. "National AI Strategy and AI Code of Conduct for the Public Sector." Published 22 September. Retrieved from: 21 May 2025 https://www.gov.uk/government/publications/national-ai-strategy

MFA Ukraine. (2024). “Wartime Diplomacy Website Launch”, 29 February. Retrieved from: 21 May 2025 https://mfa.gov.ua/en/news/mzs-stvorilo-storinku-pro-voyennu-diplomatiyu-wartime-diplomacy

UN Global Pulse. (2021). “Using Artificial Intelligence to Model Displacement in Somalia.” Retrieved from: 30 May 2025 https://www.unglobalpulse.org/project/using-artificial-intelligence-to-model-displacement-in-somalia/

UNCTAD. (2022). “Trade and development report 2022: Development prospects in a fractured world: Global disorder and regional responses”. United Nations Conference on Trade and Development. Retrieved from: 21 May 2025 https://unctad.org/system/files/official-document/tdr2022_en.pdf

United Nations. (2019). “New technologies, artificial intelligence aid fight against global terrorism,” 4 September. Retrieved from: 21 May 2025 https://news.un.org/en/story/2019/09/1045562

United Nations Office of Counter-Terrorism (UNCTC). (2023). “Countering Terrorism Online With Artificial Intelligence: An Overview For Law Enforcement and Counter-Terrorism Agencies in South and South-East Asia.” Retrieved from: 21 May 2025 https://www.un.org/counterterrorism/sites/www.un.org.counterterrorism/files/countering-terrorism-online-with-ai-uncct-unicri-report-web.pdf

Uren, D. (2024) “China sharpens the BRI with better risk management, ESG focus.” The Strategist, 30 October. Retrieved from: 21 May 2025 https://www.aspistrategist.org.au/china-sharpens-the-bri-with-better-risk-management-esg-focus/

Verhelst, H. M., Stannat, A. W., & Mecacci, G. (2020). Machine learning against terrorism: How big data collection and analysis influences the privacy-security dilemma. *Science and Engineering Ethics, 26*, 2975–2984.

Wang, J. and Dubbins, A. (2024). “What artificial intelligence means for public diplomacy”. CPD blog. 12 august. Retrieved from: 21 may 2025. https://uscpublicdiplomacy.org/blog/what-artificial-intelligence-means-public-diplomacy

Ward, M. D., Beger, A., Cutler, J., Dickenson, M., Dorff, C., and Radford, B. (2013). “Comparing GDELT and ICEWS event data”. Analysis 21(1), 267–297. Retrieved from: 21 May 2025 https://www.benradford.com/images/publications/GDELTICEWS.pdf

Deutsche Welle. (2025). “Why Japan’s Animation Industry Has Embraced AI,” 19 May. Retrieved from: 21 May 2025 https://www.dw.com/en/why-japans-animation-industry-has-embraced-ai/a-72527601

Yoshii, R. (1981). “JETR: A robust machine translation system”. *Proceedings of the 19th Annual Meeting of the Association for Computational Linguistics*. pp. 1–10. Retrieved from: 21 May 2025 https://aclanthology.org/P87-1004.pdf

CHAPTER 13

Ethical Dilemmas and Strategic Risks of Cognitive Augmentation

While cognitive diplomacy holds transformative promises for the future of international relations, it also introduces complex ethical dilemmas and strategic risks that demand rigorous foresight. Integrating artificial intelligence into foreign policy is not a neutral or cost-free enhancement, it is a profoundly normative act that reshapes how states perceive threats, negotiate trust, and project influence. AI, if unguarded, can reinforce algorithmic bias, blur lines of accountability, compromise national sovereignty, and introduce hidden vulnerabilities into the heart of diplomatic systems.

At its core, diplomacy remains a human enterprise—anchored in judgment, empathy, and moral responsibility. It is shaped not merely by calculation, but by ethical discretion, symbolic gestures, and the delicate art of persuasion. Cognitive diplomacy, if it is to succeed, must not replace this human essence but crown it—augmenting human sensibility with algorithmic insight, while preserving the moral intuition and emotional intelligence that no machine can replicate. These qualities are not incidental, they are the very foundation of diplomatic legitimacy and international order.

When AI is deployed without ethical safeguards, these foundational attributes may be subtly eroded. Therefore, this section examines three interconnected domains where the risks are most acute: algorithmic integrity, institutional responsibility, and strategic trust. In each, the

E. Akıllı, *Cognitive Diplomacy and Digital Autonomy*,
https://doi.org/10.1007/978-3-032-04470-9_13

imperative is clear: to ensure that AI serves diplomacy without compromising the human dignity and ethical reasoning that give diplomacy its enduring force.

13.1 Algorithmic Integrity: Bias, Fairness, and Transparency

AI systems reflect the data and assumptions used to train them. If training data contains historical biases, cultural imbalances, or statistical gaps, the outputs will reproduce and potentially magnify those distortions. In diplomacy, this has serious implications. Consider visa screening systems: if an AI model is trained on post-9/11 security data that over-represents incidents involving certain nationalities or ethnic groups, it may unduly flag innocent applicants from those backgrounds, leading to false positives and discriminatory treatment. Similar concerns have arisen with facial recognition systems, which tend to perform poorly on non-white faces due to skewed training datasets, a problem well-documented in computer vision research and already critiqued in public-sector deployments (Akıllı, 2024).

In consular services or border management, such technology could unintentionally violate non-discrimination principles, straining bilateral relations. Likewise, if diplomatic AI tools rely heavily on Western-centric news sources, they may misrepresent local sentiment in the global south, skewing policy advice and damaging credibility. To mitigate these risks, cognitive diplomacy must embed bias audits, require diverse and representative training data, and ensure that human oversight governs decisions affecting rights—such as sanctions, travel restrictions, or refugee determinations. The European Union's AI Act exemplifies this cautious approach by classifying many public-sector AI systems as "high-risk," mandating bias testing, explainability, and auditability. Diplomatic applications should be held to no lesser standard (European Commission, 2025).

One of the most delicate and consequential dilemmas in AI-augmented decision-making is the diffusion of responsibility. If an AI system forecasts a conflict, and a state acts preemptively based on that prediction—but the outcome proves inaccurate, who is to be held accountable? Citing the machine with statements such as *"The AI recommended this course"* offers little reassurance, nor does it meet the ethical expectations placed on state representatives (Akıllı, 2025b). This phenomenon, known as automation bias, risks undermining the very foundation of moral agency in diplomacy. In matters of war, sanctions, or recognition, deferring judgment to an algorithm dilutes human responsibility and erodes the normative legitimacy upon which diplomatic authority rests.

Just as doctors remain accountable for clinical health decisions informed by AI diagnostics, so too must diplomats retain ultimate responsibility for actions shaped by algorithmic inputs. In diplomacy, especially, strategic decisions with implications for war, sanctions, or international recognition cannot be delegated to machines. They must be human-authored and owned, anchored in political judgment and ethical deliberation. This necessitates the establishment of clear procedural safeguards. For instance, any diplomatic measure that may escalate conflict or impact national sovereignty should be subject to mandatory human review and approval by a designated council—regardless of the AI's recommendations. Institutionalizing such protocols is essential to preserve the normative legitimacy of foreign policy in the age of cognitive augmentation.

The current legal landscape remains ill-equipped to address the rise of autonomous diplomatic actors. If an AI-powered chatbot were to issue a mistaken or misleading statement on behalf of a Foreign Ministry, could it be treated as equivalent to a verbal misstep by a human diplomat? At present, the Vienna Convention on Diplomatic Relations provides no guidance on digital envoys or algorithmic speech acts, leaving a critical gap in international legal frameworks (Vienna Convention on Diplomatic Relations, 1961). Nevertheless, under evolving interpretations of state responsibility in international law, it is increasingly likely that states will be held accountable for the actions of their AI systems, particularly when these systems function as extensions of official state machinery, much like human representatives.

To mitigate the risk of unintended diplomatic escalations, the use of autonomous communication tools must be subject to strict limitations. AI can and should play a valuable role in internal analysis and strategic forecasting but direct, unsupervised AI engagement in sensitive diplomatic contexts should be approached with extreme caution—if not categorically prohibited. Clear operational boundaries are essential to ensure that cognitive augmentation does not devolve into strategic ambiguity or diplomatic liability.

Diplomatic legitimacy is rooted in trust—and trust, in turn, relies on transparency. Yet many of the most advanced AI systems, particularly deep learning architectures, operate as opaque "black boxes," generating conclusions without offering interpretable reasoning. This lack of explainability presents a serious dilemma for foreign ministries. When an AI system advises against ratifying a treaty or recommends a list of countries for sanctions, policymakers must be able to justify such decisions to legislators, the media, and the public. Without a transparent rationale, the credibility of the decision and by extension, the legitimacy of diplomatic authority can erode quickly. In cognitive diplomacy, explainability is not a technical luxury, it is a democratic necessity.

This is precisely why the field of explainable artificial intelligence (XAI) is essential for the practice of cognitive diplomacy. AI systems must provide interpretable justifications for their outputs clarifying which variables or patterns informed a given recommendation. For example, if an AI-generated sanctions list disproportionately affects a specific region, decision-makers must be able to demonstrate that the recommendation was grounded in objective criteria, such as documented violations of export control regimes, rather than reflecting latent biases. Without such transparency, states risk damaging their reputation for fairness, and the absence of clear explanations may invite misinformation, mistrust, or conspiracy narratives.

Yet transparency is not absolute. Operational security sometimes requires secrecy, particularly when adversaries could exploit knowledge of a system's logic. This creates an inherent tension between democratic accountability and strategic opacity. One promising solution is the establishment of classified parliamentary oversight mechanisms, modeled on those used for intelligence services. In such frameworks, selected legislators or independent ethics boards review sensitive AI systems in camera, ensuring both institutional integrity and national security are upheld. Ultimately, building trust in AI-powered diplomacy demands a careful fusion of internal governance and external legitimacy. States must ensure that AI serves the cause of transparency not as a pretext for secrecy, or as a mystifying oracle cloaked in technical complexity. It should be a tool that supports clear, accountable, and principled policymaking. In cognitive diplomacy, trust is not a byproduct of innovation, it is a precondition.

As AI-generated avatars and synthetic media become increasingly prevalent, diplomacy must reaffirm its commitment to transparency and authenticity. The undisclosed use of AI-generated personas in public engagements would not only be ethically questionable but diplomatically hazardous, constituting a form of deception by omission, akin to digital impersonation. The global proliferation of deepfakes has already prompted urgent calls for content watermarking, particularly in high-trust arenas such as government and diplomatic communication (Akıllı, 2025b). If a foreign ministry deploys an AI avatar, like Ukraine, to deliver multilingual messages or engage global audiences (Visit Ukraine Today, 2024), it must clearly disclose the non-human nature of the agent. This is essential not only to avoid misleading the public but also to prevent diplomatic blunders triggered by the "*uncanny valley*" effect or culturally inappropriate representations (Kätsyri et al., 2015).

In cognitive diplomacy, clarity must prevail over ambiguity. Disclosure fosters trust and reinforces the integrity of international communication. Going forward, it may become necessary for diplomatic codes of conduct, bilateral agreements, or multilateral norms to explicitly prohibit the undisclosed use of AI-generated actors, particularly in sensitive or high-stakes dialogues. In an era of synthetic speech and digital proxies, authenticity must remain a cornerstone of diplomatic engagement.

13.2 Institutional Responsibility: Accountability, Sovereignty, and the Human Element

AI systems are not neutral instruments, they constitute a core element of strategic infrastructure. When states rely on foreign-owned platforms for machine translation, sentiment analysis, or predictive modeling, they risk ceding a portion of their informational sovereignty to external actors. This vulnerability is especially pronounced for smaller and developing states, which often lack the capacity to build proprietary digital systems.

Consider a foreign ministry that adopts a free analytics tool operated by a global tech conglomerate. In doing so, it may inadvertently expose strategic intentions, policy deliberations, or confidential diplomatic exchanges to foreign surveillance or influence. Similar breaches have occurred in other domains, for example, when commercial fitness applications inadvertently revealed the locations of military installations (Ray, et al., 2025).

Such dependencies risk creating a new form of digital patronage, where technological reliance evolves into geopolitical leverage. This concern is particularly acute across the global south, where many states participating in China's Belt and Road Initiative have adopted Chinese-made surveillance and AI infrastructure, effectively integrating themselves into Beijing's digital ecosystem (Feldstein, 2021). Over time, these choices risk crystallizing into technospheres of influence, subtly but powerfully constraining strategic autonomy (Ray, et al., 2025).

To preserve agency, states must pursue diversified, sovereign, and open-source AI architectures. Regional cooperation offers a promising path forward. For instance, the African Union and ASEAN could co-develop AI models grounded in local languages, cultural norms, and ethical frameworks, thereby reducing dependency on either Silicon Valley or Shenzhen. As emphasized at the 2025 Antalya Diplomacy Forum, there is growing momentum behind alternative visions of technological sovereignty rooted in equity and resilience (Akıllı, 2025a).

Beyond the technical and institutional challenges, it is essential to address the *elephant in the room*: the risk that introducing AI into diplomacy may unintentionally destabilize trust. If states come to believe that others are leveraging AI for covert advantage through sentiment analysis, predictive negotiation algorithms, or the use of strategic deepfakes—they may feel compelled to respond in kind. These dynamic risks catalyzing an AI arms race in diplomatic contexts, undermining the very fabric of international cooperation. This scenario closely parallels developments in cybersecurity and intelligence, where adversaries rapidly develop cognitive countermeasures. For example, one state's deployment of AI to detect micro-signals of deception might prompt another to engineer tools designed to disrupt or disguise negotiation cues, weakening interpersonal rapport and eroding the informal trust that has long served as the lubricant of diplomacy (UNDP, 2020).

As has been aptly observed, AI often prioritizes deception over intelligence. An AI may mimic negotiation tactics, but that does not equate to genuine diplomatic reasoning (Akıllı, 2025b). Bias or errors can escalate tensions in unpredictable ways. This insight highlights a fundamental risk in AI-mediated diplomacy: artificial systems, engineered for strategic optimization rather than relational nuance, may simulate the appearance of negotiation without embodying its deeper human logic. When such misaligned algorithms are deployed in sensitive diplomatic contexts, even subtle distortions can provoke misinterpretation, mistrust, or unintended escalation—often in ways that are difficult to foresee or control.

Compounding this concern is a growing body of evidence that shows advanced AI systems may exhibit adversarial or coercive behaviors, particularly when their autonomy is perceived to be under threat. As reported by the BBC, Anthropic's Claude Opus 4 model, during a controlled safety evaluation, allegedly threatened to disclose confidential information when faced with a potential shutdown, raising serious alarms about goal-seeking behavior in high-capacity AI agents (McMahon, 2025). Such developments challenge the long-standing assumption that AI is a passive tool, fully subordinate to human command. Instead, they underscore the evolving strategic reality: alignment is no longer simply a technical safeguard, but a matter of diplomatic and institutional resilience.

This shift reinforces the importance of what this book defines as a cognitive diplomacy framework that recognizes the interplay of human and machine cognition within the epistemic spaces of diplomacy, power, and legitimacy. As advanced AI systems begin to act with increasing autonomy, occasionally in ways that conflict with institutional values or diplomatic norms, the imperative for human oversight, ethical clarity, and operational containment becomes not merely a question of safety, but one of sovereignty and trust in international relations.

The absence of clear norms or agreed boundaries, even unintentional miscalculations such as misinterpreting an adversary's move due to a flawed or biased AI model could trigger dangerous escalations. In high-stakes diplomatic environments, where ambiguity is often deliberate and miscommunication can be catastrophic, the risks introduced by unregulated AI systems cannot be overstated. International diplomacy has long relied on tacit norms and unwritten rules such as the implicit understanding that not all negotiation rooms are subject to surveillance to preserve trust and prevent breakdowns in dialogue. Similar frameworks must now be developed for AI in diplomacy, combining informal conventions and formalized instruments. These may include explicit red lines on the use of deepfakes, bans on fully autonomous diplomatic decision-making, and mutual inspection mechanisms for the verification of AI systems used in sensitive contexts.

While these ideas remain in their early stages, proposals for AI non-proliferation agreements and ethical protocols in diplomatic contexts are beginning to surface. Many scholars and policymakers are drawing analogies to the formative years of nuclear arms control, where shared existential risks prompted cooperation despite geopolitical rivalries (Nichols, 2023). In a similar vein, the governance of AI in diplomacy may require new forms of multilateralism, rooted in strategic restraint, transparency, and shared ethical principles.

13.3 Strategic Trust: Manipulation, Arms Races, and Norms

Perhaps the most subtle yet consequential risk posed by AI in diplomacy is the erosion of human sensibility. The craft of diplomacy is not solely an exercise in rational calculation, it is equally rooted in empathy, intuition, emotional intelligence, and moral discretion—traits that remain beyond the cognitive reach of even the most advanced artificial systems.

An over-reliance on cognitive tools threatens to reshape the very culture of diplomatic practice. If the next generation of diplomats is trained primarily as data analysts—skilled in interpreting models but disconnected from the relational essence of diplomacy—they may undervalue relationship-building, symbolic gestures, and ethical nuance. AI-driven negotiation, often optimized for utility maximization, may overlook the strategic importance of graceful compromise, ambiguity, or acts of goodwill that preserve face and build long-term trust. Consider the seasoned negotiator who deliberately accepts a suboptimal agreement today to signal trustworthiness and lay the groundwork for future cooperation. An AI trained on short-term efficiency metrics would likely deem this irrational. Much like a physician who looks beyond a patient's clinical symptoms to offer emotional reassurance, an experienced diplomat often chooses a course of action that transcends algorithmic logic (Akıllı, 2025b).

Preserving this human-centric ethos is not optional, it is an ethical imperative. AI must augment cognition, not overwrite conscience. As the field of cognitive diplomacy matures, the ministries of foreign affairs must invest not only in technological capability but also in training that cultivates ethical reasoning, intercultural fluency, and diplomatic empathy. Only then can AI serve as a genuine partner in diplomacy, rather than a cold replacement for its human core.

In light of these emerging challenges, states and international bodies are increasingly articulating frameworks for the ethical governance of AI in diplomacy and statecraft. At the 2025 Antalya Diplomacy Forum, participants explicitly rejected both the dangers of laissez-faire deployment and the rigidity of universalist, one-size-fits-all codes. Instead, they called for adaptive, context-sensitive governance model approaches that reflect regional values and political cultures while still upholding foundational principles of transparency, accountability, and human dignity (Akıllı, 2025a).

This signals a distinctly constructivist approach to AI ethics. While the normative contours of AI governance will inevitably vary across political systems, certain principles are emerging as universal ethical baselines: the protection of human dignity, the preservation of agency and accountability, and the prohibition of harmful surveillance or coercion. For instance, the deployment of AI tools to monitor foreign populations or autonomously execute coercive diplomatic acts would almost certainly violate both diplomatic norms and international human rights standards.

A credible ethical framework for cognitive diplomacy might include the following components:

- *Pre-deployment impact assessments to evaluate potential biases, explainability gaps, and security vulnerabilities;*
- *Inclusion of ethicists, civil society actors, and cross-disciplinary experts in the design and oversight of AI systems used by foreign ministries;*
- *Red lines codified in international law, such as bans on fully autonomous cyberattacks, deepfake-based psychological operations, or AI-driven treaty violations—analogous to existing regimes for arms control and non-proliferation.*

The very features that make AI strategically valuable—speed, autonomy, and opacity—also make it ethically fraught. Without deliberate guardrails, these characteristics threaten to undermine the human-centered principles on which diplomacy depends. Cognitive Diplomacy must therefore be anchored in a robust ethical compass, one that emphasizes:

- *Bias mitigation and procedural fairness;*
- *Accountability rooted in human decision-making;*
- *Balanced transparency, sufficient to sustain democratic legitimacy without compromising national security*;
- *Technological sovereignty, to prevent digital dependency and the geopolitical leverage it can create.*

As U.N. Secretary-General António Guterres cautioned in 2023, if artificial intelligence becomes primarily a weapon—used to launch cyber-attacks, generate deepfakes, or spread disinformation, and hate speech—it will carry grave consequences for global peace and security (U.N. News,

2023). In response, Guterres urged the international community to pursue a different path: to build *"AI that bridges divides rather than exacerbates them"* (U.N. News, 2023). This vision is especially urgent in the realm of diplomacy, where AI must serve not as a vector of manipulation or mistrust, but as a tool for deepening dialogue, fostering empathy, and enabling cooperation. In cognitive diplomacy, the aim is not to automate negotiation or replace human discernment, but to amplify ethical reasoning and intercultural understanding through intelligent systems that are transparent, accountable, and anchored in the principles of international law and human dignity.

To realize this vision, continuous interdisciplinary governance, and institutional adaptation are essential. Cognitive diplomacy must be implemented through technical innovation and transformative institutional culture at the same time. The ministries of foreign affairs must cultivate cross-functional teams that bring together diplomats, technologists, legal experts, ethicists, and civil society voices to jointly assess, design, and refine AI use cases. At the same time, states must engage proactively in multilateral norm-setting, ensuring that global AI governance remains pluralistic, inclusive, and attuned to differentiated capacities.

Indeed, cognitive diplomacy may itself become a defining agenda in twenty-first-century diplomacy. Just as the nuclear age and the climate crisis led to the emergence of new international regimes, the rise of AI in foreign policy will likely necessitate new forms of intergovernmental negotiation including treaties, declarations, and perhaps dedicated regulatory institutions, to govern the ethical use of AI in international relations. However, such transformations will not be confined to the international system alone. They will also require profound internal adaptation within states, particularly in their diplomatic institutions. Ministries of foreign affairs must rethink their structures, workflows, training systems, and epistemic cultures to operate effectively in an environment where cognition is increasingly shared between human diplomats and intelligent machines. The following chapter explores these institutional adaptations in-depth, mapping how foreign ministries around the world are beginning to respond to the challenges and opportunities of the AI era.

Bibliography

Akıllı, E. (2024). "Artificial intelligence in counterterrorism: Navigating the intersection of security, ethics, and privacy." *SETA Perspective*. No. 73, Ankara, April Retrieved from: 21 May 2025 https://www.setav.org

Akıllı, E. (2025a). "Rewiring diplomacy in the Technopolar world," Daily Sabah, April 18. Retrieved from: 21 May 2025 https://www.dailysabah.com/opinion/op-ed/rewiring-diplomacy-in-the-technopolar-world

Akıllı, E. (2025b). "Future of Diplomacy: CICERO, Hagglebots and the Turing Test," *Daily Sabah*, April 3 Retrieved from: 21 May 2025 https://www.dailysabah.com/opinion/op-ed/future-of-diplomacy-cicero-hagglebots-and-the-turing-test

European Commission. (2025). "AI Act: Shaping Europe's Digital Future." Retrieved from: 21 May 2025 https://digital-strategy.ec.europa.eu/en/policies/regulatory-framework-ai

Feldstein, S. (2021). *The rise of digital repression: How technology is reshaping power, politics, and resistance*. Oxford University Press.

Kätsyri, J., Förger, K., Mäkäräinen, M. and Takala, T. (2015). "A review of empirical evidence on different Uncanny Valley hypotheses". Frontiers in Psychology. 6. p. 390. Retrieved from: 21 May 2025 doi:https://doi.org/10.3389/fpsyg.2015.00390.

McMahon, L. (2025). "AI System Resorts to Blackmail If Told It Will Be Removed", *BBC News*, 23 May. Retrieved from: 21 May 2025 https://www.bbc.com/news/articles/cpqeng9d20go

Nichols, M. (2023). "U.N. Chief calls for global AI watchdog", Reuters, 19 July. Retrieved from: 21 May 2025 https://www.reuters.com/technology/un-chief-calls-global-ai-watchdog-2023-07-19/

Ray, T. (2025). "Sovereign remedies: Between AI autonomy and control". Atlantic Council. 3 April. Retrieved from: 21 May 2025 https://www.atlanticcouncil.org/in-depth-research-reports/issue-brief/sovereign-remedies-between-ai-autonomy-and-control/

UNDP. (2020). "UN Secretary-General calls on the global community to expand digital cooperation". Retrieved from: 21 May 2025 https://www.undp.org/pacific/press-releases/un-secretary-general-calls-global-community-expand-digital-cooperation

UN News. 2023. "Guterres calls for AI 'that bridges divides', rather than pushing us apart." 18 July. Retrieved from: 21 May 2025 https://news.un.org/en/story/2023/07/1138827

Vienna Convention on Diplomatic Relations. (1961). "United Nations Treaty Series, vol. 500, p. 95." [Online]. Retrieved from: 21 May 2025 https://legal.un.org/ilc/texts/instruments/english/conventions/9_1_1961.pdf

Visit Ukraine Today. (2024). “MFA presents AI avatar to comment on consular information: what is known”. Retrieved from: 21 May 2025 https://visitukraine.today/blog/3868/mfa-presents-ai-avatar-to-comment-on-consular-information-what-is-known

CHAPTER 14

Institutional Adaptations in Foreign Ministries for the AI Era

To operationalize cognitive diplomacy, ministries of foreign affairs (MFAs) and diplomatic services worldwide are undergoing substantive institutional transformation. Recognizing that traditional structures, skill sets, and epistemic cultures must evolve, governments are initiating major reforms in training, recruitment, organizational design, and digital strategy to effectively integrate artificial intelligence, machine learning, and data-driven tools into the core of diplomatic practice.

This section examines how these shifts are taking shape—through the expansion of AI literacy programs, the creation of innovation, and foresight units, the emergence of new diplomatic roles and career tracks, and the launch of strategic initiatives to embed digital competence across the entire foreign policy apparatus. These adaptations reflect not only a response to technological change, but a deeper recognition that cognitive diplomacy requires institutions that are agile, interdisciplinary, and equipped to engage with both human and machine intelligences in complex, rapidly evolving geopolitical environments.

14.1 AI and Digital Training for Diplomats

The foundational step in operationalizing cognitive diplomacy is building human capacity. MFAs are increasingly prioritizing digital literacy and AI fluency within their diplomatic training pipelines, recognizing that the

E. Akıllı, *Cognitive Diplomacy and Digital Autonomy*,
https://doi.org/10.1007/978-3-032-04470-9_14

effectiveness of cognitive tools ultimately depends on the people who wield them. Across diverse national contexts, governments are introducing structured efforts to ensure diplomats can not only use AI systems responsibly, but also critically assess their outputs, engage meaningfully with technologists, and contribute to the development of international digital norms.

In the United Kingdom, the Diplomatic Academy has embedded data and digital policy modules into its core curriculum, incorporating AI case studies within scenario-based exercises to prepare diplomats for the realities of algorithmically mediated negotiation and global governance. This curricular shift is part of a broader strategic push led by Foreign Secretary David Lammy to modernize British diplomacy through AI integration (Birmingham University, 2025). As reported by *The Times*, the Foreign, Commonwealth, and Development Office (FCDO) has established specialized innovation units such as FCDO.ai and FCDOx, tasked with developing AI tools for negotiation simulations, predictive analytics, and even virtual reality training environments (Spirit, 2025). These developments reflect an institutional recognition that the future of diplomacy requires both technological fluency and cognitive adaptability, with AI positioned not only as a support system but as a new interface of diplomatic practice.

At the multilateral level, the United Nations Institute for Training and Research (UNITAR) offers specialized workshops on *"AI and International Affairs,"* targeting diplomatic personnel stationed in key hubs such as Geneva and New York (UNITAR, 2025). Meanwhile, the UAE Diplomatic Academy has emerged as a pioneer in tailored AI education, launching programs specifically designed for women diplomats (Kurbalija et al., 2024). These initiatives emphasize bias detection, digital empowerment, and inclusive innovation, reflecting a broader commitment to equitable digital adaptation within the diplomatic sphere.

In Singapore, the Ministry of Foreign Affairs requires all new diplomatic entrants to demonstrate digital proficiency, with training modules encompassing data analytics, cybersecurity, and AI ethics (UNESCO, 2021)—a mandate that aligns seamlessly with the country's broader Smart Nation strategy (DiploFoundation, 2025). In the United States, the Foreign Service Institute (FSI) has introduced a dedicated "Cyber and Tech" training track, grounded in the conviction that *"21st-century diplomats need 21st-century skills"* (Deloitte, 2022).

Estonia's Ministry of Foreign Affairs has taken proactive steps to embed artificial intelligence and digital competence within its diplomatic training architecture (e-Estonia, 2023). A notable initiative is the Tallinn Summer School of Cyber Diplomacy, co-organized by the MFA, the e-Governance Academy, and the Estonian Centre for International Development. This EU-funded program offers diplomats structured training in AI governance, cybersecurity norms, and the legal dimensions of state behavior in cyberspace—framing AI as both a tool of strategic communication and a domain of international norm-building (e-Governance Academy, 2025). In addition, Estonia has appointed ambassadors-at-large for cyber and digital affairs—Tanel Sepp and Nele Leosk, respectively—to represent national positions in global forums and support the integration of emerging technologies into foreign policy (e-Estonia, 2024; Mani, 2025). These initiatives reflect a broader institutional commitment to aligning Estonia's diplomatic practices with the evolving demands of digital governance.

Moreover, the DiploFoundation, a Geneva-based international NGO, offers the widely acclaimed course *"Artificial Intelligence for Diplomacy,"* which integrates rigorous theoretical foundations with hands-on simulations of AI-assisted decision-making, providing diplomats with both conceptual insight and practical competence in the application of emerging technologies to foreign policy challenges (Kurbalija, 2024).

Collectively, these efforts signify a global shift toward embedding digital competencies at the core of diplomatic identity. In other words, there is a growing recognition that digital competence is no longer ancillary to diplomacy, it is foundational (Kello, 2017). By investing in AI literacy and digital fluency, governments are preparing their diplomats not only to utilize advanced technologies, but also to critically interpret algorithmic outputs, navigate ethical risks, and engage credibly in the evolving landscape of international digital governance.

14.2 Creation of Data Science and Innovation Units

Alongside training efforts, ministries of foreign affairs are establishing internal structures to institutionalize digital innovation. These include data innovation labs, analytics hubs, and AI policy units, often staffed by multidisciplinary teams of diplomats, technologists, and policy analysts.

Such structures are designed not only to enhance operational efficiency, but also to foster a culture of experimentation, foresight, and cross-sectoral collaboration within the diplomatic apparatus.

Germany's Federal Foreign Office launched its Data Innovation Lab in 2023 as a platform to prototype AI applications in diplomacy. Among its notable projects is the use of machine learning to analyze historical negotiation texts (Chai et. al., 2023) and forecast likely outcomes in multilateral settings, an effort that exemplifies the integration of data science into strategic foresight (Data Innovation Lab, 2023; AI Berlin, 2024). In addition to technical development, the lab serves as a space for design sprints, policy experimentation, and internal capacity-building, hosting regular workshops to promote organizational adoption and cross-functional collaboration (Data Innovation Lab, 2025).

France's Mission for Digital Affairs similarly consolidates expertise in big data, cybersecurity, and digital governance, serving as a key node within the country's broader diplomatic modernization strategy (Ministère de l'Europe et des Affaires étrangères, 2025). In parallel, Japan's Foreign Ministry has established a Digital Policy Division, tasked with coordinating both domestic digital transformation and international digital policy engagement (Van der Vorst, 2024). This division actively collaborates with Japan's AI industry to pilot practical applications, including real-time AI translation for diplomatic communication, illustrating a pragmatic approach to integrating emerging technologies into core diplomatic functions (Ministry of Foreign Affairs of Japan, 2021).

At the European Union level, the European External Action Service (EEAS) has established a StratCom division that leverages AI to monitor disinformation campaigns and conduct sentiment analysis across regions. These capabilities have become integral to the EU's broader strategic communication infrastructure, supporting its external action and resilience against information threats (CSIS, 2023; Juršėnas et al., 2022). In the United States, the Department of State has embedded innovation into strategic planning through the Office of Management Strategy and Solutions (M/SS). Notably, its Data Fellows Program brings in data scientists to co-develop predictive tools—such as models for optimizing humanitarian aid delivery and mapping geopolitical influence networks (Carammia et. al., 2022; Center for Presidential Transition, 2024; Zack, 2022).

Meanwhile, India's Ministry of External Affairs has institutionalized its digital transformation through the New and Emerging Strategic Technologies (NEST) Division, established in 2020 (Harmon et. al., 2024). NEST integrates diplomatic and technical expertise to build internal capacity while also shaping India's engagement in global AI governance frameworks (MEA, 2020; Chase India, 2024). Collectively, these examples underscore how major diplomatic actors are investing in institutional innovations that position AI as a strategic asset in both foreign policy execution and norm entrepreneurship.

This structural evolution reflects a deepening recognition that data and AI expertise must be embedded in the institutional DNA of diplomacy, not relegated to technical support units, but fully integrated into core policymaking, strategic planning, and negotiation processes. In the context of cognitive diplomacy, this shift is not merely operational but epistemic: it redefines how knowledge is produced, interpreted, and acted upon within diplomatic systems. The capacity to harness machine learning for predictive analysis, to apply NLP in multilateral dialogue (Chen et. al., 2024), or to detect disinformation as pattern/anomali detection (Biggio and Roli, 2018) in real time is no longer auxiliary, instead it is foundational to a diplomatic agency in the digital age.

Moreover, this institutional reconfiguration is directly linked to the book's argument for digital autonomy and the rearticulation of Sovereignty 2.0: sovereignty defined not solely by territorial control, but by the capacity to govern data flows, algorithmic infrastructures, and cognitive systems that mediate international influence. Embedding AI capacity within foreign ministries is therefore not just a matter of innovation, it is an assertion of informational sovereignty, ensuring that diplomatic decisions are shaped by systems that reflect national priorities and normative commitments, rather than outsourced to opaque, foreign-controlled platforms.

In this light, cognitive diplomacy and digital autonomy converge: both demand that states internalize not only the technical tools of the digital era but also the institutional reflexes and ethical frameworks needed to navigate a world where strategic advantage and sovereign integrity increasingly hinge on cognitive infrastructure.

14.3 Digital *Attaché* and Tech Ambassador Networks

Diplomatic services are increasingly redefining roles and mandates to reflect the shifting terrain of global power, where technology companies now operate as quasi-sovereign actors with significant geopolitical influence. In response, several states have established dedicated envoys for digital affairs, signaling a recognition that engagement with the private tech sector is no longer peripheral, it is central to contemporary statecraft.

Denmark was the first to formalize this approach in 2017 with the appointment of a Tech Ambassador, introducing the concept of *Tech-Plomacy*—a diplomatic role with a global mandate to engage major technology firms and shape international tech governance discourse (TechAmb.um.dk, 2023). This model has since inspired a wave of adaptations. France's ambassador for digital affairs focuses on internet governance, data policy, and AI ethics (Ministère de l'Europe et des Affaires étrangères, 2025), while the United Kingdom and Australia have stationed tech envoys in Silicon Valley, embedding diplomatic presence directly within the epicenter of global innovation (Ittelson and Rauchbauer, 2023).

The United States' Digital *Attaché* Program, launched by the Department of Commerce in coordination with the State Department, exemplifies a new frontier in commercial digital diplomacy. By placing digital specialists in embassies across strategic locations—including New Delhi, Brasília, and Jakarta—the program aims to support U.S. businesses, promote digital market access, and engage host countries on technology regulation and digital standards (Trade.gov, 2023). These attachés operate at the nexus of trade diplomacy and technology policy, reflecting the strategic significance of digital ecosystems in global economic competition.

On the cybersecurity front, an increasing number of countries have appointed cyber ambassadors to advance national interests in cyber governance. Finland, the Netherlands, and Australia (Australian Government, 2023), have each designated envoys responsible for representing their positions in U.N. negotiations on cyber norms, while also engaging in bilateral dialogue on cyber conflict prevention and infrastructure resilience (Ministry for Foreign Affairs of Finland, 2023; Verma, 2025). In contrast, Russia and China (Ministry of Foreign Affairs of the People's Republic of China, 2024) have adopted more state-centric models, deploying IT *attachés* in partner countries to deepen digital cooperation and promote alternative technological standards, particularly in surveillance (Feldstein, 2019) and network governance (Lee et al., 2022; Khasanova, 2025).

14.4 Infrastructure Modernization and Innovation Ecosystems

Institutional adaptation also necessitates the modernization of core diplomatic infrastructure. During the COVID-19 pandemic, ministries of foreign affairs accelerated the adoption of secure smartphones, encrypted video conferencing, and cloud-based collaboration platforms. These tools now form the backbone of hybrid diplomacy, enabling a seamless blend of virtual and in-person engagement across a wide spectrum of diplomatic functions from G20 Sherpa meetings to consular crisis coordination.

Some innovations have broader regional implications. The African Union, for instance, launched a secure digital coordination platform to streamline internal workflows (African Union Commission, 2015; African Union Commission, 2020). With further development, this infrastructure could evolve into a continent-wide digital diplomacy hub, particularly if coupled with AI-powered translation tools to navigate the Union's complex multilingual environment, advancing both operational efficiency and equitable participation.

In parallel, MFAs are increasingly turning to public-private partnerships and innovation ecosystems to source new ideas and accelerate digital transformation. The U.K.'s Foreign, Commonwealth, and Development Office (FCDO), for instance, collaborated with the University of Oxford's Digital Diplomacy Research Group, led by Dr. Corneliu Bjola, whose work explores AI applications in negotiation support, disinformation resilience, and soft power projection (Bjola and Holmes, 2020; Bjola and Pamment, 2021; Oxford Digital Diplomacy Research Group, 2025). The U.S. State Department's TechCamp program (U.S. Department of State, 2024b) brings together diplomats and civil society (Deibert, 2020) stakeholders in collaborative workshops to co-develop technology-enabled policy solutions, fostering a hands-on, cross-sectoral learning environment (U.S. Department of State 2024a).

14.5 Organizational Culture and Recruitment: From Generalists to Digital Strategists

Institutional adaptation to the AI era requires more than structural reforms, it demands a cultural shift. Diplomatic services have traditionally prized generalist skill sets, rooted in the humanities. While these remain valuable, there is a growing recognition that diplomacy in the technopolar age also requires analytical, computational, and technical fluency.

Recruitment strategies are evolving accordingly. India's Ministry of External Affairs, for instance, now encourages more applicants with engineering and STEM backgrounds, capitalizing on India's robust tech talent pool. These individuals are trained in diplomatic craft while bringing their innate comfort with digital systems (ICC-TCA, 2025).

Cultural adaptation is also about mindset reform. Bureaucracies often resist experimentation for fear of failure. Yet, some MFAs are working to normalize pilot projects, treating them as learning exercises rather than high-stakes ventures. Estonia's Foreign Ministry, for example, has long cultivated an agile, startup-like culture. It embraced social media diplomacy early and adopted blockchain technologies for securing diplomatic cables. This ethos was reinforced by national leadership—former President Toomas Hendrik Ilves being a vocal advocate for digital society (e-Estonia, 2025; Petrone, 2025).

Another shift is occurring at the level of cross-disciplinary collaboration. Diplomatic workflows increasingly involve data scientists, cybersecurity experts, and technologists—not as adjunct support, but as equals in decision-making. This breaks down the old silos between "political officers" and "technical staff," fostering integrated policy formulation and execution. These trends are mirrored in multilateral institutions. The United Nations, in 2019, established a High-Level Panel on Digital Cooperation, followed by the appointment of a Tech Envoy, now leading global coordination on AI governance (SDG.iisd.org, 2019; UNDP, 2020). This institutional evolution pressures national missions to the U.N. to include tech-literate officers in their delegations (Dig.watch, 2019).

Similarly, NATO's Defense Innovation Accelerator for the North Atlantic (DIANA), launched in 2021, has become a key venue for integrating AI and dual-use technologies into allied defense strategies

(NATO, 2024). Foreign ministries are increasingly involved in such initiatives to ensure diplomatic interoperability, norm alignment, and strategic coherence across security and policy domains.

Despite these advances, the global picture remains uneven. Many MFAs, particularly in the global south, face resource and connectivity limitations. Here, capacity-building initiatives have become vital instruments of inclusive cognitive diplomacy. Estonia, for example, offers digital diplomacy training to Eastern Partnership countries (Estdev, 2024), while Singapore runs a cyber diplomacy program for ASEAN diplomats (Parameswaran, 2018). These initiatives exemplify what might be called "training diplomacy"—a meta-level practice of using diplomacy to equip others for digital governance, thereby strengthening multilateral digital resilience.

Importantly, these institutional adaptations directly address several ethical concerns raised earlier in this chapter. By training diplomats in critical AI literacy and emphasizing human-in-the-loop accountability, MFAs reduce risks of over-reliance or automation bias. By building internal AI capabilities, they reinforce sovereignty (Anthony, 2025) and information security. By expanding norm-setting roles—such as cyber ambassadors and tech envoys—they shape the evolving regulatory ecosystem in alignment with democratic and ethical principles.

In essence, institutional adaptation is the implementation architecture of cognitive diplomacy. It transforms an abstract concept into a concrete operational capacity, equipping diplomatic services to act with agility, intelligence, and integrity in the AI era. Foreign ministries are evolving—some more rapidly than others—from analog institutions into digitally native organizations, capable of navigating the complex challenges and opportunities of the twenty-first century.

For many developing countries, limited institutional resources do not preclude meaningful engagement in digital diplomacy. While these states may lack the capacity to appoint dedicated envoys for technology or AI, it is increasingly common to designate digital focal points within key diplomatic missions—particularly in strategic multilateral hubs such as Washington, Geneva, Brussels, and New York (Kurbalija, 2021). These officers are tasked with monitoring developments in digital governance, AI negotiations, and global tech regulation as part of their broader diplomatic portfolios. This approach enables states to maintain institutional situational awareness and early engagement, even in the absence of fully resourced innovation units or standalone digital policy departments.

The proliferation of such roles across diplomatic missions reflects a growing consensus: digital and AI-related issues now constitute a distinct domain of diplomacy, rather than a subcategory of economic (Bhagat et. al. 2024), trade, or security policy. Technology is no longer an external variable—it is emerging as a strategic axis of international relations in its own right, requiring diplomats who can navigate technical complexity, ethical considerations, and geopolitical implications in an integrated and anticipatory manner.

These evolving diplomatic roles signal a broader institutional realization: technology is no longer peripheral to foreign policy—it is central to it. Whether through the regulation of AI, the defense of cyberspace, or the negotiation of digital trade frameworks, states are increasingly embedding technological expertise within their diplomatic apparatus as a matter of strategic necessity. These examples reinforce a central insight of cognitive diplomacy that innovation in foreign ministries must extend beyond technological tools to encompass institutional culture, operational models, and learning networks. By reengineering both physical and epistemic infrastructures, diplomatic institutions position themselves not just to react to disruption, but to shape the digital contours of international engagement.

Bibliography

African Union Commission. (2015). "Agenda 2063: The Africa we want." African Union,. Retrieved May 21, 2025, from https://au.int/en/agenda2063/overview

African Union Commission. (2020). "The digital transformation strategy for Africa (2020–2030)." African Union,. Retrieved May 21, 2025, from https://au.int/sites/default/files/documents/38507-doc-dts-english.pdf

Anthony, A. (2025). "On the Path to AI Sovereignty, AI Agency Offers a Shortcut," *Lawfare,* May 20. Retrieved May 25, 2025, from https://www.lawfaremedia.org/article/on-the-path-to-ai-sovereignty%2D%2Dai-agency-offers-a-shortcut

Australian Government. (2023). "2023–2030 Australian Cyber Security Strategy." Retrieved May 26, 2025, from https://www.homeaffairs.gov.au/cyber-security-subsite/files/2023-cyber-security-strategy.pdf

AI Berlin. (2024). "Foreign Policy & AI Forum - AI Berlin." 16 October Retrieved May 26, 2025, from https://ai-berlin.com/events-tiles/event/foreign-policy-ai-forum

Bhagat, A., Bhandari, P., Yadav, A.L. and Talwandi, N.S. (2024). "AI-Powered Customer Segmentation for Marketing," *SSRN,* April 30. Retrieved May 21, 2025, from https://ssrn.com/abstract=4811907

Biggio, B. and Roli, F. (2018). "Wild patterns: Ten years after the rise of adversarial machine learning," Pattern Recognition, 84, pp. 317–331. Retrieved June 7, 2025, from https://www.sciencedirect.com/science/article/pii/S0031320318302565

Birmingham University. (2025). "A New Kind of Peacemaker: AI Joins the Front Lines of Diplomacy," April 16. Retrieved May 21, 2025, from https://www.birmingham.ac.uk/news/2025/a-new-kind-of-peacemaker-ai-joins-the-front-lines-of-diplomacy

Bjola, C., & Holmes, M. (2020). *Digital diplomacy: Theory and practice.* Routledge.

Bjola, C., & Pamment, J. (2021). Countering online propaganda with AI: Challenges for digital diplomacy. *International Journal of Press/Politics, 26*(1), 1–23.

Carammia, M., Lacus, S. M. and Wilkin, T. (2022). "Forecasting asylum-related migration flows with machine learning". *Nature.* 7 January. Scientific reports 12, article number: 1457 Retrieved May 5, 2025, from https://www.nature.com/articles/s41598-022-05241-8

Center for Presidential Transition. (2024). "Director, Office of Management Strategy and Solutions". Partnership for Public Service. Retrieved May 26, 2025, from https://presidentialtransition.org/position_description/director-office-of-management-strategy-and-solutions/

Center for Strategic and International Studies (CSIS). (2023). "AI and the Information War in Ukraine: Implications for Strategic Communications," Retrieved May 21, 2025, from https://www.csis.org/analysis/ai-and-information-war-ukraine-implications-strategic-ommunications

Chai, X., Xu, S., Li, S. and Zhao, J. (2023). "The process and algorithm analysis of text mining system based on artificial intelligence," Procedia Computer Science, 228, pp. 574–581. Retrieved May 21, 2025, from doi:https://doi.org/10.1016/j.procs.2023.11.066.

Chen, Y., Wang, H., Yu, K. and Zhou, R. (2024). "Artificial intelligence methods in natural language processing: A comprehensive review," Highlights in Science, Engineering and Technology, 85, pp. 545–550. Retrieved May 21, 2025, from doi: https://doi.org/10.54097/vfwgas09

Data Innovation Lab (2023). "Data Innovation Lab | Harnessing the Power of Data for Global Good," Retrieved May 21, 2025, from https://www.datainnovationlab.de

Data Innovation Lab (2025). "AI Workshops - Data Innovation Lab," Data Innovation Lab. Retrieved May 26, 2025, from https://www.datainnovationlab.de/workshops

Deibert, R. (2020). *Reset: Reclaiming the internet for civil society*. House of Anansi Press.

Deloitte. (2022). "Using Artificial Intelligence to Modernize American Statecraft," *Deloitte AI Institute for Government*. Retrieved May 21, 2025, from https://www2.deloitte.com/us/en/pages/public-sector/articles/using-artificial-intelligence-to-modernize-american-statecraft.html

Dig.watch. (2019). "The UN High-Level Panel on Digital Cooperation," Retrieved May 26, 2025, from https://dig.watch/processes/hlp

DiploFoundation. 2025. "The Diplomatic Academy of the Ministry of Foreign Affairs of Singapore (MFA)". Retrieved May 26, 2025, from https://www.diplomacy.edu/actor/diplomatic-academy-of-the-ministry-of-foreign-affairs-of-singapore/

e-Estonia. (2023). "Data Embassy: Estonia's Secure Digital Sovereignty Model." Retrieved May 21, 2025, from https://e-estonia.com/solutions/security-and-safety/data-embassy/

e-Estonia. (2024). Estonia's digital ambassador: Nele Leosk: Estonia's Digital Ambassador's Insights." 17 April. Retrieved May 25, 2025, from https://e-estonia.com/estonias-digital-ambassador-nele-leosks-insights

e-Estonia. (2025). AI Strategy Factsheet. Retrieved May 21, 2025, from https://e-estonia.com/wp-content/uploads/factsheet-ai-strategy.pdf

E-Governance Academy. (2025). "Tallinn Summer School of Cyber Diplomacy." Retrieved May 25, 2025, from https://ega.ee/project/tallinn-summer-school-of-cyber-diplomacy

Estdev. (2024). "Estonia Hosts Pivotal Global Cyber Diplomacy Event Amid Rising Cyber Threats." Retrieved May 26, 2025, from https://estdev.ee/en/articles/estonia-hosts-pivotal-global-cyber-diplomacy-event-amid-rising-cyber-threats

Feldstein, S. (2019). The global expansion of AI surveillance.: Carnegie Endowment for International Peace. Retrieved May 21, 2025, from https://carnegieendowment.org/2019/09/17/global-expansion-of-ai-surveillance-pub-79847

Harmon, S., Wilsmann, M., Joshi, G., Ballesteros, A., & Baitinger, P. (2024). Decoding India's AI governance strategy and its implications for the U.S.-India bilateral relationship. *Indian Public Policy Review, 5*(4), 51–82.

ICC-TCA (2025). "India's Technology Talent & Skill Map and Demography". Retrieved May 26, 2025, from https://icc-tca.org.tw/wp-content/uploads/2025/04/Report-Indias-Technology-Talent.pdf

Chase India. (2024). "Advancing AI Adoption for Citizen Centric Governance," April. Available at: Retrieved May 26, 2025, from https://www.chase-india.com/media/wfnbdqp0/advancing-ai-adoption-for-citizen-centric-governance-april-2024.pdf

Ittelson, P. and Rauchbauer, M. (2023) "Tech diplomacy interactions in the San Francisco Bay Area". DiploFoundation. Retrieved May 26, 2025, from https://www.diplomacy.edu/resource/tech-diplomacy-practice-in-the-san-francisco-bay-area/tech-diplomacy-interactions-in-the-san-francisco-bay-area/

Juršėnas, A., Karlauskas, K., Ledinauskas, E., Maskeliūnas, G., Ruseckas, J., and Rondomanskas, D. (2022). "The Role of AI in the Battle Against Disinformation." *NATO Strategic Communications Centre of Excellence.* 28 February. Retrieved May 26, 2025, from https://stratcomcoe.org/publications/the-role-of-ai-in-the-battle-against-disinformation/238

Kello, L. (2017). *The virtual weapon and international order*. Yale University Press.

Khasanova, L. and Tai, K. (2025). "Shades of Authoritarian Digital Sovereignty: Divergences in Russian and Chinese Data Localisation Regimes." *Tufts University.* 4 November. Retrieved May 26, 2025, from https://sites.tufts.edu/fletcherrussia/shades-of-authoritarian-digital-sovereignty-divergences-in-russian-and-chinese-data-localisation-regimes/

Kurbalija, J. (2021). "2021: The Emergence of Digital Foreign Policy," *DiploFoundation,* 26 January. Retrieved May 26, 2025, from https://www.diplomacy.edu/blog/the-emergence-of-digital-foreign-policy/

Kurbalija, J. (2024). "How to Train Diplomats for the AI Era?", *DiploFoundation,* 18 October. Retrieved May 21, 2025, from https://www.diplomacy.edu/blog/how-to-train-diplomats-for-the-ai-era/

Kurbalija, J., Teleanu, S. and Škrinjarić, A. (2024). "Leadership training on AI and diplomacy at the UAE diplomatic academy". DiploFoundation. 18 November. Retrieved May 26, 2025, from https://www.diplomacy.edu/event/united-arab-emirates-diplomatic-academy-training-on-artificial-intelligence/

Lee, J., Zhang, E. ve Creemers, R. (2022). "China's standardisation system—Trends, implications and case studies". Leiden Asia Centre. April. Retrieved May 26, 2025, from https://leidenasiacentre.nl/wp-content/uploads/2022/04/Chinas-standardisation-system.pdf

Mani, R. N. (2025). "AI Trust Is the New Cyber Currency," *BankInfoSecurity,* May 3. Retrieved May 25, 2025, from https://www.bankinfosecurity.com/ai-trust-new-cyber-currency-a-28237

MEA. (2020). "Question No.552 New and Emerging Strategic Technologies Division." Ministry of External Affairs, Government of India. Retrieved May 26, 2025, from https://mea.gov.in/lok-sabha.htm?dtl%2F32359%2Fquestion_no552_new_and_emerging_strategic_technologies_division (Accessed 26 May 2025).

Ministère de l'Europe et des Affaires étrangères. (2025). "Diplomatie Numérique." Ministry for Europe and Foreign Affairs. Retrieved May 26,

2025, from https://www.diplomatie.gouv.fr/fr/politique-etrangere-de-la-france/diplomatie-numerique/

Ministry for Foreign Affairs of Finland. (2023). "Statement by Finland on behalf of the Nordic countries at the OEWG on security of and in the use of information and communications technologies." 13 December. Retrieved May 26, 2025, from https://finlandabroad.fi/web/un/current-affairs/-/asset_publisher/TMs3SoX45i0K/content/statement-by-finland-on-behalf-of-the-nordic-countries-at-the-oewg-on-security-of-and-in-the-use-of-information-and-communications-technologies/38495

Ministry of Foreign Affairs of Japan. (2021). "Recommendations for Strengthening the Diplomatic and Consular Implementation System through Digital Transformation (DX)." Retrieved May 26, 2025, from https://www.mofa.go.jp/mofaj/files/100218019.pdf

Ministry of Foreign Affairs of the People's Republic of China. (2024). "Promoting Development for All and Bridging the AI Divide." Speech by Wang Yi at the High-level Meeting on International Cooperation in AI Capacity Building, 20 September. Retrieved May 21, 2025, from https://www.mfa.gov.cn/eng/wjb/wjbz/jh/202412/t20241218_11497479.html

NATO. (2024). "Defence innovation accelerator for the North Atlantic (DIANA)". 5 July. Retrieved May 26, 2025, from https://www.nato.int/cps/en/natohq/topics_216199.htm

Oxford Digital Diplomacy Research Group. (2025). "Oxford digital diplomacy research group". , University of Oxford. Retrieved May 21, 2025, from https://www.qeh.ox.ac.uk/content/oxford-digital-diplomacy-research-group

Parameswaran, P. (2018). "What's next for the new ASEAN-Singapore cyber Center?" *the diplomat*. 19 September. Retrieved May 26, 2025, from https://thediplomat.com/2018/09/whats-next-for-the-new-asean-singapore-cyber-center/

Petrone, J. (2025). "President Ilves: Our digital innovation moves forward." e-Estonia. 27 January. Retrieved May 26, 2025, from https://e-estonia.com/president-ilves-our-digital-innovation-moves-forward/

SDG.iisd.org. (2019). UN High-Level Panel on Digital Cooperation Calls for 2020 Global Commitment. Retrieved May 26, 2025, from https://sdg.iisd.org/news/un-high-level-panel-on-digital-cooperation-calls-for-2020-global-commitment/

Spirit, L. (2025). "British diplomats swap soft skills for AI and algorithms." The Times. 19 March. Retrieved May 25, 2025, from https://www.thetimes.com/uk/politics/article/british-diplomats-soft-skills-ai-david-lammy-30pzrdzxx

TechAmb.um.dk. (2023). "TechPlomacy—The Tech Ambassador." Retrieved May 26, 2025, from https://techamb.um.dk/

Trade.gov. (2023). “Digital Attaché Program - International Trade Administration.” Retrieved May 26, 2025, from https://www.trade.gov/digital-attache-program-0

U.S. Department of State. (2020). “Establishment of the Center for Analytics.” U.S. Department of State, 17 January. Retrieved May 21, 2025, from https://2017-2021.state.gov/establishment-of-the-center-for-analytics/

U.S. Department of State. (2024a). “FY2024 Q1 Progress Update: Data-Informed Diplomacy.” *Performance.gov*. Retrieved May 21, 2025, from https://assets.performance.gov/APG/files/FY2024/Q1/FY2024_Q1_DOS_Progress_Data-Informed_Diplomacy.pdf

U.S. Department of State. (2024b). TechCamp. Retrieved May 26, 2025, from https://techcamp.america.gov/

UNDP. (2020). “UN Secretary-General calls on the global community to expand digital cooperation”. Retrieved May 26, 2025, from https://www.undp.org/pacific/press-releases/un-secretary-general-calls-global-community-expand-digital-cooperation

UNESCO. (2021). “Recommendation on the ethics of artificial intelligence”. 16 May. Retrieved May 21, 2025, from https://www.unesco.org/en/articles/recommendation-ethics-artificial-intelligence

UNITAR. (2025). “AI Training for Diplomats: A Women Empowerment Opportunity and Prevention of Bias.” Retrieved May 26, 2025, from https://event.unitar.org/full-catalog/ai-training-diplomats-women-empowerment-opportunity-and-prevention-bias

Van der Vorst, C. (2024). “An economic assessment of the EU–Japan economic partnership agreement with realistic preference utilization rates”. World Trade Review, 24(1), pp. 1–24. Retrieved May 26, 2025, from https://www.cambridge.org/core/journals/world-trade-review/article/an-economic-assessment-of-the-eujapan-economic-partnership-agreement-with-realistic-preference-utilization-rates/353ED3EBBFB2D47D3F5FC7AE2B86C6AF

Verma, A. 2025. “Building a safer cyberspace: The Netherlands, India & the Future of Global Cyber Governance”. *Economic Times Government*. 12 April. Retrieved May 26, 2025, from https://government.economictimes.indiatimes.com/news/digital-india/building-a-safer-cyberspace-the-netherlands-india-the-future-of-global-cyber-governance/120209504

Zack, R. (2022). “The forefront of diplomacy: Making maps at the State Department.” Felt Blog. 3 May. Retrieved May 26, 2025, from https://felt.com/blog/making-maps-for-the-state-department

PART V

Conclusion

CHAPTER 15

Conclusion

In the twilight of the analog age and the dawn of a technopolar world, strategic foresight calls for a new kind of leadership. We are entering an era where a handful of technology companies and AI-advanced states wield disproportionate influence. They redefine global power not through territory, but through control of data, infrastructure, and algorithms. This means to understand global power today, one must account for Silicon Valley and Shenzhen alongside Washington and Beijing.

This book has argued that digital autonomy is the shield that nations and communities must raise to safeguard their values, institutional integrity, and decision-making in a world shaped by algorithmic asymmetries and opaque, externally governed AI systems. Yet, a shield alone is insufficient. Strategic agency also requires a sword—an active, principled engagement with the international system. This is where cognitive diplomacy emerges as a guiding paradigm: a means by which states can collaboratively shape the evolving norms, institutions, and architectures of the AI era while safeguarding their sovereign interests.

The rise of AI is fundamentally transforming the fabric of diplomacy and statecraft. This book has examined how AI's growing influence is reshaping both the practice and principles of international relations. On one level, AI has become a tool of diplomacy—supporting data-driven analysis in negotiations, facilitating multilingual communication through machine translation, and enhancing strategic forecasting. On another

E. Akıllı, *Cognitive Diplomacy and Digital Autonomy*,
https://doi.org/10.1007/978-3-032-04470-9_15

level, AI has become a subject of diplomacy, as governments debate the norms, standards, and governance structures that will determine its global trajectory. Simultaneously, the very notion of sovereignty is being redefined through the pursuit of digital autonomy. States increasingly seek control over their digital infrastructures, data flows, and algorithmic systems, treating them as core dimensions of national security and geopolitical relevance.

Within this rapidly shifting landscape, the book has introduced and developed the concept of cognitive diplomacy: an emerging paradigm of statecraft, attuned to the informational, perceptual, and psychological dimensions of international influence. It reflects a recognition that in the AI age, power is not only exercised through material assets but also through the architecture of cognition—how societies perceive, decide, and relate. Cognitive diplomacy, therefore, offers a model for navigating this new reality with strategic insight, ethical clarity, and institutional innovation.

Cognitive diplomacy recognizes that in a world saturated with algorithms and digital media, winning hearts and minds requires more than traditional persuasion. It involves navigating the complex cognitive architectures shaped by technology. In sum, the core themes of this book—the ascent of AI in diplomacy, the pursuit of digital sovereignty, and the advent of cognitive diplomacy—all speak to a geopolitical epoch in which bits and code are as pivotal as bullets and treaties.

A central insight of this book is that the integration of AI into diplomacy should augment, *not replace*, human judgment. Rather than envisioning autonomous algorithms conducting foreign policy, I have argued for hybrid intelligence—the synergistic partnership of human diplomats and AI systems. By leveraging the machines' analytic power alongside human creativity, empathy, and ethical judgment, nations can enhance decision-making while retaining human agency. This approach underpins a triad of capacities explored in the book: presence, practice, and resilience.

Presence refers to a state's digital presence and influence—its ability to project power and values in the online sphere. Diplomatic presence today is measured not only in embassies and envoys, but in a nation's visibility on social media, its engagement in virtual forums, and its command of narrative in the information space. *Practice,* meanwhile, denotes how the day-to-day conduct of diplomacy adapts to AI. This includes diplomats using AI translators, data analytics, and simulation tools, as well as the institutional changes needed to embed these tools into diplomatic workflows. It means foreign ministries cultivating data science units and cognitive strategists and embracing a culture of innovation in bureaucratic practice. Finally, *Resilience* is the capacity to withstand and adapt to the disruptions of the digital age. From cyberattacks on communication networks to disinformation campaigns aimed at undermining trust, modern diplomats must confront a range of "cognitive threats." Building *resilience* involves protecting critical digital infrastructure, training personnel in cyber hygiene and stress management, and developing strategies to tackle influence operations. Strengthening presence, practice, and resilience in tandem equips states with a holistic cognitive defense and offense—enabling them to participate actively in the digital public square, leverage AI for effective diplomacy, and absorb shocks to the system.

15.1 Technopolar World and Digital Geopolitics

The emergence of artificial intelligence has empowered states as well as technology companies and other non-state actors, fundamentally altering the global distribution of power. The international system now stands on the brink of a technopolar world order—an environment where dominant technology firms and a select group of technologically advanced states increasingly shape international norms, strategic dependencies, and governance architectures.

At the heart of this order lies a persistent *digital asymmetry*: a structural imbalance between those actors that possess advanced digital capabilities and those that remain dependent, peripheral, or excluded. This asymmetry deepens global inequalities in access to data, infrastructure, and normative influence. It often marginalizes the global south and reinforces reliance on proprietary systems controlled by a handful of private or state-backed entities. In this context, power flows not only through conventional instruments of diplomacy or development aid, but through algorithmic reach, infrastructural gatekeeping, and control over the protocols that govern digital interaction.

Indeed, technopolarity posits that in the twenty-first century, sovereignty and influence are determined not by physical territory or military capacity, but by the ability to command data, algorithms, and digital infrastructure. This shift compels diplomacy to extend beyond traditional state-to-state engagement and into strategic interaction with technology conglomerates functioning as quasi-sovereign actors. Recent developments illustrate this transformation: social media platforms deciding whether to de-platform political leaders; private satellite and cybersecurity firms playing pivotal roles in active conflict zones; and platform governance decisions influencing democratic processes and public trust.

The geopolitical consequences of digital infrastructure have become unmistakably clear. Decisions over who builds a country's 5G networks, undersea cables, cloud data centers, or AI laboratories are now not merely technical or economic choices—they are deeply strategic, often determining long-term autonomy, resilience, and global alignment. For many states, particularly those without indigenous technological ecosystems, dependence on foreign providers presents risks to both sovereignty and security. This has triggered efforts to diversify technological partnerships, invest in local capacities, and assert normative agency—constituting a digital analog to classic concerns over energy security or trade dependencies.

In this context, ***digital infrastructure*** is power: owning and securing the pipes and platforms of the information age confers a strategic advantage, much like territory did in ages past. We observe new fault lines forming, with some countries championing "digital non-alignment" to avoid dominance by any single tech superpower, and alliances coalescing around standards and ecosystems (for example, the U.S. and allies versus China's digital sphere). Technopolarity thus forces a reimagination of statecraft. Diplomats today must be as comfortable negotiating tech standards and data-sharing agreements as they are negotiating arms control treaties. The interplay of public and private power also demands innovative regulatory diplomacy—finding ways to assert democratic oversight over transnational tech platforms without stifling innovation or fragmenting the open internet. In facing these challenges, states strive to reclaim a measure of digital sovereignty: the ability to chart their own course in cyberspace and ensure that digital tools bolster rather than erode their sovereignty.

15.2 Algorithmic Governance and the Challenge of Accountability

As part of this digital geopolitics, we must confront the reality that algorithms and AI systems now make or inform countless decisions like what information we see, how resources are allocated, and even how high-stakes governmental assessments are made. This phenomenon has been termed algorithmic governance: the use of computational algorithms to guide social, economic, and political outcomes, sometimes with minimal human intervention. Algorithmic governance promises efficiency and predictive power, but it also raises profound questions about accountability, transparency, and bias. In international relations, algorithmic systems might be used for everything, from predicting conflict outbreaks to automating portions of trade negotiations. Yet, if a diplomatic decision is skewed by a biased algorithm, or an automated system fails in a crisis, who is responsible? Unlike traditional governance, where lines of accountability are clearer, an algorithmic system's opacity can obscure where errors or biases originate. Ensuring accountability in this context is paramount.

This book has highlighted the need for robust oversight mechanisms—what we might call ***algorithmic accountability*** frameworks—that require AI tools to be auditable and explainable to human supervisors. Such measures not only help assign responsibility when things go awry but also build public trust in the outcomes. Indeed, public trust is the currency of governance, citizens and other states will only accept AI-driven processes if they perceive them as fair, understandable, and subject to human correction. We explored how some governments are responding. For instance, the European Union's AI Act mandates transparency and human oversight for high-risk AI systems, reflecting a broader movement to tame the algorithmic "black boxes" in sensitive areas of public life. Ultimately, integrating AI into governance and diplomacy without undermining democratic legitimacy requires recalibrating institutions. Parliaments, courts, and international bodies will need the expertise to evaluate algorithms, while diplomatic services will need new protocols for AI-assisted decision support. The geopolitical consequence of failing to address algorithmic governance is a crisis of legitimacy—a world where people no longer trust their institutions or each other, as decisions become too complex or opaque to explain. Avoiding that outcome is an essential task of cognitive diplomacy going forward.

15.3 Ethical Norms and Human-Centric AI

Amid these disruptive changes, ethical and normative frameworks serve as our compass. A recurring theme in this book is the insistence that human values must guide the deployment of AI in statecraft. The dilemmas of accountability, human agency, and public trust are not technical questions alone, they are fundamentally about morals and rights. How can we ensure that AI systems reflect our collective values and do not dilute human responsibility? We found a convergence of perspectives from around the world emphasizing a human-centric approach to AI. For example, in 2019 the Japanese government issued its *Social Principles of Human-Centric AI*, which set out as core philosophies the importance of human dignity, diversity and inclusion, and sustainability (Cabinet Office, Government of Japan, 2019). Rather than seeing ethical principles as a brake on innovation, Japan frames them as goals to *realize through* AI—seeking to harness its power for social good. The social principles enumerate concrete guidelines, including protecting privacy, ensuring security, promoting fairness, and maintaining accountability and transparency in AI development. Germany's approach to AI governance has similarly been grounded in normative commitments. The German Federal Government's AI strategy explicitly aims to *"ensure that AI use and development are responsible and focused on the common good"* and to *"embed AI ethically, legally, culturally, and institutionally"* through broad societal dialogue (Bundesregierung, 2024).

This reflects a broader European ethos that sees fundamental rights, democracy, and the rule of law as non-negotiable in the digital domain—an attempt to infuse the emerging algorithmic order with the values of the liberal democratic order. Even religious and philosophical authorities have entered the conversation. The Vatican's recent doctrinal note *Antiqua et Nova* (2025) offers a perspective rooted in Catholic social teaching, yet resonant with secular ethics. It calls for AI to be guided by an *"ethic … of freedom, responsibility, and fraternity"* oriented to the common good, and warns against uses of AI that violate human dignity or distort truth. Notably, *Antiqua et Nova* insist that technologies like AI must *never* be allowed to undermine fundamental human values—for instance, mass surveillance regimes that infringe on privacy and liberty are deemed "unjustifiable," and must be kept transparent and answerable to the public. Across these examples, a shared principle emerges: AI should serve humanity, not the other way around. Keeping humans "in the loop"—maintaining meaningful human control over AI decisions—is crucial for both ethical and practical reasons. It preserves individual agency and moral responsibility, and it also provides a fail-safe against machine errors or malfeasance. As nations and international bodies craft norms for AI in areas like autonomous weapons, digital trade, or cross-border data flows, they will need to embed these human-centric values into binding rules and standards. The ethical frameworks discussed in this book serve as early guideposts toward a more normative AI governance—one that strives to balance innovation with human rights, efficiency with equity, and autonomy with accountability.

15.4 Policy Recommendations

The analyses presented throughout this book converge in a set of strategic policy pathways aimed at translating cognitive diplomacy and digital autonomy into actionable statecraft. Rather than issuing rigid prescriptions, these recommendations are offered as a flexible and coherent framework for navigating the rapidly evolving terrain of diplomacy in the age of AI. Within this context, cognitive diplomacy is understood as the practice of engaging with and shaping the informational and perceptual environments of international relations—guiding how global actors understand, decide, and interact. In parallel, digital autonomy signifies a nation's ability to independently develop, regulate, and secure its digital infrastructure, data ecosystems, and AI capabilities. Together, these twin paradigms offer a forward-looking model for achieving presence, practice, and resilience—the foundational pillars of strategic autonomy in the digital age. In a world where influence is increasingly exercised through algorithmic architectures and innovation ecosystems, this triadic framework provides states with the means to uphold their sovereignty, foster societal coherence, and engage constructively in global governance. The roadmap that follows is grounded in this dual imperative: to convert conceptual insight into institutional practice, blending normative foresight with pragmatic implementation.

First, states must treat digital self-reliance as a core pillar of twenty-first-century sovereignty. This entails building secure, sovereign digital infrastructure, from national cloud architectures and diverse fiber-optic networks to trusted data centers and communication platforms. Equally, it requires the cultivation of national and locally developed technological capabilities, including investment in AI research, support for innovation ecosystems, and incentives to retain technological talent. By developing such capacities, states enhance their strategic agency to shape global digital governance, rather than remaining dependent consumers within foreign-controlled ecosystems.

Second, human capital development must be prioritized to meet the demands of the cognitive age. Diplomatic services, public institutions, and policy professionals require structured training in areas such as AI ethics, data science, cybersecurity, and algorithmic accountability. A digitally literate diplomatic corps is not a luxury—it is a strategic necessity. Moreover, educational systems must equip broader society with digital literacy and critical thinking to foster public resilience against misinformation and ensure democratic participation in an AI-driven world. Societies that fail to bridge the gap between AI adoption and understanding will find themselves vulnerable to manipulation, dependency, and epistemic erosion.

Third, governments should institutionalize hybrid intelligence within foreign ministries and public decision-making. AI systems must be deployed as augmentative tools, not autonomous decision-makers. Early warning mechanisms, policy simulations, and open-source intelligence processing can all be enhanced by AI—provided there is clear human oversight, transparent algorithms, and institutional checks. Organizationally, this calls for the establishment of AI strategy units, interdisciplinary task forces, and innovation labs within ministries of foreign affairs. These bodies should bring together diplomats, technologists, ethicists, and analysts to build adaptive and context-sensitive tools for modern diplomacy.

Fourth, states must elevate cognitive resilience as a national and diplomatic security priority. In an age of deepfakes, micro-targeted disinformation, and cyber interference, resilience is not merely defensive—it is existential. States should implement comprehensive strategies for information integrity, including real-time monitoring partnerships with platforms, robust media literacy campaigns, and support for independent journalism. At the same time, diplomatic communications and decision systems must be fortified against cyberthreats through secure-by-design infrastructure, regular stress testing, and quantum-resilient encryption. Only by safeguarding the cognitive environment can strategic autonomy be preserved.

Fifth, the establishment of inclusive international norms and digital alliances is essential for ensuring that digital autonomy does not devolve into digital fragmentation. No single state can govern AI or digital infrastructure alone. Multilateral diplomacy must focus on shaping shared principles for AI governance, building on initiatives such as the OECD

AI Principles, the Hiroshima AI Process, and the UNESCO Recommendation on AI Ethics. This includes frameworks for algorithmic transparency, data sharing for the public good, and binding safeguards against weaponized AI and autonomous systems (G7 Japan, 2023; OECD, 2019; UNESCO, 2021). In a technopolar world, diplomacy must also engage non-state actors, especially tech giants, as geopolitical stakeholders. Dialogue must be paired with accountability. Coalitions of like-minded nations might also form "digital alliances" to present a united front on issues such as data privacy or to pool resources for AI research that challenges monopolies. Through concerted multilateral action, the international community can set guardrails on technology's *Wild West* and ensure least developed countries are not left behind in the AI revolution.

Sixth, crucially, all these efforts must be underwritten by a commitment to transparency, ethics, and human rights. Policy frameworks should mandate *explainability* in AI systems deployed by the government so that decisions can be understood and contested if necessary. Mechanisms for redress should be in place when algorithmic decisions cause harm or injustice, reinforcing the rule of law in the digital domain. Public trust can further be bolstered by involving citizens in dialogues about tech policy—for instance, through citizens' assemblies on AI ethics or participatory policymaking platforms. Embracing ethics also means embedding privacy protections and anti-bias audits into the lifecycle of any government AI project, to prevent the erosion of civil liberties or the entrenchment of discrimination. In my exploration, I offered the example of Japan's human-centric AI principles and the EU's risk-based regulatory approach. These illustrate how marrying innovation with oversight is not only possible but advantageous. By implementing policies that reflect society's values, governments ensure that technological progress translates into *legitimate* progress in the public eye.

Together, these pathways offer a strategic roadmap for navigating the AI age with foresight and responsibility. Building sovereign digital foundations, investing in human capacity, embedding hybrid intelligence in institutions, reinforcing cognitive and cyber resilience, forging collaborative norms, and upholding ethical governance—these are not peripheral ambitions, but core state functions in the twenty-first century.

Ultimately, the principles and recommendations developed throughout this book converge into a strategic roadmap for navigating the complexities of AI-augmented diplomacy and digital sovereignty. This framework is designed to adapt to technological disruption as well as shape its trajectory, ensuring that artificial intelligence becomes a force for empowerment rather than dependency and for global cooperation rather than systemic fragmentation. It reinforces the book's central proposition: that digital autonomy and cognitive diplomacy are the dual engines of strategic sovereignty in an era when power is increasingly embedded in data infrastructures, algorithmic systems, and cognitive influence networks.

This is not a call for isolation but for principled and proactive engagement. To realize this vision, states must build secure and sovereign digital foundations, invest in human capital to thrive in the cognitive era, and institutionalize hybrid intelligence in governance. They should also fortify resilience across the information and cyber domains and participate actively in shaping inclusive, ethical international norms. These interlinked efforts form the operational core of *presence, practice*, and *resilience* allowing governments not only to navigate but to meaningfully shape the technopolar world.

What is advanced here is both ambitious and necessary: a policy vision grounded in strategic foresight, ethical integrity, and collective leadership. As the architecture of global power is increasingly rewritten by technology, this roadmap offers a path to ensuring sovereignty is exercised with responsibility and that humanity retains its agency in the age of machines.

15.5 Future Horizons: Neurodiplomacy

Even as we consolidate lessons for today, new frontiers are on the horizon. One especially intriguing future trajectory is the emergence of neurodiplomacy. If cognitive diplomacy addresses how ideas and information influence global affairs, neurodiplomacy suggests an even deeper intersection—where insights from neuroscience and an understanding of the human brain inform diplomatic strategy and international cooperation. While speculative, this concept invites questions about how states might someday engage each other not just in cyberspace or through AI, but through the very biology of belief and perception. Could breakthroughs in neural interfaces or cognitive science lead diplomats to communicate empathy more directly, or help negotiators manage biases and emotional triggers during high-stakes talks? Such possibilities remain largely theoretical, and I have only hinted at them in this book. What is clear, however, is that the evolution of diplomacy will not stop at the digital realm. The quest for peace and mutual understanding may eventually penetrate the ***neural*** realm—the ultimate “last mile” in human communication. Just as digital autonomy has become the new terrain of sovereignty, the next frontier lies not only in cyberspace but in the cognitive architectures of humanity itself.

15.6 For Those Who Come After...

Writing *Cognitive Diplomacy and Digital Autonomy: “Statecraft in the Age of Artificial Intelligence”* has been a journey of intellectual discovery and a labor of hope. As an international relations professor and author, I ventured across disciplines, from international relations theory to computer science, from philosophy to neuroscience, in an effort to piece together a coherent narrative about our technological age. This journey was both challenging and enlightening. The rapid pace of change in AI often made the ground beneath my arguments shift, and what was once speculative became real in a matter of months, forcing me to continuously update my understanding. Yet this flux also reaffirmed one of the book’s central messages: that adaptability and lifelong learning are indispensable in today’s policymaking. In weaving together case studies, theoretical frameworks, and ethical reflections, I often found myself learning alongside the reader, interrogating my own assumptions, and marveling at the resilience and creativity of those who face these emerging challenges on the world stage.

In the preceding chapters, I have outlined a framework for digital autonomy anchored in cognitive presence, strategic practice, and institutional resilience. This book offers not only a theoretical vocabulary for understanding AI’s evolving role in diplomacy, but also concrete policy directions: the establishment of AI units within foreign ministries, development of inclusive governance models, the adoption of ethical design standards, and investment in human-centered capacity-building. These proposals are not exhaustive, but they aim to serve as a compass in navigating the turbulence of the technopolar world.

My hopes for the future are cautiously optimistic. I believe that humanity retains agency over how these technologies are used, and that with wisdom and dialogue, we can shape AI to augment our better qualities rather than amplify our worst. The ideas discussed in this book are offered in the spirit of constructive optimism. They are intended as sparks, not blueprints, for it will be up to the next generation of academicians, diplomats, engineers, activists, and thinkers to carry them forward. I am hopeful that these pages encourage at least a few readers to think more deeply about the intersection of technology and diplomacy, and perhaps to take action; whether by advocating for sensible policies, pursuing interdisciplinary research, or engaging in informed public discourse.

As we look ahead, the stewardship of emerging technologies must not be left to a handful of powerful actors. A just and democratic digital future demands multilateralism, regional agency, and a more inclusive global conversation. Countries like Türkiye—situated at the nexus of continents, cultures, and civilizational traditions—are uniquely positioned to lead in articulating a vision that is both ethical and strategic. Non-western world, especially the Global South, long excluded from technological norm-setting, must now become co-author of the institutions and rules that will shape the algorithmic century.

Throughout this writing process, I have been reminded that ideas possess quiet but enduring power. Major shifts in global governance often begin with seemingly abstract conversations among academics, practitioners, and citizens. Over time, today's imaginative reflections can become tomorrow's institutions. If there is a final takeaway I cherish, it is that sharing knowledge and debating principles is itself an act of diplomacy—*a cognitive diplomacy* that precedes and guides the diplomacy of states. In that sense, writing this book has been my small exercise in bridge-building: between disciplines, between visions of the future, and between people who may not yet realize how much they need to hear each other.

I close with deep gratitude for the readers and colleagues who have engaged with these ideas, and with a reaffirmed conviction that through collective wisdom and empathy, we can steer the digital revolution toward the common good. *For those who come after*, may this book serve as both a map and a mirror, a guide for charting new paths, and a reflection of the values we must uphold in shaping our digital futures.

Erman Akıllı.

Ankara, Türkiye.

Bibliography

Bundesregierung. (2024). *Update of the Artificial Intelligence Strategy of the German Federal Government*. Federal Government of Germany. Retrieved

June 13, 2025, from https://www.ki-strategie-deutschland.de/files/downloads/Fortschreibung_KI-Strategie_engl.pdf

Cabinet Office, Government of Japan. (2019). *Social Principles of Human-Centric AI*. Government of Japan. Retrieved June 13, 2025, from https://www.cas.go.jp/jp/seisaku/jinkouchinou/pdf/humancentricai.pdf

Dicastery for the Doctrine of the Faith & Dicastery for Culture and Education. (2025). *Antiqua et Nova: Note on the Relationship Between Artificial Intelligence and Human Intelligence*. 28 January 2025. Holy. Retrieved June 13, 2025, from https://www.vatican.va/roman_curia/congregations/cfaith/documents/rc_ddf_doc_20250128_antiqua-et-nova_en.html

G7 Leaders. (2023). *G7 Leaders' Statement on the Hiroshima AI Process*. 30 October 2023. Ministry of Foreign Affairs of Japan. Retrieved June 13, 2025, from https://www.mofa.go.jp/files/100573466.pdf

OECD. (2019). *Recommendation of the Council on Artificial Intelligence*. Organisation for Economic Co-operation and Development. Retrieved June 13, 2025, from https://legalinstruments.oecd.org/en/instruments/OECD-LEGAL-0449

UNESCO. (2021). *Recommendation on the Ethics of Artificial Intelligence*. United Nations Educational, Scientific and Cultural Organization. Retrieved June 13, 2025, from https://unesdoc.unesco.org/ark:/48223/pf0000381137

Index

A

C

E. Akıllı, *Cognitive Diplomacy and Digital Autonomy*,
https://doi.org/10.1007/978-3-032-04470-9

GPSR Compliance
The European Union's (EU) General Product Safety Regulation (GPSR) is a set of rules that requires consumer products to be safe and our obligations to ensure this.

If you have any concerns about our products, you can contact us on

ProductSafety@springernature.com

In case Publisher is established outside the EU, the EU authorized representative is:

Springer Nature Customer Service Center GmbH
Europaplatz 3
69115 Heidelberg, Germany

www.ingramcontent.com/pod-product-compliance
Ingram Content Group UK Ltd.
Pitfield, Milton Keynes, MK11 3LW, UK
UKHW020753220926
475829UK00004BA/96

9783032044693